COLDPLAY

LOOK AT THE STARS

Phil O'Brien

Plexus, London

Text copyright © 2004 by Phil O'Brien
This edition copyright © 2004 by Plexus Publishing Limited
Published by Plexus Publishing Limited
55a Clapham Common Southside
London SW4 9BX
www.plexusbooks.com
First printing 2004

British Library Cataloguing in Publication Data

O'Brien, Phil
    Coldplay : look at the stars
    1. Coldplay (Musical group)
    2. Rock musicians - Great Britain
    - Biography
    I. Title
    782.4'2166'0922

    ISBN: 0 85965 349 8

Printed by Biddles
Cover design by Brian Flynn
Book design by Brian Flynn and Rebecca Martin
Cover photograph by LA Times/Retna
Back cover photograph by Spiros Politis/Retna

Acknowledgements

My thanks to Dr. Mark Tanner, Nikki Rosetti, Chris Allison
of Sonic 360 and Alan McGee for their interviews. Many
thanks also to my editor Dick Porter, and to Genevieve
Muinzer and Bill Godber of Turnaround Publisher Services
for further editorial advice.

There is a lot of good magazine writing about Coldplay that
greatly assisted in the research for this book – particularly
since the band does not co-operate on biographies, feeling
that they haven't done enough to merit one yet. My favourite
article of all was Michael Odell's droll piece for Q, August
2002. My heartfelt thanks also to journalists John Aizlewood,
Phil Ascot, Nicholas Barber, Mark Beaumont, Mark Blake,
Daniel Booth, Robin Bresnark, Katherine Brown, Philip
Begg, Tony Challis, Helen Dalley, Johnny Davis, Jon Dennis,
Matt Diehl, Mike Doherty, Jamie Doward, Nick Duerden,
Jean Aramis Encoule, Ben Gilbert, Jo Jo Gould, Adrian Grist,
Siobhan Grogan, Guernica, Robert Hillburn, Barney
Hoskyns, Sam Inglis, Will Jenkins, Emma Johnston, Ted
Kessler, Greg Kot, Dorian Lynsky, Lee Elliot Major, Craig
McLean, Emma Morgan, Piers Martin, Gary Mulholland,
Chris Nelson, Benjamin Nugent, James Oldham, Andre
Paine, Tracey Pepper, Alexis Petridis, Amy Raphael, Paul
Robicheau, John Robinson, Matt Sebastian, Victoria Segal,
Eva Simpson, Dave Simpson, Caroline Sullivan, Steve
Sutherland, Adam Sweeting, Jaqui Swift, Craig Tansley,
Chelsea Toon, Sam Upton, Everett True, Mark Watt, Jon
Weiderhorn, Ray Wilkinson, Scott Wilson.

And finally, to acknowledge her eternal support, thanks to my
mother who, like Will's, was called Sara and also loved the
ancient stones and green fields of the West of Ireland.

We would like to thank the following photographers and
picture agencies:

Tim Auger/Retna; Jamie Bowering/Headpress/Retna; Justin
Borucki/Retna; Jay Blakesberg/Retna; Eric Cararina/Retna;
Andrew Carruth/Retna; Mark Henderson/Retna; Edd
Westmacott/Retna; Robin Francois/Retna; Clemens
Rikken/Sunshine/Retna; Leo Sorel/Retna; Kelly A.
Swift/Retna; Spiros Politis/Retna; Rob Watkins/Retna; LA
Times/Retna; Hayley Madden/Redferns; J M
Enternational/Redferns; John Marshall/Corbis; Harry
Romero/Corbis; Andrew Winning/Corbis; Alessio/Corbis;
Tony Haresign/allactiondigital.com; Gene Weatherley/allac-
tiondigital.com; Suzan/allactiondigital.com;
morrison/haller/allactiondigital.com.

CONTENTS

ONE

MEET ME ON THE ROAD

'The raggedy man with the sky blue eyes and the three-day beard falls to his knees. He is finally still. He has done dry-humping his piano like a dog on your leg, he is done with all the gangly indie robotics. 'He peers out at the rapt gathering of loving couples packed into Earls Court in London to witness one of the best gigs they've ever seen in their lives and he licks his dry lips to speak. '"Thank you," he says. "Thank you for giving us the best job in the world."'
– Steve Sutherland, *NME*, 26 April 2003

The raggedy man is pop star Chris Martin. The vast, delirious crowd before him is here to see Chris and his band, Coldplay; the huge venue is Earls Court Arena, London, in April 2003; the concert is the culminating show of a sold-out UK stadium tour. These gigs, a small part of Coldplay's 2002-03 world tour, are only part of the global strategy that has, in just five years, made Coldplay one of the most successful new acts to break planet-wide.

Like the promotional and organisational bubble that surrounds and engulfs them, the group also have a strategy, albeit one which is much more creatively focused on songs. Songs that are achingly optimistic, like 'Yellow', or regretful and victimised, such as 'Trouble'. Songs like 'Politik', that crash forcefully into your life like a hijacked jet, and others, like 'Clocks', whose chords circle like the speeded up hands of a watch. Swooping, crooning, swaggering songs like 'In My Place' that generate rolling tides of Mexican waves around vast arenas across the globe.

These songs, captured in a small studio room in Liverpool for Coldplay's second album, *A Rush Of Blood To The Head,* immediately topped a dozen charts around the world, including Australia, Denmark, Germany, Hong Kong, Iceland, Italy, Norway, Switzerland, the United Arab Emirates and, of course, Britain. The album also debuted in the Top Ten in Austria, Finland, France, Holland and Portugal.

The album went straight to Number Five in America. It is hard to decide who has been more surprised by Coldplay's singular success there – the ailing British music industry, their American counterparts, or the band themselves. *A Rush Of Blood To The Head* is a classic album that epitomises the authority and confidence of a band at the height of their powers. It is the juxtaposition of the majesty and fragile beauty found in Coldplay's music that has attracted millions of fans. Yet the global music press has granted far less space to the music than it has to wondering about that

From the left: Guy Berryman, Jonny Buckland, Chris Martin and Will Champion. Their story begins with Chris's lonely country-boy dreams.

which is peripheral to it – the band's backgrounds and their lack of 'rock 'n' roll credentials.

This slanted emphasis is, to an extent, understandable. Coldplay's isolated 'soft-rock' success in America hangs heavy over the embattled British music industry, whose declining share of the US market plunged from 32 per cent in 1986 to 0.2 per cent in 2002. Before Coldplay's success, Britain had increasing difficulty breaking acts there. But why Coldplay? The Brits were incredulous that the unfancied quartet could make an impact upon a territory where press darlings such as Oasis and Blur had failed to flourish.

How, of all the desperately aspiring bands since the demise of Britpop, a mere year and a half after their debut as a college band in a shabby Camden pub, did Coldplay manage to break through to the seemingly impregnable US airplay lists?

One peculiarity of Coldplay's success is its rapidity and apparent ease; first in the UK and then – a mere five months later – in America. Watching their growth is like viewing time-lapse photography; the pace of change that the band has undergone in three short years has contained a lifetime's worth of experience.

Throughout this fast-forwarded development, the media has highlighted several issues central to the band and their music: first, how does their aim of creating accessible music with the broadest popular appeal distinguish itself from the crude dynamics of an exploitative, world-dominating commercial ethos?

Second, is there any sort of personal behaviour, lifestyle or background that disqualifies their music from 'authentic' rock or pop?

Also, does Chris Martin's concept of 'reverse rock 'n' roll' – simply, doing whatever the fuck you want (which in Coldplay's case means choosing not to do hard drugs, sleep with most of their fan base or wreck hotel rooms) – somehow render their creative output irrelevant?

Chris Martin's highly-charged creative nature stands in stark contrast to the subtle but solid bedrock of Will Champion, Guy Berryman and Jonny Buckland. 'We'd all like to meet the right person one day,' Chris told *Rolling Stone*, 'But in one sense in my life, I've already met the right people.'

However, this is not just another tale of four college friends who made good. Rather, Coldplay's story starts with a long period of loneliness: the artistic isolation felt by the young Chris Martin throughout his childhood and adolescence, which started a journey down a long road he had to travel before he, too, would meet the right people.

In an interview on the *A Beautiful World* fansite, Chris reminisced about the last weeks before he left home for university. 'When I left school I had just the best summer. I'd go off surfing with my brother, and then, just sit at home reading this book, listening to this classical piano music that I'd never heard before. Sounds totally pompous, but it was just brilliant. I would sit there, and this music would create this atmosphere of Victorian London. I loved it. I used to really like Sherlock Holmes. There was a time where I could . . . tell you everything about him.'

Born on 3 March 1977, Chris grew up on the great slant of a hillside looking north from his home, the village of Whitestone in Devon. Chris's family background was stable and resolutely middle-class; his father, Anthony, was a chartered accountant, whilst his mum, Alison, taught biology. The oldest boy of the Martins' brood of five, Chris has two brothers and two sisters.

Try to imagine the teenage Chris on summer nights; bent reading *The Collected Stories of Sherlock Holmes* whilst a flood of piano music provided a soundtrack to his memories of a day's idyllic surfing. An impossibly enthusiastic youth, Chris wove a powerful musical spell around himself in his room, sitting absolutely still, absorbed by Conan Doyle's foggy Victorian world. North of his family's house stretches the blank expanse of Dartmoor – the very moor that inspired the ghoulish *The Hound of the Baskervilles*.

Halfway up the north face of Whitestone's largest hill, the nearby Royal Oak pub pushes its cosy front hard into the hillside, ignoring the great valley that drops sharply behind it. Fields nestled within this basin are half covered by sprawling shadows thrown by the hill. The fields look janus-faced – half dark, half sunlit – their shadowed halves stay pale blue with frost in winter, while the opposite slopes are melted to dark green by the sun.

It was past this landscape that Chris and his younger brother were driven by his dad, *en route* to their Exeter primary school. High and swooping, the Whitestone road shoots down through ghost-train tree-tunnels, reaches flat land, and veers past the River Exe. During this journey they often played music. Sometimes it would be Chris's CD of Michael Jackson's *Bad*, or his dad might play something by the Man in Black, Johnny Cash.

The landscape they raced through was very different from the baking Arkansas fields where Cash picked cotton for a living as a ten-year-old. Chris' childhood connection with Johnny Cash shows that the world's darkest experiences don't necessarily come from the back streets. When a child has sympathy he can bring the dark or the light from himself from anywhere. Chris was profoundly struck by this musical visitation from another universe, 'He's my hero. His voice was bonkers. My dad used to put Johnny Cash on in the car and it sounded like this alien guy from America – which to me then was a million miles away – and here was this guy from the heart of it.'

'The first U2 album I ever heard was Achtung Baby. It was 1991, and I was fourteen years old . . . From that point, I worked backward – every six months, I'd get to buy a new U2 album.' – *Chris Martin*

All of a sudden the road would reach Exeter, and school: the drop-off cars swinging round by the cathedral yard. Exeter Cathedral School is built half above the site of the bathhouse of a Roman legion who once encamped there. Later, Chris would gain detailed knowledge of such antiquities when he took his degree in ancient history. Much later, he observed contemporary parallels: 'It's cool to learn about the Roman Empire. In the future they'll be unearthing statues of George Bush.'

A few roads away from the school, past the badly dissolved sandstone figures on top of the cathedral, lies the tiny, vaulted, underground Cavern Club. The distance between the two buildings can be walked in no time. Although he would scarcely have imagined it, back then Chris was taking his first steps on a twelve-year journey that would return him to the Cavern at the very height of the band's breakthrough.

In the meantime, the worrisome Chris, if he were stuck in Exeter after school, could just about walk home to Whitestone, stumbling ever upwards through the darkening lanes.

In daytime though, for an adventurous young boy, those lanes are a wicked slalom course, with green hedges instead of ice walls. Like the little deep road to Whitestone church – with murderous intent it heads straight at the parlour window of a cottage, swerving round it at the last moment and darting up to a tiny, creepy graveyard.

Naturally enough, Chris made the most of his idyllic rural environment. 'For about three years, I was very into survival stuff with my friend James. We would build camps around the garden until we found a dormouse in one of them.'

Six months after his eleventh birthday, Chris was sent off to board at Sherborne School in

Dorset. Sherborne is a powerfully beautiful and historic school - a school has stood on this site since the eighth century. The school has educationally forged such illustrious alumni as actors Jeremy Irons, John Le Mesurier and Jon Pertwee, as well as writers John Le Carre and Cecil Day-Lewis.

For any eleven-year-old, changing schools can be a frightening experience. For the sensitive Chris, facing the additional wrench of living away from home, the experience might have easily become an ordeal. Luckily, he made an invaluable friend quite quickly. A boy called Phil Harvey, ridiculously easy to talk to, was, like Chris, a huge fan of U2.

'The first U2 album I ever heard was *Achtung Baby*. It was 1991, and I was fourteen years old,' Chris later explained to *Rolling Stone*. 'Before that, I didn't even know what albums were. From that point, I worked backward – every six months, I'd get to buy a new U2 album. The sound they pioneered – the driving bass and drums underneath and those ethereal, effects-laden guitar tracks floating out from above – was nothing that had been heard before. They may be the only good anthemic rock band ever. Certainly they're the best.'

> **'My nicknames at school would generally question my sexuality . . . the homophobia can be pretty intense.'** – *Chris Martin*

As a schoolboy, Chris never dreamed that one day America's most eminent music magazine would ask *him* to write the definitive entry on U2 for its 'Immortals' feature. Right then, he was far too busy trying to fit in at Sherborne. An ungainly, nervous, skew-haired adolescent, Chris also stood out because of his obvious intelligence and boundless enthusiasm – particularly for music classes. His teacher, Mark Tanner, held progressive views; he wholly approved of pop music, and his doing so changed Chris's life. 'He dismissed the idea that you had to be some kind of minia-ture Mozart to enjoy music. He bought these Yamaha keyboards for the school,' recalled Chris. 'They were very easy to work with, everyone could have a go. You could play with one finger and have a tune so we did.'

The inspiration Chris got was not surprising: Mark Tanner is a very special kind of teach-er. He is an acclaimed professional concert pianist and a specialist on Liszt, whose work he has played at the Royal Festival Hall and on several CDs, but he is also broad enough in his sense of fun to enjoy providing accompaniment to famous British comedians such as Bruce Forsyth.

In response to Chris's newfound enthusiasm for the piano, his parents bought him a keyboard and encouraged him all the way with his music – thinking, they later confessed, that he'd grow out of it. Although Chris's father had stuck to what is arguably a dull-but-lucrative career path, he wanted Chris to have freedom of choice. 'Just finish college,' was all he asked of his oldest son.

In the stormy season of Chris's teenage enthusiasms, triumphs and disasters, he had concerns that he might be gay. Being at boarding school, it was an anxiety that he found particularly iso-lating. 'You hide your vulnerabilities aged fourteen because people will use them against you. And being gay at public school is all you'd imagine it to be – a fucking nightmare . . . I was sixteen when I finally felt confident I wasn't.'

Some of his schoolmates didn't share Chris's confidence in his heterosexuality, bullying and humiliating him. 'My nicknames at school would generally question my sexuality . . . the homo-phobia can be pretty intense.'

Chris's fey, gentle, and over-flowing nature made him especially vulnerable to the petty cru-elties of adolescent boys. Attending a British public school can be a brutal experience. It's not a place where they *need* to kick your head in – they can do the same thing with a half-smile. Spy

Singer-songwriters with acoustic guitars gave Chris Martin his early inspiration. He would echo their style, but not their solo performer status.

writer John Le Carre went to Sherborne, and often wrote about the way that shabby-hearted boarding schools can destroy human beings.

To be as eccentric (and enviably excellent) a character as Chris Martin and survive British public school, you have to be particularly tough. It seems ironic that certain sarcastic music writers have criticised him for his 'soft' upbringing. Undoubtedly, these school ordeals helped make Chris tough enough to withstand the ugly pressures of the music industry – although, from many of his comments, he doesn't seem to feel as strong as he actually is, later telling *Select*, 'I always ring my dad when I want to quit.'

Although Chris now knew that he was definitely heterosexual, this knowledge was wholly grounded in theory rather than experience. In fact, from the age of thirteen onward, he'd been turned down by every girl he'd approached – his rejection rate even worrying his devoutly Christian mother.

'Radiohead gave me hope . . . I thought, I'm a bit like them . . .'
– Chris Martin

At the age of sixteen, Chris fell in love for the first time - with a television phantasm from an Australian soap opera: Beth from the popular series, *Neighbours*, played by the beautiful teenage actress Natalie Imbruglia. She was the first in a series of brunettes to attract Chris – including his later, more earthly girlfriends, Emma Holland and Lily Sobhani. Despite his teenage shyness, Chris had a romantic nature. But his emotional reaction to life was separate, and more realistic - the two qualities combine in his songs to unique effect.

As well as U2, both Chris and best friend Phil drew great inspiration from the emergence of Radiohead and their conquest of America, which began in 1993 when their debut album, *Pablo Honey*, went gold. When the album came out, the two school friends were barely sixteen, and Radiohead instantly became one of their central influences. That the band was formed by middle-class Oxford boys soothed Chris's worry that boarding school kids couldn't be rock stars.

'Radiohead gave me hope,' he recalled, 'They were the band that gave me permission. I'm a public schoolboy from Devon and I'm not supposed to be in a band. Well, they proved I could. I thought, I'm a bit like them . . . I hate apologising because as far as I'm concerned it was a privilege to have an amazing education. I had some incredible teachers, great facilities. What a privilege! But so what? Does anyone give a shit?'

Once he began writing songs, Chris experienced his first pains of creative isolation. He felt his efforts were always *almost* good – but there was something missing from their composition. He knew that his material required a fresh perspective – the alternative viewpoints he would get if he had his own band.

With this in mind, Chris formed a number of short-lived groups with his schoolmates, such as the Pet Shop Boys-influenced Identity Crisis. His interest in forming a band, at least, made him no different from other boys throughout the western world. Being in the woefully-named soul ensemble the Rockin' Honkies meant that he learned to play 'Sittin' on the Dock of the Bay' and 'Mustang Sally' on the piano, but, 'like every keyboard player, I desperately wanted to be the front-man.' Consequently, Chris later admitted to *Melody Maker*, 'If you want to find tapes of me singing like Eddie Vedder in an early band, I'm sure you could.' At one early show, Chris borrowed an old raincoat and stomped onstage, trying to copy Bono, only to be booed off energetically. Thus gig-hardened, Chris resolved to have a 'completely normal' stage persona from then on.

Or as normal as the musically-obsessed Chris could ever be. By this time, he was applying to universities; one rejected him because on his application form he wrote that he wanted to study English, 'because it'll help my lyrics.' Instead of literature, he would finally opt for a course in ancient history. This was a kind of 'career suicide' degree – a qualification without many direct job opportunities. For Chris, his ambition was fiercely focused on finding and fronting an inspiring, passionate rock group.

Deciding where he should attend college challenged the brittle self-esteem of the anxious country boy. There was his local university at Exeter – but that route had already been travelled by Radiohead's Thom Yorke. Then, as Chris later told the *Telegraph*'s Craig McLean, one of his schoolteachers encouraged him to go to London to study. 'I thought, Me, London? I'm from the West Country. Maybe I'll go as far as Bristol, but I can't go all the way to that big place.' On the bus route from Exeter to London, though, loomed several large signposts for the road to Glastonbury – the mystical heart of English rock, the home of the illustrious festival. Chris longed to play there someday.

Such ambitions were far from Chris's mind at the end of the summer, as he sat in his room, devouring tales of Sherlock Holmes after a day's surfing. Instead, his thoughts bounced between the remembered crash of the waves and the deep fantasy of a Victorian London, whose descendant he would one day live in. His life would be utterly changed, then. His best friend Phil would disappear to Oxford to study classics, and he himself would depart for studies at University College, London.

But, on the musical front, things wouldn't happen so fast. After all, it's not as if people meet their ideal musical partners on the first day of term . . .

TWO

INDIA COLLIDES
WITH ASIA

Being an educational establishment with no campus of its own, University College, London is a somewhat unusual place of learning. Past graduates have included members of Elastica, Suede and Basement Jaxx, who have all trudged in and out of the rows of tall, blackened Victorian buildings on Gower Street – almost built from bricks of soot – that house the academic departments.

Just around the corner is the London School of Economics, where Mick Jagger once studied. Way off east lies the London Guildhall, from which Ray Davies of the Kinks graduated. Twenty minutes' walk down to the southeast of their patch at UCL lies Waterloo Bridge, the setting for his classic 'Waterloo Sunset'.

Over UCL looms a non-wonder of the London world, the Telecom Tower, with a bombed out upper level and its dreary grey sides dotted with dishes like toilet plungers. Tottenham Court Road, around the corner from the university, is a long, repetitive chain of hi-fi/computer stores and futon shops.

But still, if you are a musician and you go to UCL, you are never far from the places that might break your band. Go south, and you're queuing for a gig at the Astoria on Charing Cross Road. Go north and you're right in the thudding heart of Camden, full of pubs with bootleg quality sound systems, crammed with A&R men. A few streets away from UCL, in Portland Place, is BBC Radio One, Britain's all-important national music station – you can easily deliver your demos to the front desk by hand.

The UCL student hall of residence, Ramsey Hall on Maple Street, is built in an L shape abutting the Indian YMCA, so that, if you stand on the corner, students seem to bound into the hall in trainers and emerge from the entrance around the corner wearing turbans. But there is no surreal delight in the institutional interior.

That beautiful and extraordinary music has come out of the dreary Ramsey Hall is in itself extraordinary. The building is claustrophobic and anonymous, full of boxy student rooms. Four feet from the street, on the bedroom windowsills, you can see students' coffee mugs, their Pringles tubes and their carefully guarded bottles of vodka and scotch making dwarf skylines in their windows.

The pub that's ten steps away on the corner, The Anchor, is an overflow common room for UCL students. But away from the booze and roll-ups, back in Ramsey Hall, there's a room with a piano. The night porters were used to hearing 'that Chris who's now famous' playing it, like a blind man groping for perfect, breathtaking chords.

Cramped stairwells and dormitories were the first live venues for a student band briefly known as Starfish.

'When you go to college you've got a clean slate,' Chris recalled. 'No-one knows who you are and you've kind of decided pretty much who you want to be.'

Very early on, Chris Martin and his band had decided who they wanted to be, and how they wanted to stay. They weren't ashamed to bond over their love of music that's 'quite soulful and emotive'. 'Rock 'n' roll is about doing what the fuck you want,' asserted Chris. 'It doesn't have to be about doing huge amounts of drugs or being hedonistic. It's about not caring what anyone else thinks of you. Rock 'n' roll is about the seeking of the ultimate pleasure. For us, that means hanging around together and playing music that we all love and not being afraid to say that's why we're doing it.'

On the very first night of UCL Fresher's Week in September 1996, Jonny Buckland was standing by the college pool table. He'd come up from Mold in Flintshire to study maths and astronomy 'because I was quite good at them, and didn't want to do physics.'

('There is a correlation between maths and music,' Johnny's mother Joy explained to the *Flintshire Evening Leader*. 'And I believe Brian May, lead guitarist with Queen, did maths and astronomy. There seems to be something about the subject for musicians.')

Jonny was a pleasant-looking fresher whose character seemed to be spun out of a thousand metres of calm. He had eyelids that looked distinctly modelled, as if by a sculptor – and quite pale-coloured eyes, so that the pupils looked particularly dark and chiselled out.

> **'Meeting Jonny was like falling in love. He could make all the ideas work and we were writing two or three songs a night sometimes.'** — *Chris Martin*

Approaching Jonny was a tall bloke who looked as if he was on something, although he was drinking only Coca-Cola. He would turn out to be one of the most unique characters that the young mathematician had ever encountered – but Jonny had the *nous* to take such singularity in his stride. There would be no embarrassed side-glances here. No 'look who I'm lumbered with.' Jonny seemed at ease with anyone.

This Chris bloke was tall with a wavy mop of fair hair, and eyes like the children from John Wyndham's *The Midwich Cuckoos*. His face wouldn't stay still: sometimes it looked like a foot struggling into a sock, sometimes – with a small Cindy Crawford mole on his upper lip – it was more classically attractive, although Chris was hopeless with girls. His smile was a spread of delighted sunray teeth, and he had an intense manner that was a strange fusion of trainee vicar, jester, and the ultimate wired-up mentor.

Jonny and Chris soon got talking about music over the UCL pool table. Chris was terribly excitable, with Jonny smiling and interjecting now and then. Unlike Chris, Jonny's North Wales background had provided little in the way of local musical influences. 'It's not an area you really associate with music,' Jonny deadpanned. The area's rock heritage consists solely of Karl Wallinger of World Party and pseudo-rebel rockers The Alarm.

Jonny's father was a biology/chemistry teacher, and both Jonny and his older brother Tim went to Mold Alun High School, where each won the school physics prize five years apart. 'Jonathan was always brilliant at maths,' recalled Joy. 'I think it came easy to him.' His aunt also taught at the secondary school he attended and, perhaps unsurprisingly, Jonny grew up as the teacher's pet who privately hated school – a quietly excellent student rather than an unmissable anomaly like Chris.

The Bucklands had originally come from London, where Jonny and Tim were born. Joy, a

The starburst spotlight outshines the star, and that's how lead guitarist Jonny Buckland has always preferred it.

dance teacher, once taught at a school opposite White Hart Lane, the home of Tottenham Hotspur Football Club, thus inspiring in Jonny a lifelong devotion to the perennially under-achieving Spurs.

Music runs through the Buckland family like one of Jon's perfect guitar riffs. On his father's side, Jonny's great grandfather led the Vic Buckland Dance Band in the 1920s, and his grandfather was an accomplished violinist. Likewise, Joy's mother was a talented pianist. 'They've always had music,' says Joy of her sons, 'and in my professional experience creativity is the crux of everything. We always encouraged them to be creative.' In addition to junior school piano lessons, Jonny also had a brief flirtation with the violin, which Joy recalls as being 'hard to bear'.

Luckily for Jonny, there were also a couple of guitar maniacs in his house. Inspired by his father's treasured collection of Eric Clapton and Jimi Hendrix records, Jon began playing guitar when he was eleven. His older brother Tim also provided some influences, playing him My Bloody Valentine and Sonic Youth albums. Thus inspired, he put in a lot of early practice on his first guitar, a budget Japanese Westone that was 'amazingly loud'.

Apart from his guitar playing and founding a rap band at age ten, Jonny's main musical expression came in the form of album covers that he would design for the imaginary bands he dreamed of starting. What he lacked in concrete experience, however, he made up for with raw ability. 'I always felt he would do well. When he studied A-level music, his strength was in his composition,' said Margaret Parr, his music teacher from secondary school. 'He had an immense talent for the guitar.'

'I'm technically not very good at all,' Jonny told *Select* magazine. 'In fact I'm pretty shocking. I've got a really awful technique but I think Joe Strummer said somebody struggling with their instrument was the best thing to see.'

In contrast to Jonny's more conventional nature, Chris had the dramatic intensity of a dying class of English eccentrics; those who crusade tirelessly for a single cause, no matter how daft it may seem to anybody else. This ran in the family – Chris's great, great grandfather, William Willet, had introduced the idea of shifting the clocks forward one hour in spring to create British summertime. Martin's single cause was that he and Jonny should jam with a view to getting a band together.

'He only really had one topic of conversation and that was music,' a fellow student claimed in *Bang* magazine years later. 'It wasn't music generally, it was just *his* music, what he was doing and what he was writing. You'd try and change the subject, but he'd always manage to drag it back again.' This same fanatical mode of thought would still show up in 2001, in an interview for the *A Beautiful World* fan site:

Q: *'What did you do at uni?'*
Chris: 'History.'
Q: *'Did you like it?'*
Chris: 'I did, yeah.'
Q: *'Would you be working in history if – '*
Chris: 'No. I went to university to join a band.'
Q: *'But you enjoyed the studying, or just enjoyed the lifestyle?'*
Chris: 'I enjoyed the search for a band. I was pretty blinkered. From about the age of twelve I thought, "Right!" (Rubbing his hands together) 'That's where I want to go!'
Q: *'Did your parents support that?'*
Chris: 'Uh, yeah. My dad says now that he was like, playing along with me thinking that I'd change my mind. But unknowingly, he was encouraging me. I think that he thought that if he encouraged me that I'd probably be put off it.'

Amazingly, Chris had found a core member of what would become Coldplay as soon as he arrived in London. As for Jonny, he realised the musical significance of their sessions at once. Although Jon can make the Mona Lisa look guilty of overwrought emotion, he would be moved to say, 'From the moment I met Chris, I really did think we could go all the way.' That wasn't the only remarkable fact. The unique advantage, the great dynamic, was that although as characters Chris and Jonny were absolute opposites, they were still capable of being soul mates at the same time. Vitally, though they were both intensely clever, when they started to play guitar, they achieved a genuinely powerful musical simplicity.

'He sat on his bed,' Martin remembers, 'and I sat on a chair and he had this riff, and I started playing the melody, and I thought, "Fuckin' hell. This is it!" It was the best thing I'd ever done.' Right away, the sum of their talents was obviously much greater than their individual parts. 'There was no Plan B. Meeting Jonny was like falling in love. He could make all the ideas work and we were writing two or three songs a night sometimes,' Chris told *Q* magazine.

And so they continued throughout the year. Chris was practically teetotal, non-smoking and drug-free. He conscientiously avoided McDonalds and junk food in general. He expended some of his boundless excess energy by playing hockey for the college team. Otherwise, he studied.

In those early days at UCL Chris also had an interest in Christianity, and was often seen hunched over the Bible in UCL's library. In one sense, the Bible was a primary source for his studies of the ancient world.

'I did use to be quite a strong Christian,' he says. 'Now I'm more just into the morals. A lot of Christians are really good to people and I think that's really brilliant . . . isn't it great just to be nice? I think it's really great just to be nice.'

In addition to his gawky air, anyone meeting Chris would be rivetted by his braces. 'From the age of twenty to 22, when you're supposed to be a virile young man, I was going through my fifteen-year-old brace-aches!' he would laugh, in a later *Daily Telegraph* interview. He'd had no success with women to date, and the braces narrowed his future chances considerably, although he did briefly date Phil Harvey's sister. Phil was now studying classics at Oxford, but the two friends had remained in touch after leaving Sherborne. Chris used to go and visit him there – even, on one occasion, picking up the guitar for a jam session in the Trinity student's bedroom.

Huddled together one night back in the UCL student bar, Chris and Jonny didn't notice they had already attracted an audience of one. Looking, as *Rolling Stone* would later comment, like a floppy-haired, younger Ralph Fiennes, Guy Berryman drunkenly accosted the duo.

Guy had a number of grounds for resentment. First, they had a band. Second, he was not in their band. Third, they were not inviting him to join their band. Finally, he wanted to be in their band. 'We couldn't really say no,' recalled Jonny. Guy was 'someone I got the wrong impression of when I first met him,' remembered Chris. 'He's not as scary as he looks.'

Guy Berryman was born in Fife, Scotland, before moving south, aged twelve, to live in Canterbury with his mother and engineer father. He had chosen a degree in engineering at UCL, but was discovering that he loathed it. But he was absolutely sure about his value to the band as a bassist. His musical education had begun with learning the recorder at age eight, and culminated in appearances with a school band called Time Out who performed seventies Genesis covers – 'We played terrible, terrible stuff,' Guy recalled. 'We would agonise for hours trying to work out horrible prog rock stuff with ridiculous solos. We never got anywhere near it.'

In the cold, sober light of day, Guy turned out to be softly spoken rather than darkly brooding, and he brought his enthusiasm for funk, soul and R&B into the band's mix of musical interests. In fact, on the *Coldplay Live 2003* DVD, if you look at Guy playing encased in a pool of deep indigo light, the cut of his shirt, his nipped waist, the lapels and shoulders, the wavy mop of hair, there is a hint of the soul boy about him.

Some years later, when the band was appearing on MTV Italy, Chris told an interviewer that they

had just been reminiscing about the early days. 'It was great because we were just sitting in a little room, just writing songs all the time. And then three years later we can play them all over the world.'

'We just kind of hacked out these songs,' Guy recalled. 'When I look back, we actually went through tons of songs before the ones we recorded as singles and put on our first album. It seemed to be working out extraordinarily well.'

'We were more than capable of producing shit,' Guy told *Q* in August 2002. 'But the longer we went on, you could tell Chris had the magic. I'd given up my engineering course because I hated it and started a degree in architecture. I gave that up as well.'

The Guardian newspaper, specifically inspired by Coldplay's success and the fact that they had been to UCL, recently published a league table for universities that produced successful bands. Under its scoring system, rockers who *failed* to complete their degrees actually earned a university additional points. UCL and Manchester tied at the league top with eight points. But by an oversight, the survey failed to award any extra points to UCL for Guy's dropping out of college – his heroic gesture should by rights have pushed UCL to the top of the league.

> **'We would agonise for hours trying to work out horrible prog rock stuff with ridiculous solos. We never got anywhere near it.'**
>
> – *Guy Berryman*

After quitting his course, Guy stayed in London to be near the band. 'We all had an idea that we had a chance of "doing it". So we pushed ourselves really hard, figuring we might as well give it a crack.' Chris was also wired up with conviction, but wanted to honour his father's wishes and see his degree through.

Pushing themselves hard meant that the trio had to acquire a suitable drummer to complete their line-up. But when they played an early demo to an experienced drummer they knew at college, he turned them down point blank. 'We played him "Don't Panic" and he said, "No." We just couldn't believe it,' remembered Guy. 'Even then there was a feeling of, "But what we're doing is great. Why wouldn't you want to be part of it?"' Perhaps he just didn't like the kind of music Coldplay made. But, since the song he heard was later to become the opener on Coldplay's multi-platinum debut album, it's quite possible he now has some regrets.

Meanwhile, oblivious to the workings of fate, a student named Will Champion from Southampton was greatly enjoying his anthropology course at UCL. 'Happy times,' he later commented. 'It's my socio-biology lecturer I remember best. He was always saying he had enough material to give a six-week lecture course on the masturbatory behaviour of gorillas.' Will had followed his older brother to UCL from their native Southampton – they are both born and bred Southampton FC fans, as was apparent from Will's noisy support of former Saints star Wayne Bridge during the 2002 World Cup.

Will had not been a model student in primary school. For his secondary education he ended up at a rather tough – even brutal – comprehensive. Will went to Cantrell School, which lay on a kind of uneasy peace line between the deprived and affluent areas of Southampton. Similarly, Will's adolescent experiences were by turns thuggish and conciliatory. On one hand, he attended a Christian youth group called the Goldfish Bowl in nearby Highfield, and played with their band. A recent article from a local paper stated, 'Many ex-pupils from Cantrell who were in the same year as Will have many fond memories of him.' On the other hand, Cantrell could be quite rough: one of Will's classmates was later imprisoned for kicking somebody to death.

He keeps his legs spread and plays from the hip: bassist Guy Berryman is the band's closet soul brother.

But Will has said that he found the experience of life he gained there invaluable, and that he would have been bored stupid at a private school.

Will's parents were archaeologists at Southampton University. While he dreamt of, and actually got, a student job as a steward at the illustrious Glastonbury Festival, his parents more likely dreamt of excavating the mysteries of the nearby Glastonbury Tor. Chris once quipped that Dr. Tim Champion was 'the Michael Jackson of archaeology' – although that's probably not an analogy he would coin so blithely these days. Will's mother, Sara, was an absolutely extraordinary person, whose strength will become clear later in the story.

Will's most cherished possession was the blue Telecaster guitar in his bedroom. 'It was a conscious decision to go to college to find people to play with,' he has said, echoing Chris. He chose UCL over somewhere grittier like Manchester University, known for its short-lived 'Madchester' music scene in the early nineties, because he really liked the place and already knew it quite well. His older brother was already there, specialising, like Chris, in ancient history.

Naturally gifted, Will could play a whole variety of instruments, even the tin whistle. His mother was similarly talented, and often sang with the Southampton Philharmonic Society. Will looks like a drummer – his lips have the tight line that drummers assume when their arms are pushing out a great crescendo. But the teenage Will viewed himself as a guitarist – the last thing in his mind was a career as a drummer. However, he did room with one, and when he heard his hockey team-mate Chris moaning on about his need for a drummer, Will set Chris and the others up for a meeting with his flatmate. This is another beat keeper who is doubtless now kicking himself because, although he set up his kit, he then went down the pub, leaving Will stranded and apologising to three frustrated musicians.

Picking up the sticks himself, Will suggested that he salvage the rehearsal by thumping out time on the kit. With that casual suggestion, Coldplay secured their final line-up: the line-up that would play the Hollywood Bowl, Red Rocks, Denver, and Madison Square Garden. Thus on 6 January 1998, Coldplay began rehearsing together and, from that moment on, their journey toward success was under way.

As it turned out, the band had found a versatile musical asset in Champion. 'Will's a human juke box,' Chris explained. 'Me and Will used to sit on the stairs at our halls of residence and he'd know more songs than anyone. You name it, he'd play it.' It was a versatility that encouraged the lads to hit the streets: 'Our first musical incarnation was probably Chris and me busking and getting moved on by the police,' Will told *Maxim Blender* later. 'We did "Bare Necessities" and "Norwegian Wood".' He was also musically generous enough to hand over his Telecaster for Jonny to play, and it was this guitar that Jonny would use on many classic Coldplay recordings.

Within the first week of joining, Will had another vitally useful idea, his initiative securing the band the first gig they ever played. He went along to Camden, twenty minutes' walk north of UCL. The area has long been the centre of the vibrant pub rock scene, but the alehouse Will visited was certainly not a significant venue – rather, it was a seedy dive.

The Laurel Tree in Bayham Street is tucked down the back road behind Camden High Street. In the good old days before it was refurbished, a guide to Camden's pubs described it as looking 'like the front room of a particularly run down squat, not the sort of place you would go for a quiet drink unless you were a deranged hippie. If you headed up the stairs you arrived at the stage area, which seemed okay until you thought about what would happen if there was a fire – and came to the conclusion that everyone would be fried until crispier than a kettle chip.' Will walked in, absorbed the dank ambience, and blagged the band a booking.

Like Chris and Guy, Will had some previous musical experience, albeit strumming along with a band called Fat Hamster. The nearest the talented Jonny Buckland had ever got to playing before this was when he rehearsed with a heavy metal band who bashed out a hideous cover of the

Will Champion's adolescent experiences were by turns thuggish and conciliatory – and his drumming has the same range.

Madness hit 'Night Boat To Cairo'.

It's a good picture of the band – heaving their guitar straps onto their shoulders with the weight of past mediocrity also resting there – and then – hey presto! A beautiful transformation is witnessed. Of the six-song set, two numbers, 'Don't Panic' and 'High Speed', went on to become classics.

Chris has tried to sum it all up: 'Before this band we were all in really dodgy school bands and none of us were ever going to get anywhere even though it was our ultimate dream. But when I met Jonny at university, it was just like, I don't know, India colliding with Asia, two huge continents coming together. And when Guy and Will came on board, it was like East and West joining us. Bang! And it always feels that way for us, every time we play.'

Within just three years, this same band would be a major force in the global music arena, with a triple platinum album under their belts and their subsequent follow up topping the 'Best of 2002' lists from critics and fans alike.

But at this point, all that seemed very, very far-off and unlikely, since they were now just a one-gig band named Starfish.

THREE

CHART VIRGINS AT
NUMBER NINETY-TWO

For Coldplay, the key virtue of being at university was that 'it gave us a shed-load of time to play music,' as Will put it. Likewise, 'I was never a great attender,' Jonny laughingly declared. 'We would rehearse most evenings and I'd always put the band first.' Any time was the right time for a rehearsal. Chris ploughed on with his degree in ancient world studies, eventually writing his dissertation on ancient musical instruments like the lyre and 'lots of things made out of tortoise shells'. However, the bulk of Chris's manic energy was focused on contemporary music. 'I was starting to get more of a musical education,' he recalled.

Late at night in their rooms, the four sat around listening to music as well as writing it. They eagerly pooled all their current influences, and recounted their past musical adventures – Chris gesticulating and vocalising maniacally, Jonny replying with his usual dead calm. In response to Chris, Jonny expressed his lifelong love for various guitar bands including the Stone Roses and the Smiths.

'The Smiths, man! The Smiths woke me up to music,' Chris later exclaimed during a *Guardian* interview. 'It was "William, It Was Really Nothing". Jonny introduced me to them. He doesn't play like Johnny Marr but there is something in common . . . melodies first.' As the college terms passed, Jonny also developed a great appreciation for George Harrison (whom he considers 'really underrated') and Booker T. and the MG's guitarist Steve Cropper. Another influence on Jonny was onetime Bowie guitarist Mick Ronson, whom he describes as 'a really good player and arranger'.

Responding to a fan questionnaire, Jonny has stated that the song he most wishes he'd written is Bob Dylan's 'Subterranean Homesick Blues' – not the most emotive or melodic song; quite different from other obvious Coldplay influences. In fact, it's implicitly political and, with a half-shouted narrative, it's really like a precursor to rap.

A few years later, Chris would be shamelessly telling mainstream journalists that, back at college, he'd owned Sting's *Ten Summoner's Tales* (and facing the consequences in print). The antithesis of Sting's voice was that of Leonard Cohen – whom Chris was also listening to – and whose lyrics were romantically melancholic and wryly witty. But the performer who completely bowled Chris over was the late Jeff Buckley. Buckley's vivid and emotional voice, swooping up to falsetto and down to rust, captivated Chris until his own voice broke out into a kind of hero-worship of the singer.

Like a virgin: the ascetic Chris back in February 2000.

During their rehearsals on the stairwells at UCL, the band paid tribute to their influences, also adding elements of weird Celtic folksongs that Will Champion contributed from his strange repertoire.

Considering that Jonny had designed many imaginary album covers and dreamed up countless exotic band names, it was ironic that the name of the group was almost an afterthought. A choice wouldn't be made until well after the band had played their first gig.

After seriously considering but eventually dropping the ghastly Stepney Green, they finally settled on the Coldplay (later dropping the definite article). This was in fact a band name that had just been discarded by Tim Crompton, a fellow UCL student and musician, who found it in an anthology entitled *Child's Reflections, Cold Play* by the American poet Philip Horky. Crompton abandoned the name on the grounds that it was too depressing, later settling on the Bettina Motive for his band – who would go on to support Coldplay, Snow Patrol and The Coral. On the subject of Coldplay's name, *Select's* Ray Wilkinson later observed, 'Coldplay are a band so devoid of rock polemic they couldn't even be bothered to think up a name . . . To an almost transcendental extent, this is clearly a band with no extra-musical agenda whatsoever.'

Whatever first impression the name creates, there is no doubt that the band's musical creations and euphoric performances have rewritten its associations for a world-wide audience. The name Coldplay now conveys music that's doleful yet optimistic, sensitive, melodic and passionate, music powerful enough to fill a freezing void. Yet the band's name remains an appropriate and memorable paradox, and a strong existential statement. Many of Coldplay's early songs were written as the expression of a brittle soul contesting with a cold universe.

Eventually Chris and Jonny would move out of the fresher's ghetto of Ramsey Hall. UCL had a hall of residence at 199 Camden Road – right around the corner from Camden Town underground station. Jonny and Chris duly relocated, placing themselves in closer proximity to the local pub-rock scene. Camden is also close to the wealthy areas of Primrose Hill and Belsize Park, where a cabal of *nouveau riche* rockers had followed Oasis by buying flats and houses, including Finley Quaye and Dougie Payne of Travis.

Several months after the band's first gig at The Laurel Tree in early 1998, and after a few subsequent gigs on the outer reaches of the pub-rock circuit, the band happened to fall into a dispute with a Camden promoter. For every up-and-coming band, there's always a first occasion to be shafted. As Jonny Buckland told *Guitarist* magazine, 'We wanted to do a gig at Dingwalls in Camden and we had arranged it so we were headlining and a couple of mates' bands were also playing on the bill. Then, about two weeks before the gig, the promoter turned around and said, "Actually, there are eight bands playing, you're fifth on the bill, you've got a fifteen minute set and you don't get any money, just 10p from each flyer."'

The band turned to Chris's old school friend Phil Harvey for help. Phil was currently 'boring himself stupid studying Latin and Greek' at Trinity College, Oxford. A fresh-faced, cobble-cheeked, presentable guy, combining a flippant rhythm of speech with absolute sincerity, Phil worked a couple of nights a week in Oxford nightclubs, setting up and promoting student nights. Not that he was part of the 'Ents and Events' career path that some Oxford students calculatedly choose, where booking big acts to play at May Balls or inviting the politically powerful to speak at the Oxford Union create useful contacts for after-college life. Instead, Phil's work at the clubs 'was pretty basic stuff but it at least gave me a vague idea of what it is to hire a venue, book a band or DJ and try and make a little money,' as he told an interviewer for the *Coldplay e-zine*.

'Chris was telling me about how one of the local Camden promoters had a bit of a vice-like grip on the band and wasn't coughing up any money, so I suggested the band put on their own event.' Consequently, Phil phoned up the promoter to say the band wouldn't be playing. Then he hired out the same venue for the following night, using money he'd borrowed from 'investors'

– in other words, his father and his Oxford roommate. 'Thankfully we made it all back,' Jonny recalled. The band printed up thousands of flyers. 'I think in the end we got about 400 people in there,' Phil remembers, 'which, considering the band had only played three or four prior gigs, was a big deal.'

After this success, Phil officially became the band's manager. To the dismay of his Oxford tutor, he ended up abandoning his degree to work full time on breaking the group. 'Received wisdom would suggest that going into business with your best friend from childhood is a bad idea,' he told the *Coldplay e-zine*. 'I'm sure a couple of times near the beginning I theorised that it wasn't such a great idea.' The reality was that it worked fine. Just as they had somehow found, close at hand, the line-up that provided perfect musical affinity and personal compatibility, Coldplay had also found a manager with flair, high intelligence, the requisite cheek and absolute integrity. On their behalf, he could 'talk the good talk' and mean it, too.

Shortly after the Dingwalls success, Phil paid out £1,500 for Coldplay to make their very first recording at a small studio called Sync City, in Tottenham, north London. Over the years, the studio had counted acts as diverse as Bernard Butler, Shane McGowan and the Popes and the Bay City Rollers among its clientele. It was auspicious for Jonny that his first ever studio recording session meant a return to his family's parochial roots.

> **'[Coldplay] started up playing, and that was the highest I'd sat up in my seat in the six years that I'd been recording. The sound, first of all. Jonny's guitar sound, the songs, and then when Chris put his vocals down last of all that really was the icing on the cake.'**
>
> *– Nikki Rosetti of Sync City recording studios*

Nikki Rosetti engineered the sessions and was also credited as co-producer on all tracks on the subsequent *Safety* EP. She told me, 'They just came in like any other band, we didn't know anything about them. They hadn't been together that long, and they were called Starfish then.' It was actually during these sessions, Nikki claims, that the band changed their name to Coldplay. 'The first time you hear that name you think, *what?* And I said, ooh, don't like it, don't like it. They obviously did like it, though.

'I went through the motions of miking them up and getting things set up as you do. They certainly knew their own equipment, of which they had a fair range. Jonny had his guitar effects that he liked to use, they had various keyboards, including one old synth they'd found in a skip with the keys sticking up in the air: I think it may have been used on "Such A Rush" – at the end of the track there's a long synth sound.

'Then they started up playing, and that was the highest I'd sat up in my seat in the six years that I'd been recording.' Identifying the qualities that caught her attention so dramatically, Nikki recalled, 'The sound, first of all. Jonny's guitar sound, the songs – very much the songs – and then when Chris put his vocals down last of all that really was the icing on the cake.'

'It was really exciting,' Chris remembered. 'The first song we did – "Bigger Stronger" – just came out magic. We didn't quite know what had happened. It was only on an eight-track but it was wicked.' He later told *Time* magazine's Benjamin Nugent that 'Bigger Stronger' was something of a Radiohead copy, adding that he didn't have any problem with comparisons. 'We're both middle class, we're both interested in writing passionate songs.' Among the seven other tracks recorded at this session were 'Ode To Deodorant', 'Such A Rush', and 'No More Keeping My Feet On The Ground'.

'The second session they did was on sixteen-track,' Nikki Rosetti explained. They re-recorded 'Ode to Deodorant' and 'Brothers And Sisters', which introduced Jon's trademark ringing guitars and Chris's gentle voice. The equipment they recorded on is all still there. 'The desk we used was Alen and Heath CMC24 for both sessions. They were recorded onto digital machines, Fostex, and there was a fight between myself and Chris to control the amount of reverb they put on,' recalls Nikki. 'He wanted loads of reverb on everything and I had to keep sneaking it back off again.'

> ## 'Chris definitely always appeared as if he was on something, but obviously he wasn't. He was just a bit nervous.' –
>
> *Nikki Rosetti of Sync City recording Studios*

From his very first recording session, Chris's excitable and apologetic traits were evident. 'Chris definitely always appeared as if he was on something, but obviously he wasn't. He was just naturally a bit nervous. We'd do re-takes and the bits he wasn't happy with, he'd stop singing. And every time he stopped he'd say, "Sorry Nikki, Sorry Nikki," and it so annoyed me that after about a day of this I took him aside and told him to stop saying that.'

Irrespective of Chris's quirks, Nikki soon realised that Coldplay were unique in other ways. 'Every other band I've recorded, most of them may have talented musicians and write competent, professional, even catchy songs. Then there's always just that one thing missing that makes them, you know, great. But with Coldplay it's this feeling that they have in them, in their songs. The feeling that they're all talented to their roots. When they needed to put down a keyboard part any of them could play it, and they would all have a go, they would all try something out, they were all very talented musically. Anybody can play the guitar and write a pop song, but they won't necessarily understand the nuances of music, which is a quality that Coldplay do convey in their song writing.

'For instance, Jonny Buckland comes up with these just amazing little phrases, that's another part of what makes their sound. He just phrases wonderful guitar parts, beautiful stuff. So many guitarists just go one two three four; bash, bash, bash. His parts were thought-out, intelligent, they were there for a reason.'

Nikki wasn't the only person to be tremendously excited – Phil Harvey was absolutely blown away by the way the songs transferred onto tape. 'I remember very distinctly getting back from the *Safety* EP recording session on a Sunday evening and sitting with Chris and Jonny in their Camden Road flat listening to the unmixed music. The last track, "Such A Rush", ended and I turned to them and said something ridiculous like "I could go into any record company in London with this tape and get us whatever we wanted,"' he told the *Coldplay e-zine*. 'I hardly knew what a record company was . . . I was 100% into the music, which was enough for me to stumble through.'

However, Nikki did try to advise the band against using Phil as a manager. 'I said, "Does he have any experience?" They said, "No." I said, "Does he have any contacts?" They said, "No." So obviously I said it wasn't the wisest move in the world – but as it turned out, he's done a first class job for them.'

It seems that Phil turned out to be the innocent who knew it all. But how did he do so well with no management experience, in an industry so cutthroat? Phil explains, 'I think I've been very fortunate in that, for one reason and another, my complete and utter lack of experience has never been a problem. Without wishing to sound glib, experience can only count for so much. Infinitely more important is having enthusiasm and good people around you to give advice. Even more infinitely important is having an amazing band.'

In April 1998 Phil had the recordings from the Sync City session pressed up, and the band issued their first record. Entitled the *Safety* EP, it contained three tracks, 'Bigger Stronger', 'No More Keeping My Feet On The Ground' and 'Such A Rush'.

However, according to Nikki Rosetti, the Sync City recording session was a much more extensive affair, consisting of eight tracks in total. 'I'm the only one who has a copy of the other five tracks, not even Coldplay have a copy. They're in a safe. In my opinion they're the best Coldplay songs because they're the original Coldplay that I like. It's a lot more raw than it is these days where they have Jonny's guitar way down in the mix and Chris's voice up loud. There are a lot of tracks there that are very much in the mould of songs like "Such A Rush" that they did at the time. They later did a song on one of their albums that is based on another earlier song that I have a recording of. And there's a really nice song called "Vitamins", which is just Chris on his own with an acoustic guitar.'

From the very beginning, the band set out one of their key creative practices – that of ruthlessly discarding songs in the quest for the most effective melody, and choosing to create one killer rather than six fillers. Much later on, it was only Phil Harvey's insistence that they reconsider recording 'Clocks' for the second album that saved the now classic track from oblivion.

The *Safety* EP's title comes from the striking cover photograph chosen for the CD. It was taken by a friend of the band, Jon Hilton, who had been to secondary school in Wales with Jonny, and later shared a house in Camden with him. Jon managed to catch Chris's moving head in a long-exposure shot, right in front of the illuminated Safety Door sign at one of the band's first London gigs. It looks like a snapshot taken by a psychic research team on haunted premises.

As a collector's item, the record itself is now almost supernaturally rare.

'We did try to flog them round the University,' Will told *jackwills.com*. 'They only cost a fiver, and half are probably in the bin.' Heidi, a former UCL student who later became a member of Will's pub quiz team, turned down the chance to buy one from him at the time – 'Gutted I didn't buy one now,' she admits. The pressing was limited to 500 copies: occasional copies are now auctioned for anything up to £150 a time on Ebay.

Since the band didn't have any distribution deal for the EP, it was instead sent out, in time-honoured style, to record companies, radio stations, music publishers and journalists. As an absolute priority the band sent out a copy to DJ Steve Lamacq of BBC Radio One, whose popular *Evening Session* show played a vital role at that time in showcasing the talent of emerging British bands. Unfortunately, Coldplay's EP lay buried under the huge pile of submissions that Lamacq was gradually working his way through, and he never managed to get to it – something that Chris Martin later teased him about on the air.

In the midst of this promotional activity, the quartet continued to write and rehearse new material. According to Chris's own recollection, it was during this period that 'Shiver' was written. The song is an early monument to his teenage failures in love, but as Chris remembers it, the track was first and foremost a tribute to the most powerful musical influence on him at that time. 'That song is a direct nod to Jeff Buckley,' he told *A Beautiful World*. 'I certainly was listening to nothing but Jeff Buckley when we wrote that song.'

The *Safety* EP was a useful tool in securing some gigs for the band. However, some of these were typically rough and ready affairs. At this stage, Phil Harvey's duties 'involved me booking a couple of taxis to take the equipment from the Camden Road flat to the venue; buying batteries for Jonny's pedals; going around the pub greeting all our fans by name; desperately looking for

music industry types; arguing with the promoter over £10.'

Memorably uneasy gigs ensued. On one occasion the band played an end of term ball at Wye Farming College in Kent, backing Echo and the Bunnymen-influenced indie rockers Space. 'We were supposed to be on first before Space but there were all these problems with the fire regulations,' Jonny told *Guitarist* magazine. 'In the end Space went on first at around eleven o'clock, and then some other band and then another, and by this time it was three in the morning. When we started playing everyone was either asleep or staggering around. There were about two people watching and this man kept walking on the stage and dancing in a very bizarre way.'

> 'We were first on in a tiny little café, the lowest of the low, and we had a really arsey soundman who just wanted to go for a beer. We were like, we want to have a good sound. And he was like, "hurry up, I want a beer."' *– Jonny Buckland*

An initially more attractive idea was to perform as part of the big Manchester showcase for unsigned bands: In The City – which was billed, in a victory for over-confidence, as 'the urban Glastonbury'. The experience began disastrously when, upon their arrival, Jonny discovered with dismay that he'd left all his effects pedals down at Chris's house in Devon. Phil once again came to the rescue by finding a bizarre but workable solution – somehow, he managed to locate a long-distance lorry driver travelling up from Devon, who dropped off the pedals in Darlington. 'Phil had to drive there to pick them up the morning of the gig,' recalled Jonny. Their problems continued when they saw the venue. 'We were first on in a tiny little café, the lowest of the low, and we had a really arsey soundman who just wanted to go for a beer. We were like, we want to have a good sound. And he was like, "hurry up, I want a beer." That night I completely forgot the first part of the first song and it was downhill from then on.'

As well as getting the band some low-key gigs, *Safety* was working quite well as a break-through vehicle. Debs Wild, who was then an A&R scout for Universal Records, had come across the record and was at once tremendously enthusiastic about it. 'I was the first A&R person who wanted to sign Coldplay. Unfortunately the decision went out of my hands, but I introduced them to their eventual publishers and lawyer,' she told *musicjournal.org*. Crucially, Debs passed a copy of the EP onto A&R man Dan Keeling, who had recently begun working for Parlophone Records, part of the EMI group, with a roster that included Blur and Radiohead. She also alerted Caroline Ellery of BMG Music Publishing, whose job it was to sign up new bands.

Oblivious to these developments, Coldplay were now appearing at a multitude of central London gigs in creaky settings, vaguely-themed bars and pub back rooms. 'We also played at a few of the UCL venues like the Windeyer off Tottenham Court Road, and gigs in Camden where a lot of people from UCL saw us,' Will recalled. Besides being a source of support, UCL was now also exacting heavy demands – the lads were in their final year, and soon the sweaty cramming for their finals would begin. Jonny's parents were expecting him to work hard: 'Of course, when they're away you never know what they are doing,' commented Joy Buckland to the *Flintshire Evening Leader*, 'but we were confident he'd never compromise his studies.'

Just before Christmas 1998, Dan Keeling went along to Cairo Jack's on Beak Street, Soho, another venue just half a mile from UCL. Hearing Coldplay's music in a pub sketchily got up to

As Jonny Buckland once put it, 'We are trying to be who we are.

resemble a Middle Eastern carpetbagger's lair was perhaps not the best of introductions, though. 'I wasn't really that enamoured,' Keeling recalled. 'I thought Chris had something. But the sound wasn't there.'

Although Keeling was unconvinced, Coldplay made a positive impression upon Fierce Panda Records co-founder Simon Williams. He caught the band at Camden's Falcon pub.

The Falcon was where Blur had performed when still known as Seymour, where Travis, Suede and PJ Harvey had all gigged before making it big. It was a venue that was once described in *Select* as 'seemingly held together only by the staples affixing flyers to the walls'. Here, Phil Harvey had no need to search the room desperately for music business types. A&R men from record companies haunted The Falcon regularly, all trying for first grab at the new talent.

Williams was an energetic *NME* journalist, well known for integrity, style and panache, who had been running Fierce Panda part-time from his front room. 'The whole reason for setting up Fierce Panda in the first place was to release the *Shagging In The Streets* EP as a tribute to the New Wave of New Wave scene,' Williams told *TrakMarx.com*. 'If I'd had any idea that we'd still be bunging out records nearly a decade on, I wouldn't have called the label something as stupid as Fierce sodding Panda.'

A fiercely independent supporter and nurturer of the late nineties UK indie scene, Williams also had some clout with the mainstream industry. After seeing Coldplay perform, he immediately committed to them. Of all the breaks they were to have, this would be the most pivotal to their fortunes. Fierce Panda's method of signing bands then was spontaneously rapid, totally opposite to the usual record company caution. 'At one point . . . we were getting a good demo, phoning up the band responsible and offering a single deal on the spot,' recounted Williams. The deal he offered Coldplay was a standard one-off, for a single to be recorded and released after Christmas.

> **'We stand there aghast with our jaws hitting the floor as Coldplay play to 40 people. I was speechless. You see groups who you think might be good in three months, or six months, or even a year, but Coldplay were the finished article.'** – *Steve Lamacq, BBC Radio One DJ*

Simon Williams quickly became an even bigger catalyst for Coldplay's fortunes. A close friend of Steve Lamacq, Williams urged the DJ to go and see his new band. Having convinced his friend Mark to make the trek to see a group that neither of them knew anything about, Lamacq stood in the back room at the Camden Falcon as Coldplay came on: 'And honestly, and this doesn't happen very often, but honestly we stand there aghast with our jaws hitting the floor as Coldplay play to 40 people,' he told the *Coldplay e-zine*. 'Finally Mark says, "Excuse me if I'm wrong, but are they the best thing I've seen in months . . ." I was speechless. You see groups who you think might be good in three months, or six months, or even a year, but Coldplay were the finished article.'

Steve went back into Radio One and started a campaign to get Coldplay on the air. He eventually found the *Safety* EP amongst the mountains of submissions. 'I still don't think I would have been as excited about the band though if I hadn't of seen them live, because it was their composure and humour and general stage presence that helped make them what they were at the start,' he explained. To some of Chris's fellow students, who were used to listening patiently while he obsessed over Coldplay in the ULU bar, this sudden turn of events was a real surprise. 'It was only when he said his demo was going to be played on Radio One that anyone thought his band might

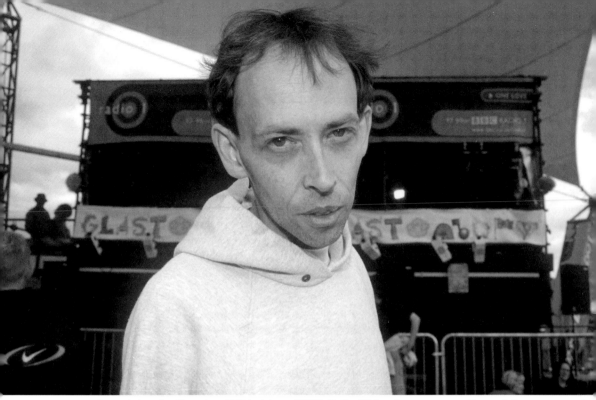

Ignore the imposing Glastonbury 2000 backdrop – BBC Radio One DJ Steve Lamacq was arguably more influential in Coldplay's early success.

actually be good,' an unnamed classmate told *Bang*.

Williams also named the band as one of his tips for success in the 2 January 1999 edition of *NME*. Coldplay were listed sixth among twenty bands, other notables including Bellatrix and Gay Dad. Williams wrote, 'Mesmerising foursome in the big-hearted Jeff Buckley mould. Already masters of both the epic chorus and the insular weep-out, they are blessed with many fine virtues, notably the fact that their singer actually demonstrates a sense of humour onstage. "Bigger Stronger" was their no-key debut release last year on their own label. Expect copies of it to be worth a couple of heavy mortgages come near Christmas.'

Following such high-profile praise, throughout early 1999 the band played a number of gigs on the pub circuit – in particular at The Bull and Gate in Kentish Town, an established pub showcase where Nirvana once played. 'From that moment on you couldn't move at our gigs for record company A&R men. The power of the press,' Phil marvelled.

Steve Lamacq also came good on his promise of coverage, first of all with a live session for *Lamacq Live* on BBC Radio One, which he emphasised 'was the first time we'd ever had an unsigned band on that show.' After that, Coldplay recorded a set for the *Evening Session*, which Lamacq described as 'a chilling first set. A real spine-tingler.'

Then, in February, at Station Studios, the band recorded 'Brothers And Sisters' with co-producer Mike Beever. Backed with 'Easy To Please' and 'Only Superstition', the three songs were completed in just four days. These tracks were mastered at Abbey Road, the studio immortalised by the Beatles album of the same name. Fierce Panda pressed 2,500 copies for release on 26 April 1999 – just shortly before Chris, Will and Jonny screwed their heads into the books for final exams at UCL.

Lamacq pushed Coldplay on the air as a band to watch for, playing 'Brothers And Sisters' in heavy rotation on the *Evening Session*. The EP even took them into the British charts for the first time – albeit to the dizzy heights of Number 92. It was an exciting first for the band in an era where everything was new – such as Chris giving his first ever interview, to a college newspaper. 'I was so excited I ended up snogging the interviewer', he later told the *Guardian*.

The interviewer, Emma Holland, was a young student journalist from Oxford with whom Chris subsequently had a brief flirtation. After the interview, she and Chris had kissed a little. A few days later he came to her dorm room and, as she lay pretending to be asleep, smoothed her hair before tiptoeing out. However, a full-blown relationship failed to materialise. Chris often claimed his romances crash because he, in his own words, 'behaves like a twat'.

It seemed that Coldplay had the happy knack of arriving on the music scene in the right place and at the right time. 'The difference between many raw unsigned bands and bands like Coldplay is very small,' Will later commented. 'Much of it comes down to luck. We were lucky that the right people heard us when they did. It could have happened differently.' But Lamacq disagrees, having viewed their rise from the backrooms of pubs, and through myriad letters received from his listeners. 'I think Coldplay were still a little out of time when they started getting noticed. I mean various A&R types passed on them because they couldn't see where the band fitted in . . . and when we started playing the record there was some dissent from listeners who really didn't get it at all.'

> **'The difference between many raw unsigned bands and bands like Coldplay is very small. Much of it comes down to luck. We were lucky that the right people heard us when they did.'** *– Will Champion*

However, the music press got it first time, and the band scored a warm review in *Melody Maker* in mid-April, where that week's reviewer, TV presenter Jayne Middlemiss, called the record 'Really Rather Ace, actually. Albeit in a Radiohead-with-Jeff-Buckley-on-vocals "bloody good music" type of way . . . Usually, I prefer things to be a little bit harder than that,' burbled Middlemiss, 'but it was interesting. I can see why all the A & R men are chasing them, I can imagine them being huge. Is the singer good-looking?'

After a Fierce Panda showcase on 31 March at the Bull and Gate, the band were described by *NME*'s Siobhan Grogan as 'currently the focus of an A&R frenzy'. In addition to reporting that Coldplay were preparing for their Oxford finals, Grogan was immediately struck by Chris's vocals. 'Beneath Chris's cheeky exterior . . . is a voice somewhere between Thom Yorke's most angelic moments and Jeff Buckley's most gorgeous inflections. It's the focus for both wonderful wisps of uplifting folk like Shiver and the more grandiose epic tracks played tonight. Current Panda single "Brothers And Sisters" is the most impressive of the latter . . . Judging by the record company pack assembled here tonight . . . Coldplay have few worries about a future beyond the exams.'

The idea that a number of labels were interested in the band proved a valuable promotional tool for Phil, in that journalists could report the rivalry and increase the buzz about Coldplay. As for any bidding war, 'We didn't have much to do with it; we were all still in college, so our manager sorted it all out. We just played the gigs,' Chris recalls. 'And to be honest, you can't see anything from the stage, so we could have been playing to a bunch of butchers or a bunch of A&R men.'

The offer that Coldplay ultimately accepted was from Dan Keeling at Parlophone, the very same A&R man who had been nonplussed by their Cairo Jack's gig. It was 'Brothers And Sisters' that finally convinced Keeling to make his move. 'It just overwhelmed me. I wanted to stay cool but I could only hold off calling until Saturday morning.' The record came out at the end of April – in May, finals started. Subsequently, when Keeling requested a meeting, Phil jumped at the opportunity, but Chris couldn't go along because he was in an exam hall.

Chris's single-mindedness, so important to the band's future success, also secured him a first-class pass. Will and Jonny also did extremely well, gaining higher seconds in anthropology and maths with astronomy respectively. Professor Danny Miller, head of the Anthropology department at UCL, formulated the following anthropological law: 'We shouldn't be surprised in the band stating they never really did much work at uni. Frankly, appearing to have done pretty well, while disclaiming any suggestion that you worked hard in order to get the result, has always been one kind of cool.'

But now it was time for Coldplay to put academia behind them. What had been a necessary stage in their lives was now a closed chapter. The students' digs they lived in were now just their London digs. They were a band with a publishing deal to sign, with BMG Music Publishing – which they did in a rowboat on the Serpentine in Hyde Park, with Chris claiming, fisherman's tale fashion, 'we only had enough money for fifteen minutes on the boat so we had to do it sharpish.' Most important of all, they had a record contract with EMI to sign – which they did in the middle of Trafalgar Square.

The euphoric adrenalin that had powered the band through the ordeal of exams was now focused on new, exciting goals. One was the chance to play in the New Bands tent at the upcoming Glastonbury Festival – the most hyped British festival of the year. They also now had the chance to go into a studio and start building up tracks for their first album.

FOUR

DON'T PANIC

With the adrenalin rush provided by signing their recording and publishing contracts fading, post-exam exhaustion set in. Daily, Coldplay would struggle down to Orinoco Studios at the Elephant and Castle, south London. 'That was a really depressing time,' recalled Jonny in an interview with *Guitarist* magazine. 'It was boiling hot that summer, the trains were screwed, and it was taking an hour and a half to get to the studio. We were so excited, and it started off well, but by the end we were tearing our hair out, getting nothing achieved.' Chris concurred, 'I think signing for a major label, you get a bit overwhelmed at first. There's a lot of stuff you have to think about that you never had to think about before.'

These transport problems amplified what was already a period of transitional uncertainty for the band. For Chris, Jon and Will, reminders of the old college life still dogged them; forwarded requests to return library books, bushels of lecture notes still to be binned. However, they now had to focus on the tasks before them – recording their first major label EP and producing new material for their debut album.

For the first time, the band were experiencing difficulties in harmonising their musical vision, a situation compounded by their professional inexperience and the pressure to produce that accompanies the advance cheque. Specific problems arose from their inexperience of *being produced*, rather than co-producing, and in this case the production desk was manned by Beta Band producer Chris Allison.

Speaking to *Guitarist*'s Phil Ascot, Jonny described the situation with his usual economy. 'We had a producer who was pulling us in a certain direction and we were kind of pulling against it. Half pulling against it and half going, "Well at least he's got a sound!"'

Looking back on the sessions, Allison remembers, 'I met Coldplay with their A&R man Dan Keeling, with the whole band present. The one thing they really said that they wanted was someone to come in and give the band a bit of a direction sound wise. Both the band and the A&R department – both parties wanted that.

'They knew my background in producing pretty forward-looking artists . . . the Beta Band is one of the most experimental bands the UK has ever come up with. One of the first albums I ever produced was the *George Best* album by the Wedding Present. So I was known in the industry for working with artists who were trying to do something different. I had seen the band play live and I saw it as a case of capturing their fairly classic sound while adding some new instruments. This

Coldplay in June 2000. Bemused by the narrow street that is success, and the endless touring and promotional work that comes with it.

is what was discussed with the band and that was what was agreed from the outset.'

Things got off to a productive start. The first track Chris and Coldplay worked on was 'High Speed', which ultimately proved good enough to make it onto the first album. Allison describes it thus: 'You'll notice it is quite a bit different to other tracks, because there are other sounds going on in it: we wanted to mix a soundscape in with the classic rock sound on that particular track. To give it a slightly different perspective I guess, with the full willingness and understanding of the band. I thought "High Speed" was a really good marriage between the classic rock sound and the new sound that was developing out of it, something that was more atmospheric.

'The record company came down and really loved it: Dan Keeling came down, Miles Leonard, the Head of A&R, came down. So the label were happy with the way things were going and we were allowed to carry on. They asked me to carry on working on more tracks, which is what we went and did.'

In creative terms, Chris Allison was pretty much his own liaison man with Parlophone. The person fulfilling that role for Coldplay was Phil Harvey. After signing to a major label, Phil's job changed as drastically as the band's. Up until now, his whole *raison d'etre* had been to bag a record deal, while using any cash from one gig to finance the gap until the next. His every move had been calculated to convey the group's allure to music corporations as a desirable package.

Now that Coldplay were Parlophone's investment, Phil found he was playing a completely different game – that of *continuing* to ensure that the record company was hopeful about the band's prospects. As with all major record companies EMI/Parlophone were not simply placing faith in the band's musical abilities, but in their capability of transforming their talent into hard cash.

After signing for a major label, the role of any band is transformed – they become a gambling chip in the hands of a hierarchy of personnel: the group makes those employees look good; it makes them look like achievers; it means that those employees can demand a flow of cash from company coffers for their protégés, which in turn demonstrates their own power within the company. Or else the band may simply retain their services for another six months. From the bipolar perspective of the record company, the band are initially the best thing that's ever happened but if they then don't 'happen' fast enough, they're rapidly dumped.

An effective liaison between the band and the company is absolutely crucial. And Phil was only a 22-year-old dropout. The manager is fundamental to how the band's potential is perceived by the company, down to the manner in which he returns minor paperwork and requests money for additional expenses. This investment means that they must justify the expenses to the next tier of management, and provides an even stronger motive to work hard to break the band and prove all the expense was worth it. But if the company invests at too great a rate early on, their enthusiasm may be worn out before the band actually breaks, and may then opt to cut their losses.

A constant hard sell from a manager therefore requires a lot of skill, and even then it generally does not work. For a manager, every decision is hair-raising – there are a thousand tactical mistakes a band can make at the early stage. So if, as Parlophone's Miles Leonard did, the Head of A&R visits the studio and pronounces himself pleased with the producer's role in the recording, it's a very positive and important step in the dynamic between band and company.

But despite this cause for optimism, Coldplay were beginning to feel some unease regarding their collaboration with Chris Allison. There is a fine line between a producer adding something unique that the band feels will amplify their natural qualities and adding something alien to the group's music. The history of rock 'n' roll is littered with examples of a producer's distortion of a young group's musical identity. This conflict is often intensified by technical inexperience and the Lucifer-like pride that any good new band possesses in abundance.

Coldplay were used to being told by the likes of Steve Lamacq that they had a great, energetic live sound. They were all musically gifted, particularly Will, who had a natural aptitude that enabled him to pick up a variety of instruments. But now, away from the spontaneity and passion of their live gigs, in the strip-light sterility of Orinoco Studios, Will's lack of experience showed up startlingly.

'A problem with the drums is a very real problem if you're trying to get a live sound,' Chris Allison emphasised. 'You need the drummer to be able to play all the way through the song rather than your editing it all together in a computer where it starts to sound chopped-up.'

An inexperienced drummer in this situation can be likened to a trainee jockey asked to race in the Grand National. Horseracing is essentially kicking, kicking, kicking your mount forward as hard as you can, never able to rest for one beat or you'll lose. Will was subjected to the same kind of exertion in the studio. In the words of a song, 'He was scared, he was tired and underprepared.' Such stresses were absolutely nothing, however, to those he was experiencing domestically. For his mother, Sara, had been diagnosed with cancer, and was losing her valiant struggle to overcome the disease.

'I spent quite a bit of time with Will,' recalls Allison, 'but I still found that I had to start chopping up on the drums to try and make the track stay in time. So after we started off so well, the work process was really slowing down.'

> **'I think signing for a major label, you get a bit overwhelmed at first. There's a lot of stuff you have to think about that you never had to think about before.'** – *Chris Martin*

The pressure of the situation affected Chris to an extreme degree. Most people, including Will, Guy and Jonny, can choose to have three or four beers at the end of the night to wind them down. Chris Martin is different: he chooses not to drink, nor wind down, even at the end of days dominated by the most gruelling schedule.

Fate had presented Chris with the opportunity he had always dreamed of. Now it was up to him to make it happen. The danger was that this long-held dream would not be realised. That Chris and Coldplay were not up to the challenge. Given the frontman's inner state, one of the most exhausting things for Chris Allison was coping with his anxious personality, and harnessing his currently hysterical talent. Allison, who had won a reputation for coaxing the best from difficult artistic temperaments, says that he had never encountered the like before:

'Chris was extremely dynamic, like "Let's do this, let's do this, everything is going to go down this route *right now!*" And everyone would sort of have to jump to it. The idea I got about the other members of the band was that they were being sort of pulled along by Chris. Pulled along by the passion, the extraordinary energy that he had towards everything. It seemed to me that he had created this whole entity that was Coldplay, from the songs, to his lyrics, to the image he was going to project, with the fact that they had all seemingly been mates at school.'

Much of this dynamism, Allison felt, was extremely positive. 'I love this side of Chris, that he has a raw determination, and vision, and commitment. He would say, over and over again, "Come on guys, we could be the biggest band in the world, we're going to be fantastic, we're going to do the most amazing music, we can do it, we've been given this opportunity and we can't mess it up." So on that level, he had a tremendous amount of commitment. He lived and breathed it 24 hours a day, seven days a week – way more so than the other members of the band.

'But then we got the very odd sort of behaviour where he would ask me what on earth he was doing here, over and over again,' Allison revealed. 'Chris was very paranoiac about his vocals. He

kept repeating, "Chris, Chris, my vocals are shite, what am I doing here?" I'd put a lot of sincere effort into reassuring him, but fifteen minutes afterwards he'd be coming back again saying, "Chris, Chris, no really, my vocals are crap, I don't know what I'm doing here." This was a kind of enormously contradictory behaviour that I'd never, ever come across before. Whatever you said to him, it was impossible to make him feel any different on a permanent basis.' Chris's change of mood was some kind of strange process unaffected by external support.

'Chris would be very on the edge and finally Jonny would tell him to shut up – but it would take a long while before Jonny would be that direct. That would be the timing of it. And Chris would ask Jonny's opinion a lot: what he thought about this, what he thought about that.'

The experience left a vivid impression on Allison. 'I liked Chris Martin; we seemed to get on very well. He was a very warm, very inclusive sort of person which, again, was unusual to come across – we had a lot of interesting conversations.'

As producer, Allison was being asked to play a number of different roles: to be a father figure, friend and industry ally, musical innovator, and deliverer of product. But somehow in the midst of all this complex interplay, the recording sessions continued and results were achieved. 'Some tracks were completed okay, and others we were having to leave because of problems with drums. But still there was that commitment from the record company, that the band should definitely continue working at it. The experience was just seen by the band and by the record label as them learning, because they were very, very green.'

Chris Allison was not, as he remembers it, aware of the dynamic within the band where Chris Martin was showering a tremendous amount of negative criticism on his bandmates. Unfortunately, it was Will that often bore the brunt of Chris's anxious fervour to get things right, 'He'd be out of time once and I'd be telling him he was shit,' the vocalist later told *Q*.

Given that Chris is usually the anxious type that sidles up to you an hour after you've bought him dinner saying, 'I hope you're not pissed off with me for having a Coke *as well* as a pudding,' this sudden outpouring of negativity came as a terrible shock to the rest of the band. It was what Guy described as 'a horrible time I could never go through again.' Chris has long since taken all the blame for this unfortunate, short-lived phase: 'I was so nervous about our fucking up our chance I'd become obsessed with whether we were a technically good band or not.'

But at the time, Will was hardly in any condition to cope with Chris's behaviour. Eviscerated by personal and professional traumas, he simply walked out. Chris had not envisaged that. In an instant, Coldplay disappeared. There were no drums, no sessions, and, it seemed, no future.

'It was an awful time. For a week, Coldplay didn't exist, and it was all my fault. I thought to myself, "You fucking twat,"' recalled Chris to *Q*'s Michael Odell. It was a great shock that all the years of work, obsession and passion, and all of Phil's intense hustling could be negated so utterly by a single abrupt event. As for Will, it was a risky tactic for a drummer who wasn't doing well on the job to walk out – he could have been immediately replaced. But perhaps he was just too pissed off to care at that point.

'We certainly wouldn't be as good a band if we weren't mates first,' Will explained to *Vanguard Online*. 'We'd never let anything get in the way of us being mates. We're all very honest with each other and if someone is being a tosser, we just say, "you're being a tosser." I think if we bottled it all up we'd explode. Honesty is definitely the best policy.'

The band's internal disputes became apparent to Allison only when Will announced he was going away. He was also apparently unaware of Will's mother's illness. 'As I remember it, Will announced after we'd done a lot of work on the drums that he was going on holiday,' he recalled. 'Obviously, to be suddenly told that at very short notice as a producer, with all the money already spent on studio time that you can't cancel, obviously there's a considerable pressure in that kind of situation.

If Chris actually were on something, would he then look completely sober?

'To have the drummer you are already having problems with suddenly leave – the drums being the backbone of the track, how can you do anything without the drums there in place? It's like a Catch-22 almost, because no one else in the band particularly played drums, and the idea of bringing in a session player was not the kind of thing I would consider.'

Neither was it an option from Chris Martin's point of view – for the crisis made him recognise Will's importance to their music. 'Going through that experience made me realise that our chemistry is special. I can't do it without them – all of them – and vice versa.'

Sometime during that miserable week, Chris apologised to Will. Typically, for Chris, merely apologising wasn't enough – he insisted on performing some ritual act of contrition to atone for his behaviour, and did so by getting drunk.

> **'I was so nervous about our fucking up our chance I'd become obsessed with whether we were a technically good band or not.'**
>
> *– Chris Martin*

This dramatic act of penance, performed in Guy's flat, involved tanking up his already stressed-out body with a non-stop stream of vodka and beer. As Chris told *NME* later, 'To mark the end of this bad, bad week, the worst week ever, I decided I'd get hammered just to make myself more miserable. It was Guy, Guy was feeding me.'

Presently the hungry bassist went out for some chips, and when he returned he found a prone Chris begging for mercy in his purple vomit-strewn bathroom. 'I don't know what it was,' Chris said, 'all I remember is playing harmonica on the street trying to eat his chips and just sleeping on the bathroom floor with all this weird red stuff. What was that red stuff? Vodka and cranberry?' ('Ribena,' replied Guy.) 'And then just feeling really not great and trying to sleep in Will's room 'cos he wasn't there. And it was freezing cold.'

Chris's wretched spree can be viewed in various ways – as a desperate effort to become more at one with the others, by giving up the role of teetotaller, or perhaps as a way of paying penance by doing the thing he hated most: becoming unconscious of all life's compelling stimuli. What is certain is that getting drunk was a means of subverting his repressive control over the band. Previously, Chris had laid down strict rules about substance use.

As Guy explained to *Q*, 'We're not a druggy band, but basically there was a time when Chris was following Thom Yorke very closely and he read something he said and suddenly it was, "If anyone does coke they're out."' Later Chris admitted that he had been very dogmatic and confrontational with his edict: 'I just get these passions about things.'

Viewed with hindsight, the quarrel was a very useful row to have had sooner, rather than later: the catalyst that led to the setting up of some valuable new ground rules, which certainly helped the band avoid further crises. It was at this point that Chris introduced the policy that all four band-members should share songwriting credits and royalties equally, despite the fact that he often comes up with the melodies in addition to being Coldplay's lyricist.

'I don't want all the fucking money,' Chris almost exploded to *Q*, 'I don't want any more than the others. Do I really want to spend two weeks in court some way down the line arguing with my closest mates about who wrote what?' In an interview with *Esquire* in 2003 he exhorted, '*Bands* write songs. You know. The Beatles would not be anything without Ringo Starr . . . It drives me fucking insane. Radiohead, REM, U2 – all their songs say "written by the band". Coldplay is our band. Our gang. Not *my* band.'

'A complete royalty split is a very bright and admirable thing to do,' Chris Allison observed, 'because often problems with a band arise from unequal earnings. I don't remember that decision. I don't know if it happened in one of our breaks from recording and they didn't really mention it to me.'

According to Martin Roach, Bono's decision to split royalties with the rest of his group has personally cost him over £30 million. But this was a necessary form of insurance for band longevity. U2 have been around for two-and-a-half decades, and Chris Martin held similar aspirations for the embryonic Coldplay.

Some relief from the stress of labouring long hours in the studio came when the band thankfully got out and played some live shows. Their most important gig to date came when they got to support Catatonia at London's Kentish Town Forum on 5 April 1999. Will told *MusicZine* that this gig was 'sort of like a landmark, our first big support.'

As one of the organisers of this Radio One event, it was Steve Lamacq who championed the band to appear despite resistance from the Welsh headliners. 'Originally Catatonia didn't want a support band, or wanted to pick their own. So we had to dig our heels in to get them on,' he told the *Coldplay e-zine*. Lamacq's industry clout and the promotional leverage of his radio show were certainly factors in Catatonia's acquiescence. Once again, Coldplay owed the DJ big time. Particularly as the gig provided them with their first ever substantial live review, which appeared in *Melody Maker* on 17 April.

'Last time Coldplay played Kentish Town, it was at the pip-squeaking Bull and Gate,' wrote Robin Bresnark. 'Tonight two weeks later, they're supporting Catatonia down the road at the cavernous Forum. Next month, no doubt, Coldplay are pencilled in to play Shea Stadium, followed by a short tour taking in Nuremberg, the Sahara Desert (sold out) and the Mir Space Station. Going places? Oh yes.'

'That was incredible, it was huge,' Jonny told *Guitarist* magazine, 'It was one of our best gigs and we were amazed at the size of their rider. They had JD and tequila, it really gave us something to aspire to.' Through this great swathe of hospitality swept Catatonia's then-diva Cerys Matthews, commanding Chris to hold her cigarette while she went to the loo. Characteristically polite, Chris did was he was told.

Bresnark's highly positive review immediately laid the foundations for the interminable perception of the band as 'nice boys'. 'Imagine the nicest, kindest, sharpest new band in Britain. But why imagine? Just book that ticket for Mir, and go see.'

After such effusive coverage, the band's first ever appearance at the Glastonbury Festival was confirmed. There is no greater endorsement for a British band than to appear at Glastonbury. For more than 30 years, it has provided British rock with a spiritual home in the fields of founding farmer Michael Eavis. It's a key target for any new band to secure a gig as part of Glastonbury's customarily, muddy, rainy and hectically musical weekend.

This was the gig that really earned the band fans on a major scale. One such was *Vanguard Online* contributor Guernica, who reported, 'I first saw Coldplay grinning from ear to ear in disbelief at a straggled mid-afternoon crowd in the New Bands Tent at Glastonbury 1999. They played a confident set of sumptuous, instantly accessible guitar songs rasped and uplifted by the tender, tired voice of Chris Martin.'

Coldplay's Glastonbury set also became Steve Lamacq's favourite gig from the band's early period: 'It was gorgeous. It was Chris's day really. In-between songs he was a) a bit cheeky, b) a bit cocky and c) the most self-effacing singer on the planet,' he told *Coldplay e-zine*. 'It was a perfect Glastonbury appearance, which basically said, "We're good, and that's why we're here on this stage, but actually we're no different to you lot watching us."'

Such overwhelmingly positive live experiences gave the band a sense that they were pushing forward, not running on the spot as they had been in the studio. Live success counterbalanced recording difficulties – and, importantly, conveyed a vitally favourable impression to their record company.

However, both band and producer were being pressured by Parlophone to prepare material for an EP release. The tracks they had completed by this point were 'Don't Panic', 'See You Soon' and 'High Speed'. Fortunately, the long hours in the studio were beginning to bear fruit as the band established a sound way of turning inspirations into rounded creations.

Generally, Coldplay create their songs as a group, after Chris has worked out a piano sketch. Jonny adds his unique, essential guitar melodies and riffs, and then the quartet work out the arrangements. As for the final musical choices, democracy generally prevails and Chris's opinions are sometimes overruled by the others.

'Another thing I was quite surprised at was that Chris didn't seem to have a massive knowledge of music,' revealed Allison. 'Most of the artists I have worked with have a real understanding of the history of music and different artists and they can name this artist or that obscure artist. But seemingly not Chris Martin.

'I don't know how much difference from a songwriting perspective that background of knowledge makes. But the reason I mention it is because a band kind of hones down a sound for themselves after they've heard so many other different types of bands. Slowly that sound gets refined down into a sound that is more unique to the artist. And I think having that musical frame of reference helps with that process of making the sound a band has. Not with the actual songwriting, but their distinct sound.

'Chris's songs came over as pretty damn pure, that's for sure, because he just played the piano or a guitar. I was always knocked out by what he came up with; he'd just start strumming a new song. He'd just come into the studio and strum it out, and it would be really melodic. They were writing a lot more songs than ended up on the EP we produced.

'At this stage, the band actually wanted me to work with them even though we still hadn't resolved the situation with the drums. After two or three months I remember, we had a definite break and that break was supposed to be used by the band to write the rest of the album. Then after that, we were supposed to start pre-production of the album on a particular date.

'On that date I turned up as arranged at the rooms where they were rehearsing . . . They started up playing in the rehearsal room and they really just weren't together at all. I don't know what had happened to them, or what on earth had been going on during that break, but now, their playing really wasn't together.

'And I was very honest with them, I just sort of said, "Look, this simply isn't good enough," and explained to them that they needed to take a lot more time to rehearse before we went into the studio. Then the band went off with their manager to have a bit of a discussion. And the next morning I got a call saying, "Chris Allison won't be doing the album any more." I was totally, totally shocked, because as far as I was concerned, I was producing the album.

'To this day I don't know what happened and exactly why I didn't do that album. And that was the last time I saw the band, that day in the rehearsal room.'

To persuade Parlophone's A&R department that the band could not, and would not, work with Allison was no easy task. Coldplay were not in the best position to lay down the law. After spending several months and much money in the studio, nothing in the way of saleable product had been produced.

On the other hand, this very low level of productivity and the insistence that musical incompatibility had caused it gave Coldplay a strong case for discarding producers. Their vow to co-produce all recordings henceforth was an astute and resolute way to maintain control over their musical destiny. That Parlophone – a label with an international reputation for rapidly fading enthu-

Chris as the angelic leader of the gang.

siasms – should let an essentially unknown group exert such creative control is a little more surprising. It's a testament to the band's self-belief and powers of persuasion.

Chris Allison adds, 'The interesting, the most significant thing that did occur out of the fact that we didn't end up starting the album on that day of the rehearsal was that, as far as I knew, Chris Martin had not written "Yellow" by that time. I remember seeing that track when they played it first at Glastonbury 2000, and I thought it was a really great track, along with everybody else. It was very fresh, great delivery, good lyrics. I don't know how many bands come along where they're signed to major record labels and they make great albums, but they always just lack that one hit like "Yellow" that's going to propel them forward into universal recognition.

'Although, having said that, going back to Chris Martin's character, with his extreme commitment and extreme drive, probably whatever he turned his hand to, he was going to do very well at.'

THE UNCERTAINTY PRINCIPLE

Wresting away responsibility for their own record production was creatively desirable, but it also intensified the pressure on the band to push out some music onto the market.

Although a three-track single would have been a perfectly marketable slab of product for Parlophone, the quartet insisted on the plan of producing an EP. Centrally important was the fact that a five-track extended play CD would not be eligible for the British charts, and this showed much caution on Coldplay's part. 'We didn't want to look like we were just trying to get a chart place, we're not really bothered by that . . . well, we are bothered, but we didn't want to have a big major label push on our first EP,' Chris explained to *Total Guitar* magazine.

'We're very keen, and so is our record company, not to be one of those over-hyped new bands, just to build things slowly,' he told *Vanguard Online*'s Guernica, who noted, 'They could count the number of interviews they had done on one hand and Chris simply couldn't believe that being in a band meant he'd get his pizza for free.' This interview typified Chris's weird fusion of diffidence and ambition: 'We want to be Number One, but we don't want to jump the gun.'

Work on the EP filled up the remainder of the summer, but then a welcome interruption came when Coldplay hit the festival circuit for a second time. Over the August 1999 Bank Holiday weekend, the band made their debut at the Reading festival, which this year had expanded to include a second leg at Leeds. Once again, Steve Lamacq's support brought dividends – Coldplay were to appear on the Radio One *Evening Session* Stage, alongside headliners Luscious Jackson and the Flaming Lips. As at Glastonbury, the group went down well, although they received little more than a namecheck in the music press.

Maintaining the pace, Coldplay returned to the studio to complete their major label debut. *The Blue Room* EP spliced 'Don't Panic', 'See You Soon' and 'High Speed' with two tracks from *Safety*, 'Bigger Stronger' and 'Such A Rush'. Despite the time and money spent on recording sessions, these were the only tracks that the perfectionist quartet were prepared to have the public hear.

Nine days before *The Blue Room*'s official release, promotional copies picked up immediate airplay on Radio One and London's XFM. Lamacq's championing of the band gained pace when Jo Whiley continually played their EP. Whiley's career in radio was built on her affinity with 'indie' music, but her support for Coldplay was also centrally important because she hosted a daytime nationwide show on Radio One.

Released as a pressing of 5,000 on 25 October 1999, the EP won Coldplay their first taste of

No sympathy for the Devil. Chris's frontman persona is mildly eccentric – but wholesome, too.

media interviews set up by a record company press office, rather than scraped together by the ever-toiling Phil. It was a coup for them to feature centrally in the *Guardian*'s 'Guide to New Bands' series, but, being complete novices, they were more open than wise. Intriguingly, Dave Simpson noted, 'Apparently they're less than happy with the sheen-like production, which is unusual for a newly-signed group, who usually proclaim, "The record company are such nice chaps! They love our music . . ." before being ceremoniously dumped a year later.'

Unlike Liam Gallagher, rather than engaging in headline-hogging haranguing of their rock peers, Coldplay preferred introspective analysis from the start. Chris Martin would rarely put any-one down without including himself in the criticism.

> **'We're very keen, and so is our record company, not to be one of those over-hyped new bands, just to build things slowly.'**
>
> *– Chris Martin*

Coldplay were a band that had been bought to be fattened up for market over time. So any record company would take a dim view of musicians who, at a critical moment, knock their own product as they publicise it – a product invested with money, resources and expectations. Music journalism is a niche market for sarcasm, and what Fierce Panda's Simon Williams has called the 'loathe 'em or loathe 'em' style of writing. So why give journalists any encouragement to turn the oxygen of publicity into laughing gas at the expense of their Parlophone debut?

With Coldplay it was a case of compulsive honesty at any price, self-deprecation in the quest for musical perfection. The band themselves highlighted their flaws to be addressed as they gained experience. Also, Chris's self-criticism was also a subtle subversion drawn from his discomfort with what he saw as the vulgarity of marketing. Criticism of *The Blue Room* was a small but significant way of distancing themselves from surviving elements of Chris Allison's production, and com-municating that they would do better next time.

Luckily, the buzz about Coldplay was big enough that they could get away with putting them-selves down. They were assured crucial Radio One coverage and were not entirely dependent on Parlophone's pluggers. They were 'already being touted as next year's Next Big Thing,' as the *Guardian*'s Dave Simpson pointed out, adding, 'not by us, though – a young band needs a tag like that like a 130lb anvil falling on them.'

NME continued to endorse Coldplay powerfully, declaring that *The Blue Room* 'hinted at the band's potential for stadium-destined greatness with a wholly civilised and dramatic take on the Radiohead/Jeff Buckley melancholic acoustic method of mass seduction.'

While the overall critical reaction was positive, inevitably the band received some lukewarm reviews. A headline in *Select* magazine trumpeted, 'Supposed miserablists and guitar revivalists – Be prepared for plenty of Radiohead comparisons.' The accusation that the band were derivative of Radiohead, and to a lesser extent Travis, was quickly established as a recurring media theme. Similarly, Dave Simpson recommended, '*Don't buy if:* You can't stand Radiohead, the Verve or any of their numerous offspring of whinging, musically incontinent, miserable buggers.'

Coldplay were dismayed by being labelled as depressing; as *Select* noted, the accusation of being miserablists 'disgusts them'. 'All our songs have very simple emotions,' explained Chris. 'They're either very happy or very sad, but never miserable . . . Oh all right, the last track, "Such A Rush" is pretty damn depressing. But the rest aren't, I promise.'

That last blip of self-deprecation hinted at Chris's comic touch. But journalists didn't know the band well enough yet to recognise the contrast between Chris's bounding personality and his sad, scrupulous songs. There was a general assumption that Chris was another straight-faced Thom Yorke. Time would change this impression, of course, but the band and those around them were not to know that they'd ever get more than this split-second chance of stereotyping.

On 27 October, Coldplay set out on tour to promote *The Blue Room*. For most of the gigs, the band were to co-headline with Icelandic quartet Bellatrix, although the eight-date trek was broken by two nights at London's Shepherd's Bush Empire in support of Scouse indie-rockers Shack.

But as the tour began, Coldplay were still urgently looking for a co-producer for their next studio project – a full album. To hurry this along, Dan Keeling sent promos to a number of likely candidates, one of whom was Liverpool based producer/engineer Ken Nelson, who had recently cut himself a reputation through his work on Gomez's first two albums, *Bring It On* and *Liquid Skin*.

Fortunately, on the opening night of their tour, Coldplay were booked to support Gomez at Liverpool's Royal Court Theatre – with the concert beamed out live on Radio One. By now Ken Nelson was familiar with the EP, and had been immediately impressed. 'As soon as I heard Chris Martin's voice, I realised that he was something special,' he told *Sound on Sound*. Nelson arranged to hook up with the band at the Royal Court, and was offered the job of co-producer. Despite Coldplay's nerves being reflected in their rushed performance, Nelson reckoned that 'they just need to calm down', and accepted.

> **'All our songs have very simple emotions. They're either very happy or very sad, but never miserable . . .'** – *Chris Martin*

What made Nelson ideal for Coldplay was his central philosophy that as producer he functioned simply to help a band to realise their own ideas, rather than imposing his own. All his projects are intrinsically co-productions, he notes. 'It says that on the sleeve and we talked about that early on and, to be honest, I think that's what possibly got me the job, because they could have worked with anybody.'

Nelson and the band talked through their basic ground rules, and found themselves in accord. Catching that feel of a live performance on tape was crucial in Ken's eyes. 'That was the plan when we first got together: they wanted it to be as organic as possible, and I think that's a good policy.' Also from the outset, 'We decided that we weren't going to use lots of trickery.' Significantly, from the rhythm point of view, they decided not to use a click-track as a straitjacket on the beat: 'I like a song to ebb and flow, and the band are the same.'

It seemed to be a marriage of minds, and so the collaboration began. To help the band focus on generating an album's worth of material, Keeling booked Coldplay into the residential Rockfield Studios near Monmouth, in South Wales,

'Soul!' 'Passion!' 'Emotion!' 'Energy!' Chris dashed around the neutral studio rooms taping up key words on the walls. 'It sounds really naff, like a business management course,' he laughed, 'but at the time, it was all very important.' Coldplay vowed to make their first album a really uplifting record, or die in the attempt.

Regardless of the band's eagerness and Nelson's straightforward approach, the total recording period dragged on for over six months. 'We started in the middle of November, and it was finished towards the beginning of May, but they had two tours in the middle of that, one was for about a month, and the other about three weeks – so there were probably about nine or ten weeks of recording,' Nelson explained.

This was clearly a make or break time for Coldplay – the band knew that if this album didn't work well they'd be quickly dumped by Parlophone. Jonny told *Select*'s Dorian Lynskey that the long studio sessions were 'horribly tense', adding, 'We thought it could be the last record we ever made, so we might as well put everything into it. That's why we were so fraught – no second chances.'

The next six months were desperately hard work. 'Well, not hard work like being a miner, but in terms of music it was the hardest thing we've ever had to do, in terms of our friendship and commitment. It was more a case of frustration,' revealed Jonny. Speaking to *Melody Maker*, Chris stressed, 'We don't think of the album in terms of 42 minutes of music. We think in terms of nine weeks of argument and pain.' Will told *Select*, 'If you spent six months with us in the studio you wouldn't think we were nice boys. Fucking fierce rows, big strops, smashing things.' With all the sweating, arguing, and, even in the vicarly Chris's case, swearing – 'Oh, *fuck* yeah,' grinned Will – the band regularly lost perspective, caught up in a torrent of argument over technical minutiae. 'A lot of times we thought we'd got it then we'd listen to it a week later and it was no good, there was a lot of going around in circles,' Guy told *MusicZine*.

'I like bands who play live,' Nelson told *Sound on Sound* magazine, 'And in the end, that's basically what we did. We'd go through every song and get them to learn how to play it live, get them to learn what tempo to play the song at, and so on – and I think that's why the album sounds so organic.' He added, 'Most of the tracks would be laid down with an acoustic guitar or piano . . . drums and bass. We'd tend to redo the bass, but if we could, we'd keep as much of that original first take as possible.'

Most of the vocals were also done in one complete take. Chris's confidence in his performance had increased since the hot anxious Orinoco sessions. 'Chris has got that attitude of, "It's a great take; it's got that line there that's not great, but let's keep it as one take," ' observed Nelson. 'It's a brave thing to do, but it seems to have worked.'

> **'We thought it could be the last record we ever made, so we might as well put everything into it. That's why we were so fraught – no second chances.'** — *Johnny Buckland*

Describing Nelson in an interview with *RealAudio*, Will explained, 'It was just like having a fifth member of the band . . . He was someone who knew more about the technology behind [the process] and the actual sort of way to make things work and the functions of everything. But also someone who knew the songs and could tell us when something good had been done. We just trusted him implicitly with being able to tell what was good and what wasn't.'

Capturing live spontaneity on record demanded a lot of planning and many takes – 'Spies' was the perfect case in point. Recorded at Rockfield, it took three full days' playing to achieve a backing track that pleased everyone. Nelson moved around, snapping his mics into their stands with butch deftness. He put the excited Chris in a tiny cubby hole, placed Guy and his bass beside the mixing desk and Will in another room, his kit surrounded by a press conference-worth of mics that Nelson employed to cover every mixing possibility.

'Spies' begins with Chris's bleak, desolate open strumming – like America's 'A Horse With No Name' – and one discordant note threaded throughout the needling chords that accompany the melody line. The vocal comes in, then Jonny's guitar effect shudders across the soundscape.

The dreamlike guitar notes and Chris's falsetto outcry, 'They're all spies,' resolves into a syncopated, rocking refrain.

Nelson concentrated on enforcing his clean and direct production methods, 'The shorter the signal path, the better,' was his mantra. However, although he was an effects-miser, Nelson certainly wasn't a knob-hog at the mixing desk. 'If someone wants to have a tweak on the EQ, that's fine by me, and sometimes good will come of it . . . As long as I know where it was so I can put it back! Or I might say, "I know another way you can get that and there'll be slightly less noise." I don't keep any secrets.'

> **'If you spent six months with us in the studio you wouldn't think we were nice boys. Fucking fierce rows, big strops, smashing things.'** – *Will Champion*

Although the chemistry between Nelson and Coldplay worked, Dan Keeling felt that the product didn't. When the band rushed their 'Shiver' tape to Keeling in London, he was disappointed and mystified. All the vigour of their earlier EPs had disappeared.

'It didn't have any of their passion, their energy. It was just limp. I drove straight down to Wales and had a very tense meeting. Chris didn't like what we had to say, which was basically, "Do it again."' The wall of silence from the band made Keeling realise, for the first time, that under opposition Coldplay were, as *The Guardian* observed, 'a fearsomely tight unit'. 'They don't like people sticking their noses in,' he reflected.

During the previous studio trouble, Coldplay's producer had been sacked within 24 hours. Although this new crisis didn't do much for Ken Nelson, the band were now the only candidates for imminent firing. With one producer fired, there was no shield left, and the problem was not one that young Phil Harvey could pleasantly talk away. And so Coldplay continued working, both demoralised by Keeling's lack of enthusiasm for their track, and galvanised by the increased pressure.

Night after night, the band waited in headphones for the countdown to their takes. Songs that were later hailed as classics were stopped and started again and again. Throughout, Ken Nelson doggedly sustained his role as collaborative psycho-diplomat and high technician, and provided a counter-current of soothing continuity.

One tricky proviso from the band was that no track would end up on the album unless all four members approved it. Such democracy was wildly affecting the schedule. Jonny later told *Pollstar.com*, 'We wanted to finish it in two weeks . . . In the end, it took ten weeks to record and mix. The original idea was just to put everything down live, but then we realised that we didn't have enough songs that all of us liked.'

But out of endless, tortuous arguments, tracks were gradually polished until the band could finally see their album coalescing. The selected tracks fulfilled a simple brief, 'Just songs that we liked that fitted together,' Jonny recalled. This simple formula reflected the way that songs 'just arrived' in Chris's imagination. Ken Nelson recalled one such memorable epiphany: 'The studio we were in was called the Quadrangle Studio – the studio is along one side of an open courtyard about fifty yards square, and we went out one night, and because there were so few lights, the stars were amazing.' At this moment all unhappiness and aggravation lifted, and a lighter mood came over the band, inspiring a creative incident that changed their future forever.

The band stood outside to take in the evening's magic. 'Just absolutely clear sky. It was just an amazing setting,' Will told *mtv.com*. Out of the blue, Chris suddenly struck up his de-tuned

The rest of the band look pretty 'street', but Chris just looks quizzical.

guitar and belted out a falsetto Neil Young parody, 'Look at the stars. . .' These were the most obvious, improvised lyrics: 'See how they shine for you/And everything you do,' but somehow they also had the authority of timeless simplicity.

'It started out as a joke, really, ' said Chris to *coldplayitalia.it*, 'I started trying to sing like Neil Young, just 'cos the song had the word "stars" and that seemed like a word you should sing in a Neil Young voice. It's funny how things happen.' Chris got a chord pattern, and he kept it pinned down while Jonny's guitar jumped in. The song started out slow, Will recalled, 'but when Jonny started playing on it and started throwing ideas in, he had that riff, and it sort of got a bit heavier.' However, the song's lyrics would not reveal themselves. Chris was instinctively sure that the song needed one specific word to focus the music on. And there, written down somewhere in the studio he saw the word 'yellow'. Although Chris wasn't really that keen on the colour, it nonetheless triggered his euphoric flow.

Guy and Will pounced upon the track in their turn, and they all worked on it through the night. As Guy pointed out to New Zealand's *Pavement* magazine, 'Writing and recording is like a production line. It starts with a little seed and then a chemical process and a song grows from that. It's like a chain reaction.' Chris couldn't believe what had happened: 'When "Yellow" arrived, I thought, "Bloody hell. I can't believe we've got that song. That'll be a single."'

Integral to the song's powerful arrangement were the specific guitar tunings Jonny and Chris used, as Jonny explained. 'When Chris plays chords he does a lot more tuning. It can make a chord sound a hell of a lot better if you mess the tuning up a bit just to get the key you're playing in, lots of open strings and stuff. If you play "Yellow" in normal tuning it sounds terrible, it sounds like the most boring song ever. Just a couple of notes tuned makes a huge difference.'

Christmas came, and the band escaped from the cramped studio confines. However, the holiday had a terrible sense of finality for Will. This was to be his mother's last Christmas – she was losing her hard-fought two-year battle against breast cancer. It was the second time she had been seriously ill, yet she had always battled on – her forceful nature refusing to die.

Sara Champion was an archaeologist, and a woman of 'unreal energy' as a colleague described her, 'truly wonderful and extremely popular.' She had been eagerly athletic when young, a formidable runner on the sports field – something Will inherited from her – and also a beautiful singer with the Southampton Philharmonic Choir. She loved organising her very male household of two equally energetic sons (one with a loud Telecaster guitar), and her professor husband Tim. An advocate of early, unrecognised women archaeologists, whose research she broadcast on the radio, Sara also belonged to a women's studies group. She led summer excavations to megalithic sites in the West of Ireland, and camped out in her office at college late into the night to organise her students' research projects. In 1995 Sara co-founded the most extensive internet collection of archaeological links. During Christmas festivities past, she would think nothing of cooking up a big meal for dozens of friends, students and colleagues. The only event beyond Sara's prodigious organisational abilities was her own recovery.

A happier event marked the new millennium for Chris, who finally had his braces removed. His beaming smile was now chrome-free.

Coldplay spent the first month of 2000 on the *NME*/Carling Premier Tour of Britain, dubbed the 'Annual Brats Tour' – alongside Shack, Campaq Velocet and Les Rythmes Digitales. Between 17-30 January, they played ten university dates in Glasgow, Leeds, Newcastle, Manchester, Sheffield, Cardiff, Bristol, Oxford and Norwich, with a final showcase at London's Astoria. 'It was a real cross-section of bands,' Chris told *Total Guitar*'s Helen Dalley. First to play every night, Coldplay were the youngest and least experienced of the four acts. As Chris quipped, 'We'd get on stage and people didn't know whether we were the cleaners or the band. But it's a good challenge for us . . . we like trying to win people over.'

'We want to be Number One, but we don't want to jump the gun.' *– Chris Martin*

Their less than successful attempts culminated in the Sheffield leg of the tour, where *Vanguard Online*'s Guernica was the only person to watch them tune up. 'Coldplay went on first and nobody bothered to turn up in time to hear Chris announce he had just written a new song, which the band then played for only the second time. That song was 'Yellow'.'

After the tour, February was free from gigging commitments and Coldplay headed back to the studio to continue work on their debut album. But instead of returning to Rockfield, the band travelled to Parr Street Studios in Liverpool. This was Ken Nelson's 'home studio', and had hosted sessions by local boys Echo and the Bunnymen, as well as the Charlatans, Diana Ross and Barry Manilow.

Immediately, the songs started to flow. 'We only had a week in the studio but we got three songs recorded exactly how we wanted them and really surprised ourselves,' remembered Jonny. Coldplay had suddenly found the knack. That kind of knowledge, like riding a bicycle, would never be substantially reversed – although general insecurities about recording would periodically resurface. Jonny concluded, 'It was still a bit of a struggle from there but it was much better. The recording was broken up with a tour in the middle, which helped, but things seemed to be coming together. We were much happier.'

'Everything's Not Lost', which had been left in limbo since the early days of the Rockfield sessions, was finally put on tape in the last week of recording in Liverpool. In fact it was the last track to be recorded for the album. With its opening series of gentle chords that seem to say, 'Pause . . Think . . Pause,' the track showed an emphatic Flaming Lips influence. 'We wanted to get that really roomy drum sound they have, all that power,' Chris explained to *Melody Maker*. 'When I saw the Flaming Lips live a few months ago, they were so intense and sincere. That's the feeling I want to capture with Coldplay.'

In February 2000, the band's first ever Parlophone single, 'Shiver', was released. The track that had given them so much trouble at Rockfield just a few months before had since been re-worked at Parr Street. Chris sang superbly. His voice seemed to click into guitar effects in a piercing contrast. 'He recorded more than one take, but the one we picked was one take, warts and all,' Ken Nelson pointed out – but there are few warts evident, just a remarkable performance. Jonny's guitar line sings out as a voice, a great pure wail of emotion as he repeats the plaintive but slugging refrain, plucking out the vocal doo-wahs that shudder behind the lyrics. 'From the moment I wake – to the moment I sleep . . .'

The single's B-side, 'For You', had been recorded on the spot to keep up the momentum of the album sessions. But 'Shiver' had originally been written two years previously, during the period when the band first recorded at Sync City. It conjures up images of a lovelorn Chris, composing a letter for the object of his affection, a letter wrapped in rhyme and melody.

Refusing to be drawn about the woman who inspired his lyrics, Chris stalled, 'I just find all this really funny. It's just a song. I've got nothing to say about these songs.' He later declared that the woman serenaded in 'Shiver' was Australian soap star turned singer-songwriter Natalie Imbruglia, but later retracted. '"Shiver" is a bit of a stalking song,' Chris observed in *NME*'s 'Kicking & Live Special'. 'That's in the mix, really. It's a very aggressive mix.'

Irrespective of Chris's 'stalking' analogy, there is little stealth in the song's overpowering delivery. You can hear Chris, energised by Dan Keeling's accusations of lifelessness, grabbing the melody in his voice box and belting it out for everyone, everywhere. As with most Coldplay songs, 'Shiver' is a duet for two voices – Chris's vocal and the concise, but commanding voice of Jonny's guitar.

The press greeted the single enthusiastically. '"Shiver" stamps their ambitious talent and marks them out as future stars,' proclaimed *NME,* who listed the song at Number One in their 'Turn On' chart. Further excitement arose for the band when MTV gave the song a good shove, as did several prominent radio stations that playlisted it.

Released on 6 March, 'Shiver' crept into the UK Top 40, peaking at Number 35, which boosted the band's standing with Parlophone. Even so, the band did feel some disappointment that the track had not charted higher. Still, this placing was a very good result for a band that had hardly toured, and had not yet played a set longer than 45 minutes.

Guy spoke critically to *Melody Maker* about being in the contemporary charts compared to those that had inspired him as a child. Guy has always been Coldplay's unofficial musical archivist, with a huge collection of old vinyl and an affinity with soul music. He now broke out and expressed his views. 'The biggest shame about the charts, if you are into music and of a young age, is having all that thrust brainwashing whole generations. More individual taste in music isn't nurtured via the charts . . . when I first got into music there was so much Stock, Aitken and Waterman.' Guy pointed out that a record's progress toward the Number One slot is very different these days. Records now are promoted 'so far in advance of release that when they come out there's this rush to buy the song. Time was when you watched a song make its way up the charts, like a team or the football league divisions.' Guy was keen that Coldplay show their superiority over manufactured hits: 'I want us to beat all the rubbish. To get to Number 35 with "Shiver" was great!'

Following a support with Ocean Colour Scene at the Astoria on 13 March, Coldplay set out on tour with Terris, a Welsh band who had recently been cover-featured by *NME*. This was organised by Metropolis Music, co-promoter for the V-Festival and tours by Britain's most successful acts, such as Oasis, Radiohead and the Prodigy. Kicking off in Leicester on 15 April, the twenty dates took in moderately-sized venues such as King Tut's in Glasgow, Lomax in Liverpool, or The Forum, Tunbridge Wells.

One venue the band played in, typical of many on the tour, was an arts centre in a converted church, in Colchester, Essex. A *Dotmusic* reviewer saw the joint musical soundfest and pronounced Coldplay the winners. 'Despite their similarities with other anthemic, epic rock bands, Coldplay have the tunes to pull it off. Their sound is both despairing and uplifting; resembling a rainy morning in Blackpool, replaced with the warm glow of the sun in the afternoon.' The review held up Chris's humorous, self-deprecating repartee as a display of 'relaxed confidence'.

> **'Most of the tracks would be laid down with an acoustic guitar or piano . . . drums and bass. We'd tend to redo the bass, but if we could, we'd keep as much of that original first take as possible.'** – *Ken Nelson, Producer/Engineer*

What boded particularly well for Coldplay was the musical variety of their set, the reviewer felt, from the piano-driven epic of 'Brothers And Sisters' to solo acoustic guitar to the syncopated folk of 'Shiver'. The final opinion was that, 'whilst Coldplay produce nothing outrageously original, with their versatile sound the future looks bright.'

The following night, 18 March, was particularly significant for Chris as the tour reached his old Exeter haunt the Cavern Club – where the band received a sweaty and enthusiastic homecoming reception.

The tour ended its journey with a show at London's ULU on 7 April and immediately Coldplay returned to Parr Street to begin the final phase of work on the album material. It was during these sessions that the group finally nailed 'Yellow'. 'It was really difficult to record, because it worked at about five or six different tempos,' Will explained to *RealAudio*. 'It was a tough choice choosing which tempo to play, because sometimes it sounded too rushed, and sometimes it sounded as if it was dragging.'

Beat was exceptionally important to the success of 'Yellow' because the song works off a counterpoint of utter sweetness and a mesmerically cutting beat. 'It was quite difficult to sort of hit it on the head, but eventually we had a great take and it happened from there,' Will remembered.

While Coldplay worked, finished tracks from the album were spirited away for mixing in the States. 'Originally what the record company wanted to do was pick the singles and just have those mixed by a mix engineer,' explained Nelson. 'The mix engineer they wanted to use wasn't around, so they picked Michael Brauer.' Brauer was immensely experienced, with credits including Bob Dylan's *Bringing It All Back Home,* Paul McCartney's *Driving Rain Tour* album, and Jeff Buckley's *Live at Sine.* Since Brauer was based in New York, Coldplay flew over to hear his mix in progress and to record tracks for the single's B-side – 'Help Is Round The Corner' and 'No More Keeping My Feet On The Ground.' The quartet didn't see much of New York, but Chris later enthused about 'some outstanding meals'.

At the beginning of May, Coldplay made their debut on the BBC music show, *Later with Jools*

Holland. The band had supported Jools at their Trinity College, Oxford gig the previous year and the former Squeeze keyboardist got the band in to appear on his long-running show. The studio audience applauded enthusiastically after 'Shiver' and 'Yellow', which got its first TV airing. But as Will later told *Q*, the band were more concerned with the sound quality than audience reaction, 'We weren't really happy with the Jools Holland thing . . . It was just appalling. Worst sound I've ever heard. On any band, ever! Yeah, that was really annoying but it didn't really do us much harm 'cos more people seemed to hear us.'

Back at Parr Street, with the album finally complete, Coldplay's future direction suddenly showed itself when out of nowhere, as the band packed their gear away, Chris wrote 'In My Place'. 'I was just sat at this organ that my friend had lent me; this pump organ that you have to sit and peddle which was really designed for sea shanties and drunken sailors, and I wasn't either,' he told *Shekenstir* magazine. 'So I suggested we try a sea shanty and these chords just came out. It was a time when we were late for the last record and we suddenly discovered things like Jimmy Cliff and even 'Whiter Shade of Pale''. This little two-and-a-half octave keyboard was also used on 'Don't Panic'.

> **'We'd get on stage and people didn't know whether we were the cleaners or the band. But it's a good challenge for us . . . we like trying to win people over.'** – *Chris Martin*

Although 'In My Place' was written too late for inclusion, Chris declared to *NME* that he was very happy with the finished LP. 'Some of the album's really good . . . The most important thing is every song, we've got a feeling into it. And that's the first priority.' The meanings of all those key words taped to the studio wall had made it onto Coldplay's tape, in the end.

When he listened to the album for the first time, on his headphones in Battersea Park, Phil Harvey was overwhelmed. 'Even though I hadn't contributed a note it was still an amazing feeling of pride and fulfilment,' he announced in the band's *e-zine*. All the songs he'd heard in rehearsals, or the back rooms of pubs, were now fixed for posterity.

Tragically, on the very day the album was completed, Sara Champion finally succumbed to cancer. That Sara, who clung to life throughout the whole saga of the album's recording, died just an instant before her son's big breakthrough – that she missed this literally by a mere exhalation of breath, was almost too much to bear. But with dignity and character, Will channelled his suffering by taking on most of the band's promotional interviews over the next months. 'I can't say I had a harsh childhood but I've had a lot of things to deal with, especially in the last year,' Will later told *Select*, pointedly responding to journalists who claimed the band had had life too easy. 'People say, "You haven't suffered." It's like, "Fuck you, you don't know what I've been through."'

Eventually a new common room at Southampton University was dedicated to Will's mother by the Home Secretary, David Blunkett. The National Prehistoric Society established a yearly Sara Champion Lecture. And a dedication on Coldplay's longplay debut reads simply, 'This album is for Sara Champion.'

Emotional redemption was a theme behind the LP's name. The band decided on *Parachutes* as a title because, as Chris pointed out to the *NME*, they provide rescue and deliverance. In a world resonant with vertigo, where people feel they are free-falling through life, rescue is the ultimate aim of even Coldplay's most desolate songs: 'They get you out of a bad situation. So do some of our songs – you'll jump out of a plane and everything looks bleak, you know, and then you pull the parachute and you enjoy it: "Aahhh, it's not so bad.'"

Chris paused and then, with a typically mercurial about-turn, denied his whole explanation. 'But that is bollocks. It's called *Parachutes* because we had to decide a title. But it works, it fits. Often the things that fit best are things that have to be decided very quickly, or are a bit of an accident. A good analogy is when you've got to rush out of the house and get something to wear, you often pick up the first thing that looks any good and it sticks.' The same applied to the eponymous album track.

The track 'Parachutes' creates a kind of fine agony for the listener. Its sweet, pure melody, sung in a lulling voice hardly louder than the sound of Chris's thumb on the strings, stops just before any defining chorus, with a feeling of missed opportunity. In the same way, the final hidden track, 'Live Is For Living' – a brief, aching waltz danced to the wheeze of a prairie organ, with a drum like the brass boom of some band standing below a gallows in a western – is another beautiful song that Coldplay chose not to sing in full.

Otherwise the disc was mainly comprised of tracks that were familiar to fans of Coldplay's live shows and early releases. *Parachutes'* opener, 'Don't Panic', had first appeared on *The Blue Room* EP. 'Shiver' was the band's first single, followed on the album by 'Sparks' and the soon-to-be-massive 'Yellow'. Next came 'Trouble', 'Parachutes' and 'High Speed', which had also appeared on *The Blue Room*. The album closes with 'We Never Change' and 'Everything's Not Lost' before the final hidden song.

Continuing their policy of total artistic control, the band created the album cover with help from Mark Tappin at Blue Source, with photography by Tom Sheehan and Sarah Lee. The cover image was an arresting photograph of the glowing globe that they regularly placed on their piano during gigs. 'That represents our sense of ambition,' Chris explained in an interview with *Select's* Ray Wilkinson. 'It's also a little nod to the Flaming Lips. When they play they set out to make as many people in the room as happy as possible. Seeing the Flaming Lips just gave me the manifesto I wanted – unbridled togetherness. Wayne Coyne can sing sad things and you're like "Oh I feel a bit sad." But then he can make everyone feel happy. There's this unifying thing with their music. It's all embracing. I love that.'

In keeping with the rescue motif conveyed by *Parachutes*, the album dissipated some of the unease between the band and their label. Just under a year after signing, they now had a complete and rather promising album in the can. 'Our record company target was to sell 30,000 copies of *Parachutes*,' Guy later told *coldplaying.com*.

It was universally agreed that 'Yellow' was the ideal single to promote the album: a smiling attack on critics who had declared the band to be miserablists. With this object in mind, the band took complete control over the accompanying video. They decided they would find a beach – an incredibly beautiful beach – and flood it with lots of extras, then film the whole band there in a beautiful panoramic setting.

Under the helm of directorial duo Alex Smith and James Frost, whose previous credits included the Beatings, Six By Seven and the Beta Band, the ideal location was found – Studland Bay on England's south coast, a few miles north of Swanage. Everything was meticulously arranged for a shoot on 23 May.

The planned video was never made: Sara Champion's funeral had to take place on the same day. On the day of the shoot the crew descended on the beach with Chris, but Will and the rest of Coldplay were all further along the same coast in Southampton, where his mother was being laid to rest. The band had already decided Chris would salvage the shoot by performing the song alone. 'We found out about Chris being the only member a couple of days before, so we had time to change how we planned on shooting it,' James Frost told *Coldplay e-zine*. But sadly, the band's total artistic control did not include the weather. It was pouring. The directors suggested sending everyone home, but Chris insisted that the band needed to have a video by the end of the day. James remembered, 'We initially tried to carry out our original concept, but the weather got so bad we had to completely re-think how best to approach it . . . Alex, Chris and I stood under a tent, and Alex said, "Let's just film Chris walking in front of the camera." I suggested the beach and it quickly evolved into what you see on the screen.'

Quickly the directors filmed Chris lip-synching whilst walking along the drenched shore. Meanwhile, the hired throng trooped away from the beach like a procession of sodden mourners. Over in Southampton, crowds left Sara Champion's funeral like a procession of rain-drenched extras.

The whole shoot took twenty minutes. 'It looks like "Bittersweet Symphony", on the beach, in the rain!' Guy observed. But the video worked. 'It was a fluke at the end, but a happy fluke,' Will told MTV's David Basham. 'If you watch it again, knowing what's in the back of Chris's mind as he joyously trills along, it puts a lump in your throat,' wrote Dorian Lynskey. Fate had focused the cameras on Chris, singling him out as the band's most charismatic figure

Around this time, Chris cut his hair into what has become its trademark crop. He'd always worried about losing his hair. Paradoxically, hair had always looked faintly ludicrous on him, an unlikely mess of bubbly curls. The haircut *revealed* Chris Martin for the first time, showing his features with perfect clarity. 'Has he been recognised in the street since his haircut?' *MusicZine* asked Will. 'Not in the street, but outside gigs he always gets little girlies flocking round him,' came the reply. This interview was conducted to promote the band's next tour – supporting UK pomp-metallers Muse – but before that, Coldplay played a gig that strikingly showed their escalating popularity.

> **'Writing and recording is like a production line. It starts with a little seed and then a chemical process and a song grows from that. It's like a chain reaction.'** – *Guy Berryman*

On 25 May Coldplay appeared at Harlow Square in Essex. The gig was another benefit of their tie-in with Steve Lamacq and was again broadcast on his *Evening Session*. For the DJ, it was the live highlight of his association with the band. 'I used to live in Harlow, and the Square used to be my local venue, so going back there was quite a big deal for me,' he told *Coldplay e-zine*. 'And not a lot of people knew them at that time, but the gig sold out a couple of weeks in advance, and that was when I knew it was beginning to take off.'

The day before the gig, Phil Harvey seriously aggravated his charges in pursuit of their immediate interests, and wrote it up in a diary he'd began keeping for the official Coldplay website. 'The band have one day to rehearse. To intensify the situation even more, it is Will's first day back since a family bereavement . . . I have also arranged for Channel 4 to be here to make a fifteen-minute documentary about the band. They plan to film the entire rehearsal and need interviews and specially coordinated performances. Did I mention that I really hadn't told the band about this?'

'Yellow' was due for release in a week, and there had been an immense amount of radio play, particularly on Radio One, as Steve Lamacq again picked up the single and carried it. For the first time ever, the more conservative regional radio stations play-listed the song, acknowledging Coldplay's arrival in the mainstream. The rain-soaked 'Yellow' video was powering sales from its heavy rotation on MTV and countless other music channels. This exposure was creating a head-of-steam momentum ready for the moment the single hit the shops.

This gig in Oslo, Norway, one of myriad promotional concerts in the year 2000, was videotaped for TV.

But Phil couldn't pass up the opportunity of giving the band one further push. To get another TV slot – any TV slot – within a month of the new album's release really was a marvellous coup. But the nervous band, just reunited after bereavement, the day before a gig in a tough venue that could go disastrously wrong, didn't see it that way.

'Everyone is seriously pissed off with me,' wrote Phil. The band's immediate response was to evict the camera crew from the rehearsal room, so that they sat around waiting for four hours. 'Inside, the rehearsal continues without the flicker of a smile,' the worried manager continued, 'I'm praying the crew will be allowed back in – they've spent over £10,000 putting this together.' When the band eventually let the camera crew back in, Phil's relief was palpable.

The next day the band headed off for Harlow. 'By this point, there was a huge buzz about the band,' remembered Harlow Square's then promoter, Des Wiltshire – who had previously booked Blur and Oasis. The 275-capacity club, part of the UK tour circuit for bands working their way up the ladder, the Square is a nursery ordeal for musicians with most of their blood, sweat and tears still ahead of them. The nondescript council building has floors tacky from lager, black walls rag-rolled with roll-up smoke, and a munchkin-high stage. 'Coldplay were down-to-earth, normal people who were just interested in getting up on the stage and doing their thing – no egos, no "silly things" in the dressing room, no massive riders,' Wiltshire told *Bang* magazine.

Right away, local wags taunted the band with cries of 'Sunshine bus!' as they came on stage wearing trainers and deeply uncool shirts. Chris, with his huge-eyed grin and bright sunflowers on his guitar straps, provoked this irresistible jibe that Coldplay had come here on a Sunshine coach trip for handicapped kids. After fronting the gig with his usual boundless energy, Chris introduced 'Shiver' with equally typical restraint: 'This was our only ever hit single and it wasn't really much of a hit.' At that point, the same sneering yobs started singing along fervently and knew all the words.

Coldplay's rider for the gig was also modest by general standards: two bottles of red wine, 24 strong continental lagers, soft drinks, bottles of mineral water, two litres of apple juice, fresh fruit, stamped, local postcards (to send to friends and family), hot meal for eight people, and tea, coffee and sandwiches at the load in. And it was only six months since Chris had marvelled at getting free pizza along with his gig. A couple of bottles of spirits had been crossed off the list though – clearly the band didn't feel they had quite reached the rock 'n' roll heights they had seen Catatonia enjoy.

Steve Lamacq later gave his verdict on the gig: 'They still had a lot to prove, but the mixture of affability and tenacious songwriting won the crowd over and if they could do that in Harlow, they could do anything.'

Four days afterwards, Coldplay began a short but important seven-date tour with Muse. It was a marked step up from touring with Terris – a clear sign that the band were making progress. Beginning on 29 May at The Pyramid, Portsmouth, and travelling on to Liverpool, Newcastle, Glasgow, Sheffield, Wolverhampton and culminating with the Astoria, London, on 6 June, the tour was the ideal build-up for *Parachutes'* release.

The two bands found plenty of common ground while touring. 'They were really cool,' Will told *MusicZine*, 'they came into our dressing room and gave us a couple of bottles of champagne as a "Hello!" sort of thing.' As well as sharing Chris's Devonian heritage, Muse mainstay Matt Bellamy also enjoyed outdoor sports. Bellamy's latest acquisition was a Paramotor: a propeller-operated 'jet pack' that attaches to the back. He planned to soar, 007-style, over the Devon coast, possibly to out-do any heroic image of Chris below him surfing on the waves.

'This tour will be really good for us 'cos a lot of Muse fans have actually heard of us and quite like us too, and the two gigs we've played already have been really really good,' enthused Will. The drummer's optimism was proven right; a gig at Newcastle Student's Union swung round in their favour when Chris stood in front of an angry, restless crowd of Muse fans and said very simply, 'We've had a really shit day so we just want to enjoy this as much as possible!'

During this short tour, *Melody Maker* interviewed the band and lewdly enquired as to Chris's attitudes to love and sex. Mark Beaumont asked if he had a favourite sexual fantasy. Chris replied, 'I always liked the idea of falling in love with one of your teachers, who is a lady, and just running off. Somewhere sort of Robinson Crusoe-like with no stuff, living in the wild, like Tarzan and Jane. I love that.' Warming to his theme, Beaumont asked whether Chris had ever fancied somebody of the same sex. 'Not really, no. I don't think so. There was one time I looked at a girl and thought "She's nice" and it was a boy! So I put on a low voice and walked away.'

These responses from Chris – not exactly boiling with eroticism – established his reputation as a shy bungler. *Melody Maker*'s article indicated that Chris said he'd like a one-night stand with Hillary Woods from JJ72 – in an interview with *MusicZine,* Will denied that Chris ever said this: 'The guy asked about one-night stands, if there was anyone in the pop world he'd like to have a one-night stand with, and Chris said, holding his hand over the tape recorder, and basically said the bass player from JJ72's really pretty, and they printed it! It's just one of those things, one of those spur of the moment things I think!'

This interview of Chris's with *Melody Maker* for *Parachutes* catches his mood just before success hit him. Notably, he showed an obvious naivety about the band's obligations to Parlophone if the album should succeed. 'After this album, we're not planning to do any interviews at all. Either because we won't have to – because we'll be so massive – or because we'll have been dropped. I'm fully expecting the album to be panned, because we've put so much blood and guts into it . . . It's upsetting, but it makes you more determined.'

Just as Chris feared, an *NME* review of 'Yellow' began caustically, 'Coldplay are the Sunday

School kids brought in to provide a little heart-warming interdenominational harmony.'

'As albatrosses go, I suppose it's a minor one,' Chris later told *Q*, 'but it does get a bit tiring reading that we are such nice, humble chaps all the time.' Chris was equally unimpressed when the *NME*'s Piers Martin pointed out to him that 'Chris Martin' is an anagram of 'Mr Christian'.

However, *NME* couldn't keep up the jaded pose for very long: 'It's amazing how they get away with this. There's something undeniably enchanting about them. Whatever moves "Yellow" beyond the drippy Thom-Buckley pastiche, it's a true gift.' And a good review from the oft-acidic *NME* was a true gift for the band.

When asked by *Melody Maker* what it was like to be on the verge of fame, Chris shot back, 'I don't think of it like that. It's impossible to predict things like that. One night, I get treated like a regular gig-goer at the Astoria – the next, I'm allowed to go everywhere because I'm the singer with the new "Travis" or something. It's bollocks, isn't it? Especially when you realise that stars like Nick Drake weren't recognised when they should've been. It's impossible to tell whether we're going to be a massive success. There are better bands than us who haven't been signed, I'm sure.'

> **'More individual taste in music isn't nurtured via the charts . . .**
> **when I first got into music there was so much**
> **Stock, Aitken and Waterman.'** – *Guy Berryman*

Never one to miss out on a sleepless night, Chris confessed, 'I was terrified ['Yellow'] would go in at number 60.' Particularly and joyously nerve-wracking was that they were about to embark on their first ever headline tour – beginning at the Leeds Cockpit on 8 June and taking in small-ish venues in Oxford, Southampton, Exeter, Leicester, Manchester, London and Bristol. Support was provided by Mercedes, a quartet signed to Fierce Panda.

As the band headed out as headliners, an expensive crew of roadies fell in behind them. These included a student friend of Jonny's called Matt, who later became his personal guitar tech. At the head of all roadies was a highly expert tour manager, the bespectacled Jeff: so formidable that you'd be afraid to go in the tour bus loo *before* him, let alone after him. A bloke called Hoppy was now Chris's guitar roadie and, although there's something of the East End geezer about Hoppy, he also looks strangely like a blond, box-jawed, Disney caricature American.

Phil Harvey was responsible for assembling this road crew – a really nerve-wracking task for a 22-year-old who still often felt like a teenager. If he didn't choose the right dependable personnel, gigs could be ruined. Doubtless Phil's last thought at night, sometimes, was that just one 'teenage' decision from him could make everything go haywire. 'Roadies are a breed of their own,' mused Guy, while drinking with the crew in a Manchester pub after a gig. 'They may not even be from this planet.'

In his review of Coldplay's Leeds Cockpit concert, *The Guardian*'s Dave Simpson realised that 'what nobody predicted is that their live performances can induce unabashed joy and merriment: there isn't a soul who doesn't leave this marvellous gig grinning from ear to ear.' He pointed to Chris's knack for self-deprecation as a key reason: 'The man is a master of deadpan wit, self-mocking hilarity and genuine warmth. The contrast with the band's spellbinding melancholia could not be more profound . . . It becomes apparent that we're witnessing something very special. Nobody goes to the bar; before long the staff actually abandon their posts to join the throng. Eventually, Martin cuts himself some slack to cry, "Remember this as a little secret between us when we come back next year and we're massive.'''

On 14 June Chris made another return to the Cavern Club in Exeter. To play to a cramped cave full of familiar hometown faces was an emotional experience. In *NME*, Victoria Segal noted the 'eager audience members clutching silver marker pens and ready-to-sign CDs', plus 'the excitable way in which Chris declares that this is his hometown gig or asks everyone to say hellos to his parents.' She described the gig as 'a one band pitch for the Hope Revivalist tent' and Coldplay as a group offering a 'chance to cut free of cynicism, ridiculous optimists to the last.' The concert buoyed Coldplay up, showing just how far they had come, in the eyes of the press, their loved ones, and, most importantly, themselves.

'We're made up! This is the first tour we're not losing money on. Apart from the first show, they've been sold out, sold out, sold out! Wicked!' Chris crowed to *NME* scribe Piers Martin in an ensuing piece predictably called 'Yellow Fever'. 'Can't believe it! You know, we got to Manchester yesterday and the student union was dead 'cos no one was there but it was sold out! Wicked! It's very exciting you know.' It *was* exciting, even for Phil Harvey, who had nail-bitten his way through financing the previous tours and was already in the early planning stages of expensive shows in exotic destinations like Australia or Japan.

> **'Listen to the vocals – too quiet. That's our philosophy: never happy, always aiming for more.'** – *Chris Martin*

Along with *Q* journalist Nick Duerden, Coldplay met up at the Lucas Arms in King's Cross just before their Scala gig on 19 June, when a white van pulled up, blaring 'Yellow' from its stereo. Chris's reaction was instant. 'Listen to the vocals – too quiet. That's our philosophy: never happy, always aiming for more.'

Coldplay returned to Glastonbury with their profile significantly raised from twelve months earlier. That also raised their place on the bill – promoted from the New Bands Tent to a mid-afternoon set, squeezed in between Toploader and David Gray, on the more prestigious Other Stage. A flesh forest of raised, clasped hands met their performance, and Guy told *Melody Maker*, 'It was amazing to play in front of that many people on such a nice day. I was really nervous for about the first three songs, but then I started feeling really comfortable with it. It was so nice looking over to the horizon and seeing all those people in front of us.'

'We really wanted to play "Yellow" well, with a bit of soul, 'cos we knew there'd be a lot of attention on it,' explained Chris. 'The last couple of times we played it were absolutely rubbish.' He needn't have worried. The set – virtually the whole of *Parachutes* – was triumphant; any doubts about the impact of softer numbers on such a huge event were dispelled. 'The slower, more acoustic stuff sounded impressively *big* and marked an improvement in the band's live set over the last couple of months,' noted *Melody Maker*.

Halfway through the set, Chris Martin demanded that Coldplay be higher on the bill next time. 'Chances are he will get exactly what he wants,' observed *Dotmusic*'s Ben Gilbert. However, such bravado could be risky, for on Monday, 'Yellow' would be released – and if it charted very low Chris's demand might return to haunt him in the press. Coldplay's solemn goodbye to the Glastonbury crowd was a cover of 'You Only Live Twice.' 'This is our tribute to Robbie Williams,' Chris announced, cheekily referencing Williams' sampling of the melody for his hit 'Millennium'.

On 26 May, two days after Glastonbury, 'Yellow' came out. This coincided with some of

Coldplay's first European dates, a one-off performance in Hilversum, Holland followed by an appearance at *Les Eurockeenes* Festival in France. The band knew that 'Yellow' would either appear in the following week's chart, or it would sink, whereupon the buzz about them at Parlophone would be abruptly silenced.

By the middle of the week, the band heard that early sales figures suggested 'Yellow' would make the Top Ten by the weekend. Braced for disappointment, though, the band agreed that even Top Twenty would be an excellent improvement on 'Shiver'. After the Hilversum show Phil put his head in the dressing room door with some rather good news. 'It's number four. We've gone straight into the UK charts at number four.'

The band were stunned, astounded and jubilant. They had arrived. But now a new nagging fear replaced the old. Would they be just a one-hit wonder? Would they be forever known as the 'Yellow' men?

YOU DON'T
KNOW ME

'Number Four – shit! ' wrote Phil in his website diary.

'Something odd definitely happened on 26 June this year,' ran a piece in *Select*. 'Travis had just taken the Saturday night Glastonbury headlining slot originally pencilled in for Oasis, Badly Drawn Boy released his debut album which won widespread acclaim; Richard Ashcroft released his solo album, which didn't, and Coldplay released "Yellow". Beautifully simple, hauntingly happy, "Yellow" was the perfect soundtrack to the year's musical spring-clean: out with self-important posturing, in with good tunes and chummy patter.'

'It has taken something as simple as a catchy tune for Coldplay to totally hog the limelight,' marvelled *Melody Maker*'s Emma Johnston. She described 'Yellow' as 'Coldplay giving us a kick up the charts.' Chris, declaring that the chart position was 'amazing', completely agreed. 'A victory for indie music. It's just good songs coming back.'

For the band, the charting of 'Yellow' was an immense, if surprising breakthrough. 'We thought, if we were lucky, we might scrape into the Top Twenty, but this was beyond our wildest dreams,' said Guy, 'It's quite a lot to live up to.'

Writing in his web-diary, Phil observed, 'I do know the ramifications will go on for years . . . "Yellow" is a proper, cross-over hit which means the album will probably chart fairly high, which means the profile will go up loads, which means that I and the band will be much busier than we've ever been before.'

Phil was dead right. Almost immediately, Coldplay were in demand. The first of these 'ramifications' came in the form of an invitation to appear on BBC1's weekly chart showcase *Top of the Pops*. An instant landmark in any band's career, after an appearance on *TOTP* your parents can't deny you're famous, and must stop whingeing that you're wasting your time.

The line-up for the show broadcast on 7 July included Kylie Minogue, Eminem, Vengaboys, Lonyo, Samantha Mumba and Robbie Williams. Furthermore, across from Coldplay's dressing room lay the temporary boudoir of Victoria Beckham, Posh Spice, attended by her husband, David. Being surrounded by such pseudo-royalty did not impress Coldplay. 'The day we had a dressing room at *TOTP* opposite Posh 'n' Becks, I thought, being a celebrity doesn't make you any better than anyone,' Chris told *Melody Maker*.

The band had felt far more honoured by an invitation to play at Glastonbury founder Michael Eavis's annual placatory event for local people whose lives were so disrupted during June. Called

Capturing the tedium of promotional work: 'I'd rather talk about Fair Trade than the colour of my socks,' as Chris once put it.

the Pilton Village Fete, this customarily took place a month or two after the actual festival. The invitation had very exciting implications for Coldplay as tradition held that bands who were asked to appear at the fete often got invited to be Glastonbury headliners the following year.

On the eve of *Parachutes'* release, Coldplay travelled to Kinross in Scotland for the T in the Park festival, which took place amidst pouring rain. (Luckily, they were performing in a tent.) Other acts included Travis, Muse, the Flaming Lips, Macy Gray and Iggy Pop. The year before, Coldplay probably couldn't afford a ticket. Now, they were received with adulation by the tightly packed and gently steaming throng.

> ## 'The day we had a dressing room at TOTP opposite Posh 'n' Becks, I thought, being a celebrity doesn't make you any better than anyone.' – *Chris Martin*

'When we peeked through the curtains and saw the tent was rammed, we realised it was something special,' Will told *Melody Maker*'s Daniel Booth. 'You end up feeling so many emotions at once that it feels almost numbing,' added Guy. As the band emerged through the curtains to a rapturous reception, Chris shouted, 'Does anyone remember the Deep Blue Something? That's how we feel. Next year, we'll probably be somebody's roadies.' The crowd had been pulled in 'by possibly the most beautiful song ever written about jaundice,' joked *Melody Maker*'s Mark Beaumont. 'But knowing that they wouldn't end up a one hit wonder within the space of this set, they set their wares out with a vengeance.'

After the show, Daniel Booth waylaid Chris to ask, 'So many people have said your set was the weekend's highlight. Did it feel like that for you?' 'It was the most overwhelming thing I've ever done. I'm still gobsmacked. Speechless. I went to the microphone to say something. But I was speechless.'

Booth pointed out that this year's headliners Travis had played a similar slot last year – 'Ooh that's dangerous talk,' demurred Chris. 'We're Coldplay, not Travis . . . at the moment we're being told, quite rightly, to take each day as it comes, otherwise everything's gonna be a letdown. We're perfectly happy with the reception we got today.'

10 July 2000 was a date with a huge red ring around it on Coldplay's calendar – the album's release date. This was the day that the effort, expense and, particularly in Chris's case, the non-stop worry would be either validated or exposed as a monumental folly. In order to ensure that the album would succeed, the band now submitted to a promotional treadmill that, amazingly, would keep trundling right until the end of the following year.

To mark the release of *Parachutes,* Coldplay landed smack in the middle of London at HMV's mammoth flagship store in Oxford Street with a promotional gig to commemorate the album's birth. 'We were absolutely up to our limit capacity-wise, and I had to turn fans around outside,' said HMV spokesman Simon Winter. Tight, exhilarating music pushed between the heads of the jam-packed crowd of press, industry types, and 700 Coldplay fans. The set list included 'Spies', 'Don't Panic', 'Trouble,' 'Bigger Stronger,' 'Yellow' and 'Everything's Not Lost'. Although the store had hosted many gigs, Coldplay's was hailed as one of the best ever seen. Virtually everyone who came along also bought signed albums. 'Sales today suggest they could be number one by a long shot,' predicted Winter.

Immediately after the HMV show, Coldplay departed for a string of one-off shows and festival dates in Europe that would have the band repeatedly crossing the channel throughout July and

August. Following a gig at La Scala in Paris, the Coldplay roadshow travelled to Italy for a pair of outdoor engagements. For the second of these, the band headed to Verona to for the Roccaforte Festival, which took place beside an imposing castle.

Coldplay were yet to make any kind of impact in Italy, and their performance went largely unnoticed alongside the din of Italian noise rock acts such as Marlene Kuntz. 'There were 50 people there – you wouldn't call it an audience,' Will told MTV. 'There was our record company and a few drunks,' added Chris. 'The thing is that we don't know if anyone outside of England knows anything about our band. So, it's quite scary for we never know if we're popular or unpopular; or if people like our songs, or if they hate our songs. And if there weren't many people. But it was OK, it's an amazing place.'

A week's return to the UK in mid-July revealed that all the promotion Coldplay had done for *Parachutes* had now bourne fruit in the form of generally positive reviews. In a *Guardian* interview with Chris, Dave Simpson explored the polarised critical reaction to the band during their eighteen-month career, either championed as the great white hopes of guitar revivalism, or ridiculed as a bleak-spirited Radiohead tribute act.

'The thing about those comparisons, that was all started by one of our early songs called "Bigger, Stronger",' explained Chris. 'Once something like that is thrown at you it's really hard to shake off. Because every interviewer reads up what the last person has said. It's Chinese whispers.'

> 'After the Gallagher model of boorish self-aggrandising rock-star behaviour, Martin's modesty is refreshing. But he certainly doesn't lack for ambition.' – Dave Simpson, *The Guardian*

'Few would describe Chris Martin as a moaning minny after an hour in his company,' Simpson wrote, adding, 'They are all "nice middle-class boys", but Martin feels he shouldn't apologise for this any more than the Happy Mondays should have made excuses for being underclass lowlife.' Capturing the steel within Chris's nature, Simpson observed, 'After the Gallagher model of boorish self-aggrandising rock-star behaviour, Martin's modesty is refreshing. But he certainly doesn't lack for ambition.' He also made an entirely accurate prediction: 'Now Martin's band have an album up their sleeves which should finally bury all accusations of mere copyism.'

Sure enough, a torrent of positive press ensued. In the *NME*, Siobhan Grogan wrote, 'Chris has poured every thought, every feeling he's had in the last two years into this record. It's like reading one long, intimate love letter. Some moments here indicate there's more to him than anyone knows.' *Q*'s Mark Blake similarly recognised the album's intensely personal nature: 'You can only wonder what well of emotional trauma has been dredged for some of what's on offer here. Halls of residence will echo with this record for months to come, but the rest of the world could do worse than listen.' Meanwhile *Uncut*'s James Oldham called *Parachutes* 'a sensational opening gambit and one that more than justifies the plaudits heaped upon them by the weekly music press.'

Some records get great reviews and exposure and don't sell. Some records sell millions and don't deserve to. But with *Parachutes*, the record buying public was not nearly as savagely indifferent as they sometimes can be. On release day, it moved over 20,000 units at big and small stores throughout the UK. By the week's end, another 50,000 units sent it straight in at Number One. Parlophone's sales target of 30,000 had been surpassed in the very first week of release.

Afterwards, the band had to sift through a mass of feeling about their achievement and its

Dazed and dazzled by the crowd response at T in the Park, 2000.

implications. 'Yellow' and *Parachutes* were becoming the defining music of the new millennium's first summer. Coldplay knew they had made it. They would always occupy a place in the public consciousness – even if only as has-beens – and they knew that they had earned their place in the musical pantheon. On the other hand, they also realised that they now had a crushing global workload.

And yet, they were still plagued by doubts. It was hard to believe that such massive success had been borne of a recording process that had been agonising for all concerned. 'Everything is like this incredible schoolboy dream,' Chris told *Melody Maker*. 'But we know the success and the hype and everything isn't going to last, so we're just enjoying it.'

For Steve Lamacq, the news about the album topping the UK chart triggered an ambivalent reaction: 'The weird thing about *Parachutes* was that I was in America when it went to Number One, and for a couple of days I genuinely thought that I should resign from Radio One there and then. I probably was a bit mad, but in my own head I thought, "Here's a band we've championed from nothing to Number One in the album charts and nothing will ever be this good again."'

Although delighted with the album's success, Phil Harvey quickly discovered that the band's increased profile came with a proportional jump in workload. 'All of a sudden I was working sixteen hours a day with three phone lines ringing constantly. I didn't have an assistant or anything so there was no one to take any of the load off my shoulders. I got on top of things in the end and for nearly a year got through on sheer adrenalin . . . I got incredibly stressed and was convinced I'd got in over my head.'

It never occurred to the conscientious and brilliant manager to delegate any of this mass of work. An enormously approachable, energetic chap, Phil had a compulsive need to tie up all loose ends personally. As a manager he clearly wanted to leave nothing to chance.

Like Phil, Coldplay were totally thrown by the relentless pace imposed by rocketing success. 'I hate bands who moan, but there was no learning curve. It was a vertical gradient,' said Guy, who also felt the album was 'not that great considering what we're capable of.' He shortly became so suspicious and so confused by success that he started telling Chris he thought the album was a shambles.

'Fame is a little bit of a sham when it's huge after only one album,' said Jonny's mother Joy. 'The rapidity freaked them out at first. It was destabilising. When you have fame thrust on you like that, you wonder if you deserve it – like anyone would.'

Q's Nick Duerden added a less maternal perspective: 'Overnight, they became the New Radiohead, only catchy and friendly, the new Jeff Buckley, only alive and with sales. Critics started calling them "The Men Who", the inference being that what Travis did in 1999, Coldplay will do this year.'

After a return visit to the BBC's Maida Vale studios for another *Evening Session* performance on 24 July, Coldplay played *La Zeleste* Festival in Barcelona, where they won some new converts despite the poor sound. They then returned to Britain to play some smaller one-off dates, which included the group's first acoustic-only gig at Ronnie Scott's in Birmingham. On 1 August, Coldplay also taped a set in Camden's tiny Monarch pub for *The Barfly Sessions* on Channel 4.

That same day, the band signed a US deal with EMI subsidiary Nettwerk Records, who announced that they would be releasing *Parachutes* in early November. The label, home to Ron Sexsmith, Neil Finn and David Gray, had been convinced of Coldplay's worth by the album's impressive sales, and the announcement, a week earlier, that the disc had been nominated for the Mercury Music Prize.

In addition to *Parachutes*, the Mercury panel had nominated albums by Badly Drawn Boy, Richard Ashcroft, the Delgados, Death In Vegas and Leftfield. Major UK betting chain William Hill installed Coldplay's LP as the 3-1 favourite to win: 'It's just because it's a bit more commercial than the others, and it's in the charts,' a spokesperson told *Melody Maker*. 'Lots of people are expecting an outsider to win.' The music paper held a poll asking who should win, and 73 per cent of the votes went to Coldplay.

The band were cautiously thrilled by their nomination – this was an award for serious musicianship, bringing with it national exposure. 'Well, that's um, that's nice,' Chris told *Q*. 'What I mean is, it's a nice surprise. Not that I don't think we deserve it, because we do. In a way, it's a bit like a surprise birthday party. It's your birthday, so it's perfectly feasible that someone will throw you a party, right? And if they don't tell you about it beforehand, then it will be a surprise, but not really much of one because, well, you know . . . Does that make any sense?'

At the Mercury Music Prize press conference on 25 July the Chairman of the Judges had declared that *Parachutes* was full of 'elegant songs, classic guitars and gorgeous singing. One of the year's most uplifting albums.'

Coldplay sidestepped this tribute and issued a rather bashful statement in reply: 'We put a lot of effort into making a record that we are proud of and happy with, so it's nice to know that other people quite like it too. We always hoped our record would mean as much to other people as our favourite records mean to us. Our vote would go to Badly Drawn Boy because he is brilliant.'

The new Badly Drawn Boy album, *The Hour Of Bewilderbeast*, had been 'welded' to Will's stereo since its release. In addition to guaranteed mainstream media exposure, a square meal and a good night out, the Mercury Music Prize also promised a £25,000 cheque for the winner. This would be presented at a gala in the Grosvenor House Hotel in early September.

Stressing the relative importance of this award, Alan McGee observed, 'The Mercury Prize is important because everyone on that list will sell 30,000 more records.' McGee knew what he was talking about, he had discovered and signed Oasis, and promoted a whole crowd of other acts, including the Jesus and Mary Chain, Primal Scream and My Bloody Valentine.

'Mercury Judges Are Prize Fools', read a headline in *The Guardian* a day later. An accompanying piece by Jon Dennis attacked the unadventurous nature of the panel's selections: 'Most predictable of all are Britain's indie guitar bands, who always make up a disproportionately large chunk of the Mercury shortlist, this despite the fact that the rest of the world has managed to resist our increasingly conservative indie bands for many a year now.' Dennis directly attacked Coldplay as an 'off-the-peg indie band', describing them as 'this year's Travis'.

This set the agenda for another *Guardian* piece a few days later, written by the formidable McGee himself. 'Looking down at the list of Mercury Music Prize nominees, my first thought is where have all the characters gone in music? Where are the Lee Perrys, the Johnny Rottens?' Turning his focus to today's acts, he observed, 'Top of Mercury's list is Coldplay: bedwetters' music. They're Jeff Buckley-lite, the band that you're supposed to like if you're a student. This is what frustrates me about the current music scene.'

McGee had coined an unforgettable phrase – 'bedwetters' music' – that would run and run in the UK tabloids, becoming a permanent tag, a derisive reference point in future press coverage of Coldplay. McGee's attack on the band was reminiscent of the press campaign waged against Blur by the Oasis camp. As Damon Albarn later recalled, 'We got so utterly misrepresented during the Britpop era and just fucking bullied out of town by Oasis and everyone who went on their side.'

> **'All of a sudden I was working sixteen hours a day with three phone lines ringing constantly . . . I got incredibly stressed and was convinced I'd got in over my head.'** – *Phil Harvey, manager*

Guy had complained about success being 'a sheer vertical gradient'. In parallel, the nastier, the more wounding the statement, the more publicity it got. McGee couldn't lose. 'The insult stuck, despite the fact that McGee's own 1980s indie band Biff Bang Pow wrote such bedwetters' anthems as "If You Don't Love Me Now You Never Will" and "Hug Me Honey",' noted *Guardian* rock critic Alexis Petridis.

A month later, McGee raised his polemic agression in *Melody Maker* while describing Courtney Love: 'She's about real punk rock, she's what it's all about, not like those twats in Coldplay. Coldplay are like something from an ice cream advert, just complete careerists. They might as well be saying, "bend me over the desk and fuck me up the arse." It's pathetic.'

The insecure psyche of Chris Martin had produced beautiful song ideas and sensitive lyrics. But now, this evident vulnerability was being used as a basis for condemnation. For Chris, it was agonising; he was always heavy on self-criticism, but dealing with it from others was another matter.

Will told *The Sunday Telegraph*. 'Obviously Chris gets the brunt of the pressure because he's the frontman and he writes the songs.' Chris added, 'People were saying, "Oh, they're just a careerist, major label band," that really, really hurt us.'

'Yes, he's just an old punk, isn't he?' Chris countered to *Q*. 'We're not sure how we feel about the nomination just yet. It's a strange position to be in, isn't it? We're hardly pushing boundaries, but then it's not been a good year for great albums, so of course we should be there.'

Ultimately, the band managed to muster a defensive combination of goodwill and defiance. Chris continued, 'I would like to shake Alan McGee by the hand. Quite right of him to give us a kick up the arse. I say, bring it on, because it makes me think, "I'll show you." ' Jonny added, 'I think Primal Scream should have been nominated, that last album was excellent.' 'You don't mean that, Jon,' Chris chided, 'You're just rattled by what Alan McGee said, that's all. Since when did you like Primal Scream?'

'I've always liked them, and I mean it,' said Jonny, tranquilly, '*XTRMNTR* is a great record.' 'Rubbish,' countered Chris. An awkward silence followed. 'Sorry, I didn't mean that. I just didn't know you liked Primal Scream, that's all.' Then Chris turned, embarrassed, to the journalist, as if this tiny spat had been a major row: 'Don't put that in, will you?'

> **'We put a lot of effort into making a record that we are proud of and happy with, so it's nice to know that other people quite like it too.'** — *Coldplay*

It wasn't until a year later that Chris admitted publicly to having had very different feelings from the ones he had previously expressed. Walking across St. James Park with Ted Kessler of *The Observer*, buying chestnuts and slugging from a water bottle, he finally admitted that the public attack had made him very afraid that McGee might be right. 'I'd always hoped that writing good songs that mean something would be enough. And here was a guy who'd put out really important records by the likes of Oasis and Primal Scream saying, "No it isn't you loser." '

'I'd think: "Gosh, I'm just some public-school boy with my house colours. I've got a degree. I'm from a middle-class family in Devon . . . I can't be compared to Liam Gallagher or the Sex Pistols, or anyone real. I haven't got any experiences as valid as the Wu Tang Clan." I was incredibly insecure about it.'

A year previously, just after Coldplay signed to Parlophone, Chris's father went to a big family dinner where a female relation addressed him in a pitying voice: 'Anthony, ah, I'm so sorry. All that money wasted.'

'What do you mean?' Chris's father asked.

'Well, you know, Christopher wasting all that money on this ridiculous thing.'

'Nah, it's brilliant!' he replied.

As a father, Anthony Martin had tried above all to encourage Chris to reach for a more spontaneous choice of career than his own, 'because my dad comes from a generation when you were given a job and that's what you did,' Chris noted. Anthony's feeling when he was told about the media attack on his son's music can only be imagined.

Beneath the bluster, McGee's favourite artists and Coldplay all had a great deal in common. They were all making great music, and they were all generating controversy. The arbitrary rudeness of Oasis, the uncompromising artistry of Primal Scream, the uncensored vulnerability of Coldplay, all came at a price. Each of these bands had been inspired by the music of others. And their work would combine to influence music in the future. These similarities represented a more profound dynamic within music than any public slanging match. Besides attacking Coldplay, McGee had also made some more all-inclusive statements about the record industry as a whole arguing that, 'Record companies are only interested in taking the character out of bands. Individualism is on the wane, corporate globalisation is on the up.'

Phil was quick to slam McGee's comments on the band's website: 'What are you talking about, man? You've made millions and millions of pounds doing exactly the same thing. In fact, your behaviour was infinitely more corporate and profit-driven than anything we could imagine in our bed-wetting dreams. You criticised us at a time when simultaneously we were the hottest band in the country and you were floating your new record company on the stock exchange. I fear to fucking think how many millions our name and music made you with that one well-timed remark.'

'Rock 'n' roll is about doing what the fuck you want,' insisted Chris in *Melody Maker*. 'It doesn't have to be about doing huge amounts of drugs or being hedonistic. It's about not caring what anyone else thinks of you. Rock 'n' roll is about the seeking of the ultimate pleasure. For us, that means hanging around together and playing music that we all love and not being afraid to say that's why we're doing it. We just get on with doing it. We don't want to live up to anybody else's cliché.'

While the Coldplay/McGee spat was occupying the music press, the band flew to Japan for the Summer Sonic Festival: a newly-established rival to the Fuji Rock Festival, held in a pine forest at the base of Mount Fuji, and featuring such other notables as Muse, Sigur Ros, the Flaming Lips and the Jon Spencer Blues Explosion.

'It's good that we have the opportunity to take our music to other countries, but it also feels weird, like we're travelling salesmen,' Chris told *Q*'s Nick Duerden. However strange it may have seemed, the clamour for their autographs provided proof, even to their worrisome frontman, that Coldplay had attained celebrity status far from home. Despite the intense schedule that was building up in the wake of *Parachutes'* success, their Japanese trip provided the band with a rare moment of quiet reflection. 'Me, Jonny and Will couldn't sleep one night, and so we came down to the bar in the hotel and chatted away with these really amazing barmen looking out of the windows at this great big volcano, eating chocolate.'

> ## 'Rock 'n' roll is about doing what the fuck you want. It doesn't have to be about doing huge amounts of drugs or being hedonistic.' – *Chris Martin*

Upon returning to England, the band were immediately confronted by their rapidly arriving future. Relaxing in front of a television, they were stunned by expensive adverts for *Parachutes*. They had no idea that their songs were being advertised on TV. 'I suppose, ultimately, it's a good thing, because we're getting our music to as wide an audience as possible. And it is good music, after all,' reflected Chris.

Within a week, the band departed for Portugal's Paredes de Coura festival – 'the most horrible gig we've played,' in front of a crowd mainly drawn from the global fraternity of metal-worshippers. The audience's persistent silence drove Chris to new depths of self-deprecation, introducing 'Trouble' as 'soppy' and apologising, by saying, 'I'm sorry we're not very heavy rock.'

Their stay in Portugal had begun in hectic confusion. On reaching the arrivals barrier they finally figured out that a youth with a banner saying 'Gold Pray' was their driver. 'We're still at the stage where people get our name wrong,' Chris grinned. The band screeched off into temporary anonymity, driving through rattling rain and wind with Chris asking *Select*'s Mark Beaumont, 'Are you okay? Are you okay?' every two minutes. In the kitschy hotel foyer the band went off into a huddle among the palm trees, from whence forceful murmurings about 'keeping sane' could be heard.

'Hey! It's the Cold Plays!' A grinning Wayne Coyne of the Flaming Lips greeted Coldplay at Paredes de Coura. Coyne was a welcome sight for the group, who were great admirers of both him and his merry band. The Lips were playing the slot immediately after them, and suddenly, a basic hunger for fun returned as they dashed around helping blow up colourful balloons for the Lips' stage

Chris at the band's HMV Oxford Street promo gig for the release of Parachutes. *This shot gives the illusion of space, but the gig was packed solid.*

finale. The mutual affection between the bands was strong. Will wistfully regretted that Coldplay's career hadn't mirrored the Flaming Lips' measured ascent. 'There's something enviable about the way the Lips have done it and stayed so credible. It's not as if we asked to be thrust up there.'

But now that they were 'up there', Coldplay worked hard to maintain their position. The new American deal meant there would be a US tour to promote the release of *Parachutes*. This was to be followed by a Scandinavian tour, an autumn tour of Britain, the UK release of the new single 'Trouble' in October, and gigs were already firmed up in Australia for the start of 2001.

Additionally, it emerged that EMI's strategy for *Parachutes* meant that Coldplay would be stuck promoting the album throughout 2001, across the entire globe. Chris and Guy, however, were determined that all promotional work should cease at Christmas. They didn't want to exhaust the public appetite for the band. '. . . It would just kill us. We don't want to get on any-one's nerves,' stressed Chris.

'Coldplay used to think they could record an album, do a bit of promotion, then get back to the studio and make another,' Beaumont observed wryly. 'Now they realise the second LP will have to wait and their self-confessed awkwardness with the press is suddenly more of a problem.'

This schedule, the band realised, would prevent a follow up to the *Parachutes* album for well over a year.

Next on the summer festival itinerary was a trip to Germany for the Bizarre Festival, held near Cologne, where the band appeared alongside Beck, Moby, Placebo, Muse and the Rollins Band. The following day, 19 August, Coldplay were back in the UK to appear at the two-legged V2000 Festival, which took place at Hylands Park in Staffordshire and at Chelmsford, Essex.

At Chelmsford, Coldplay pulled one of the crowds of the weekend, despite appearing on the sec-ond stage before Moby, Joe Strummer, Feeder and the Dandy Warhols. Chris took the opportuni-ty to thank the panoramic crowd for sending them to Number One. 'The charts don't mean shit to us,' he proclaimed. 'But it does feel great to beat the Corrs!'

'I love you!' screamed a girl.

'You don't know me, I'm a twat,' Chris countered.

The V Festival crowd greeted 'Yellow' with a great growling cheer that made Chris cry out, 'It's great to be back! In charge!' Coldplay chose to end their set with what *Dotmusic*'s reviewer called 'the little sad trickling piano' of 'Everything's Not Lost'.

> **'It's good that we have the opportunity to take our music to other countries, but it also feels weird, like we're travelling salesmen.'** — *Chris Martin*

The only major UK festival Coldplay couldn't play that summer was the Reading/Leeds event because - quaintly - the dates clashed with a big match for Chris's father's village cricket team. The band had missed it the previous year, and felt they couldn't let him down again.

This decision might also have come from a desire to slow down. 'I've been on the road now for just over 48 hours and boy am I tired,' gasped Phil. 'There is simply no let up – and I'm not even doing anything. I have merely trailed the boys for the last three days as they have gone from TV show to face to face press interview to radio acoustic session to gig to aftershow to tourbus to airport to hotel to TV show to radio show . . . you get the idea.' Each day brought the band a fresh maelstrom of interviews, in-store signings and radio promotions. Nights generally demanded that all their passion be summoned anew for another gig.

Success was something Coldplay could only really measure once they were onstage. From city to city, they hurried down breezeblock corridors or out of Portakabins, then made their way around the speakers into audience view. Only then would it become clear whether they were known to that particular crowd. Each night involved the same guessing game.

By day, the band tried to find ways to relax and occupy themselves as they travelled for long hours on their purple and cyclamen tour bus. Trying to read an 'absorbing' book was difficult, Jonny found. The novel he had brought along, *Das Boot,* told the famous tale of psychological decline aboard a claustrophobic WWII U-boat. Almost inevitably, the tour bus was christened 'Das Bus'. A clear consequence of this rigourous touring came when Jonny suddenly came down with a short, but severe bout of glandular fever.

The band were very worried by this, *Playlouder* reported, and had cancelled their Scandinavian tour. 'They're scared,' one source said, 'This is the most important stage of their career so far, and this could really fuck things up.' Within days, Coldplay were due to perform at the Mercury Awards ceremony – a frontline gig if ever there was one. The prospect of playing in front of Alan McGee and other doubters was already intimidating. With Jonny ill, it was possible that they would have to cancel and face a further torrent of criticism.

Will recalled this harrowing period in a later interview with *Select*. 'Johnny was completely laid up in bed, Chris was going through mad paranoia and everybody was fucking worried. It was just soul-destroying. Guy was going mad, Chris was going mad, and I was a one-man promotional machine. I think we realised our priorities were all wrong. This is not what we got into a band to do.'

With the horizontal Jonny now only capable of making feeble hand-signals, the band was now reduced to a trio. They now had to decide what they should do about playing at the all-important Pilton Village Fete in Glastonbury on 1 September. The event could make or break their status as future Glastonbury headliners.

On the day, the crowd was surprised to see Chris Martin climb up onstage alone with his acoustic guitar. His body language gave an impression of acute anxiety, his face stretched tight with fear. He put his lips right onto the mic, and muttered with an intensity that filled the huge tent, 'If you want me to stay I'll stay, if you want me to go I'll fuck off.' Then he struck up 'Shiver'.

Coldplay's music, if not the rest of the band, was now with him onstage. It was enough. *nme.com* later described the transformation: 'Stripped to its bones, "Shiver" gives him the chance to perform all kinds of tricks with his voice. He fills this cavernous tent with ease, sometimes singing falsetto where a guitar line should be, at other times just letting the ever-swelling crowd do the work for him. Two songs in, and his smile is as big as the reception he's getting. Martin has gone from being as rigid as a board to waltzing around the stage to his guitar in five minutes.'

Coldplay's music did more than just salvage this particular gig. Chris claimed that one song in particular kept the band together during this very shaky time: 'In My Place'. 'That was the one thing on the horizon that we thought, "We must stay together for that,"' confessed Chris to *VH1*'s Weiderhorn. 'And we did, and that's why we're still here. We were suddenly taken aback by everything, and we didn't know if we were coming or going. But when we wrote "In My Place", it was nice to know that we had at least one more album in us.'

> **'The charts don't mean shit to us. But it does feel great to beat the Corrs!'** — *Chris Martin*

During the summer of 2001, Emma Holland, the young student journalist from Oxford, turned up at a Coldplay gig. Emma found Chris transformed, 'he looked healthy and tanned, clean-shaven with gel-styled hair. With his braces gone his smile wasn't goofy any more – it was sexy.' Afterwards she went backstage and stood there with no college reporter's notebook as a comfortable prop. Chris strode towards her. 'Before I knew it, he planted a kiss on my cheek. "What are you doing afterwards?"' Chris asked.

'I admit it, where before he'd irritated me, I now felt flattered,' wrote Emma. 'I felt closer to him than ever. We were alone and, regardless of all that had happened, he still wanted to be with me. We made our way back to a friend's house for a night together.' However, a few days later, her telephone rang. 'It was Chris, but this time his tone wasn't affectionate. He said he felt bad about what happened that night because it had been "shallow", that he'd only wanted something he couldn't have before.'

Emma subsequently sold her story to *Elle* magazine, and versions of it later appeared in some tabloids. At the time, she was studying journalism in London, and may have seen writing her confessional memoir as a means to gaining a foothold in the industry. Conversely, Chris has maintained silence about the matter. But his later general comments made in an interview with *Q* provide some insight into his reaction to meeting Emma again: 'There's a dichotomy between the wannabe rock star in me and the son of my mother. I think girls are amazing but I also feel really guilty about doing stuff with someone that you don't really like. I don't believe there is such a thing as casual sex. Someone always gets hurt. And I hate that feeling.'

Later that summer, Chris met radio executive and Bettina Motive manager Lily Sobhani. On their first date he must have appeared quite the rock star, 'While we were out, I did get recognised for the very first time in my life. Not once, but twice!' Chris told *Q*, 'Between you and me, I think she was pretty impressed.' The frontman's feelings developed quickly. 'It was a time in my life when I thought, "this is it" and I thought I'd better start looking for a ring,' he told *The Sun*'s Jaqui Swift.

Hello, were Coldplay.
It was a great
pleasure to be
the first band on
at the Bizarre festival
especially because
it's our first time
in Germany! Thanks
to everyone who
watched us. Hope
to see you soon
in Germany.
Guy - Jonny, Chris

A note of thanks to the German organisers and audience of the Bizarre Festival.

Lily and Chris began a relationship that was to last a year, and their break-up inspired the song 'Warning Sign' that would appear on Coldplay's second album. Lily sometimes came along on the tour bus, and passed many hours quietly playing Scrabble with Chris.

Lily had hooked up with Chris just as fame was breaking, and this fact led to a surprising disclosure that intensified Coldplay's uniquely innocent public image. In a *Melody Maker* interview, journalist Everett True examined what it was like to grow up insecure and unloved: 'Themes which seem sort of appropriate to Coldplay's star-struck, solemn, moody, guitar-led music.' When True revealed that he himself had been a virgin at the age of 23, Chris piped up, 'I was a virgin at 22 and since then I've only been with one person and . . . ' Immediately Chris regretted his words, and scrambled frantically to rewind the tape recorder, 'Shit! You can't print that.' 'Keep it!' laughed Jonny, as Chris held his head in his hands: 'I swear if you repeat that, I would . . . seriously . . . I would just kill myself.'

Undeterred by his threat, *The Sun* later devoted an entire page to Chris's revelations. and, following that, *Melody Maker*'s Andre Paine asked Chris if he'd been embarrassed by such nation-wide exposure of his late deflowering. 'Yeah!' Chris paused. 'No, I don't even give a shit; I'll talk about it until the cows come home. It was just funny. Why would anyone be interested?'

'You were single when you wrote "Yellow", and now you have a girlfriend. Will that affect your songwriting?' asked Paine. 'Yes, no . . . I dunno. The darkest thing I've written is since I've been going out with someone. But then some of the lightest things we've written have been since then as well. "Yellow" is about people, it's not about a girl. It could be about you!'

Beyond the innocent games of Scrabble, Chris and Lily also found an affinity in their interest in humanitarian concerns. Even after they broke up, when Lily, together with Emily Eavis, daughter of Glastonbury founder Michael, organised a protest gig against the 2003 invasion of Iraq, Chris readily agreed to perform.

The day of the Mercury Awards Ceremony at Grosvenor House Hotel came hurrying along. With Jonny still seriously ill, the band opted to play 'Yellow' as a three-piece. Their performance, just before the judges' decision was announced, was a live test in front of the whole industry. The nervous trio knew that they would certainly be dissected by their fiercest critics. The spotlight of fame now doubled as an interrogator's lamp. Chris told *Select*, 'I felt extremely paranoid. I thought my hair was falling out.'

In any event, Coldplay's performance was no embarrassment, but as it turned out, the award went to the candidate that Coldplay themselves had championed: Badly Drawn Boy. During his acceptance speech, singer-songwriter Damon Gough generously thanked Coldplay for their gracious support of his work. It was a welcome, yet anti-climactic moment for the band.

Chris was only temporarily discouraged by such minor disappointments, yet his deep-rooted insecurities meant little chance of fame going to his head. Despite his extraordinary talent, Chris's reactions to criticism and adulation were resolutely ordinary. Caught in a media crossfire of praise and vitriol, the frontman understandably became paranoid and distressed. 'We're starting to feel that everyone's out to get us,' he told the *Independent on Sunday*'s Nicolas Barber. 'The more people that like us, the more people seem to hate us, and it's something nobody tells you how to deal with. A lot of people seem to take it personally that we're doing well, and I hate that. I hate being criticised for just doing songs. It's utterly pointless, because that's what we love and that's what people like about us. We're not evil politicians trying to swindle the whole world.'

But the band's rejection of the traditional rock 'n' roll lifestyle of excess and rebellion, in favour of the more intangible goal of 'moving people', was sometimes a media liability in itself. Chris admitted this to *Select*'s Mark Beaumont: 'We come on a bit earnest. A bit Honest John. [in a simpleton's voice] "All we know how to do is play songs." But I worry about our image becoming more important than the music. I like seeing posters for the LP on the Tube because it's our album being famous, not us for going out with the Appleton sisters.'

In *Melody Maker*, Emma Johnston was encouraged by the sudden rise of Coldplay and several other bands, seeing this as the end of 'almost a year of suffering under UK Garage', and delighting in 'the realisation that there were enough good bands to fight back and win'.

But when she met Chris in the run up to Coldplay's October headline tour, Johnston observed an individual struggling to cope. 'Sitting in the EMI offices in London, he's stressed, tired and worried. He says his eye is hurting and he's starting to fret about his hair falling out.' Asked if he was looking forward to going to America early next year, Chris's fatigue flashed out: 'No. I shouldn't have said that, should I? Right now, I just wanna go to bed, whether it's a bed in America or Hawaii or wherever.'

With Chris and Guy exhibiting the burnt-out behaviour of the seriously exhausted, and Jonny still sick, Will Champion lived up to his surname by taking responsibility for virtually all the band's promotional interviews. Many of these were done by phone, including a lot of press for the forthcoming single 'Trouble', which Will identified as 'our favourite on the album, but we don't expect it to outshine "Yellow".'

Will quickly proved extremely adept at pre-empting misconceived views of the album, and was quick to point out that *Parachutes* wasn't quite the dark, morose offering that some critics had tagged it. 'A lot of the songs are quite moody and are telling of bad things or whatever, especially lyrically. But there's a lot of twists that imply optimism and stuff like that,' he stressed to *mtv.com*. 'For example, in "Spies" there's a little twist at the end of the lyrics which is kind of contrary to the music. The music sounds really dark, but the lyrics are quite positive at the very end . . . The lyrics are beautiful and they're really, really happy, but the music is really, really sad.' Continuing his upbeat theme, Will even gave a cheerful interview about filming the 'Yellow' video, suppressing the painful memory of his mother's funeral.

The drummer was fielding most of the promotional press for the American market. A massive undertaking – but it was vital to collaborate with their US label all the way. 'Yeah, it's hard,' Will admitted during a phone conversation with *Vanguard Online*'s Guernica. 'Really hard work. I've been sitting here from nine o'clock this morning doing phone interviews. We obviously wanted to get our music across to people, but this is a tricky period. Our priorities are not our priorities at the moment.' Trapped in this cycle of press calls, Will had only been out of the house four times in the past week or so. At least this confinement allowed him to catch up on some football. Even this early in the season, his beloved Southampton were trying to avoid relegation.

Finally, Jonny walked back onto the musical battlefield just in time to take part in the filming of a video for their upcoming single, 'Trouble', on 25 September.

Directed by Tim Hope, (whose credits included the 'I Walk The Earth' promo for psych-poppers King Biscuit Time), the all night shoot took place in London's Kings Cross. This was still a notorious district for drugs and prostitution, even after the police had introduced a zero-tolerance policy and saturated the place with security cameras.

'At about eleven o'clock we heard an awful wailing sound coming from across the road,' Will told *Coldplay.com*. 'We looked out to see an old man, a girl and "youth" involved in a scuffle. The old man was being viciously beaten up by the younger bloke, and all we could hear was this piercing screeching coming from the old man.' With that, some of the crew intervened, pulling the scuffling men apart. The police turned up and the full situation was revealed. 'It turns out the girl and the boy were working together, the girl posing as a prostitute lured the old man round the corner where her accomplice beat him up and stole his wallet.'

Despite this distraction, the band completed their part in the shoot, with Will and Jonny staying up until seven a.m. to see the project through. Later that day, the band were to perform at the Millennium Dome as part of a specially filmed series of concerts for Japanese TV. It was an odd assortment on that night's bill, including Reef, Toploader, Placebo and Mansun. *Dotmusic* reported that Coldplay created the biggest, most impressive sound of the night in the vast, impersonal Dome, and that 'hearing their tender songs burst to life makes the venue feel warm and pleasant.'

On 2 October Coldplay embarked on a major headline tour of Britain, supported by low-fi indie trio, Lowgold. Starting at the Junction in Cambridge, the offensive took up almost the entire month and visited such destinations as Belfast, Dublin, Glasgow and Manchester *en route* to a trio of showcase gigs at London's Shepherd's Bush Empire. A 'big scary, fame-boosted headline tour,' *Melody Maker* helpfully dubbed it. No pressure.

There was enough tension in the Coldplay entourage to suspend them all from a high wire, because this odyssey would either affirm or dissipate the band's popularity in their homeland. *Melody Maker*'s Emma Johnston set out the stakes: 'This tour is a balancing act. For the first time, people are here purely for Coldplay, to try and work out if they care about them beyond "Yellow" . . . The question is, are Coldplay anyone's favourite band? And would Coldplay want success if it meant more people would only *quite like* their songs?'

At Cambridge, Emma Johnston observed that 'a strong, alcohol-laced tension' pervaded the gig as the band prepared to come on. On came the band and straight away sliced through 'Spies' with huge quaking drums and gorgeous guitar slides – to a guarded response from the audience.

Looking edgy, Chris chanced a smile. 'Now that we're headlining, we don't know what to say. So we'll just sing,' he announced. 'Bigger Stronger' was the next powerful number, and also representative of Chris's mood, as he bantered the crowd into good spirits. 'Just because we've got people to cook our food and clean our teeth, I don't want you to think we've got bigheaded. There's a bit of a tense atmosphere, can you lighten up a bit? If you want you can buy a t-shirt, we're *that* big.' This shattered the ice-wall between band and crowd, and by the time the quartet plunged into the set-closing 'In My Place' (described by Johnston as a 'big hearted, big bottomed anthem'), the Cambridge crowd had transformed into Coldplay zealots.

The Shepherds Bush Empire show on 21 October was Coldplay's biggest headlining gig to date. They safely negotiated 'Spies', presenting it as a great, smoking fire of a song. Chris then bounded to the electronic piano to play 'Trouble'. The piano, however, remained silent. Chris celebrated the glitch by mock-banging his head on the keys, then jumped up and ran forward strumming his guitar, while behind him roadies crawled around grappling with wires. Such assurance in the face of high farce was a far cry from the sort of panic that would have ensued a few months earlier, when Chris was wracked by doubts.

The band had been working in some new songs on this tour, and the response to them was emphatic. 'The new songs are a lot more wide-ranging than those on *Parachutes*,' observed Emma Johnston. '"Animals", for example, is much more paranoid than usual, with a huge bassline and stark guitars and Chris uncharacteristically realising, "I could die." "Careful Where You Stand" . . . [surprises us] with earburstingly high-pitched noises, and an REM jangle.'

The gig went brilliantly, gathering serious critical praise. 'The band constantly lift their material with cunning arrangements and purposeful musicianship. Their best songs have a distinctive colour that sticks in the mind, whether it's the keening, trebly guitar that Jon Buckland sends gliding above "Don't Panic", Martin's stately piano figure in "Trouble" or Guy Berryman's bassline in "Sparks". Almost everywhere, Will Champion's restless, hustling drum patterns give the music an urgency that its slow tempos and melancholy melodies might otherwise lack,' enthused *Guardian* journalist Adam Sweeting.

Throughout the gig, Chris made theatrical dashes along the stage, allowing people to clutch his clothes, satirising the idea of the musician as an icon. 'His tendency towards self-deprecation is beginning to become a live trademark of the band,' *Dotmusic* commented. 'Self-consciously starting stories and stopping halfway through because he's talking bollocks, or apologising because he isn't sufficiently rock 'n' roll.' This gently laddish, squawk-box banter created moments of humorous warmth within the music's rocking melancholy.

As for Coldplay, they felt a startling sense of role reversal because in the dimly lit and absolutely attentive crowd stood many celebrities. Liam Gallagher, Kylie Minogue and the teenage Chris's object of desire, Natalie Imbruglia, were all in attendance. Chris may mock his celebrity onstage, but the world's celebrities were now closing in on him.

> **'A lot of the songs are quite moody and are telling of bad things . . . But there's a lot of twists that imply optimism.'** *– Will Champion*

'These are people we've never associated ourselves with because they've always been "famous people". Now they're in our dressing room. It's a bit unreal,' Guy later commented to *Select*. The bassist was naturally very keen to see if Liam Gallagher was as he'd imagined him (he was), and it was an adventure to greet 'Beth from *Neighbours*'. 'I don't feel famous at all,' Will exulted, 'I like the way the name of the band is becoming more known, but I can put my hat on after a gig and slip into anonymity.'

Backstage, Liam Gallagher told Chris that 'Yellow' had made him want to write songs, for example, the beautiful 'Songbird' – the lyrics of which he gently sang into Chris's ear. Further music to Chris's ears was the Gallaghers' take on the Mercury Prize controversy: 'Don't worry 'bout fookin' McGee. We like ya.'

The surreal experience of meeting one of his adolescent icons made Chris marvel to *The Observer*'s Ted Kessler, 'Dreams do come true. They really do! I grew up watching *Neighbours* and I was totally fixated by this one character, Beth. I really fell in love with her. Years later I'm in a band and who do I meet? Beth, Natalie Imbruglia, and she's a fan. Of me, well, of our music . . . That's amazing. She's a mate of mine. She's my friend. It's too strange.' But when Kessler asked whether Chris had told her that he fell in love with her as a teenager, Chris scoffed, 'You don't really think I can talk about that with you, do you?'

On 29 October, six days after its release, 'Trouble' barged into the UK chart at Number Ten, and as Chris said, transformed Coldplay from 'a one-hit wonder to a two-hit wonder'. Not everyone liked the single, though. In *Melody Maker*, 'Trouble' was featured in 'The Dumper' – a weekly feature whereby a guest reviewer (on this occasion duff-metallers King Adora) identifies their 'absolute stinker' from current single releases. Interestingly, the column's uncredited introduction concisely nailed Coldplay's reputation: 'Already in their short career Coldplay are pretty much beyond reviewing. You've made up your mind, I've made up my mind and King Adora have definitely made up their mind.' They certainly had. 'There's no real ache in his voice, whatsoever . . . sadness with no real emotion is the worst thing on earth,' wailed the longhairs.

At the beginning of November, Coldplay made a return visit to the *Top of the Pops* studios in the esteemed company of U2, Doves, and JJ72. Phil Harvey got to meet U2's manager, Paul McGuinness, whom he had long viewed as a management role model. When McGuinness introduced U2 guitarist The Edge, Phil got a surprise: 'I was trying to think of something suitably reverential to say but before I had a chance to speak Edge was going, "Oh, so you're Phil Harvey, I was reading about you in the paper at the weekend." Very weird.'

Once again, the experience of being on *TOTP* helped to heal Chris's alienated sense of being little more than a provincial boarding school boy who could never belong to the rock musicians' gang. 'You start meeting these people and you realize they're just humans like you, like me,' he later told *The Observer*. 'We're all ordinary, it's what we make that makes us extraordinary. Why be scared of anyone because of where you're from or what you do? When I realised that, it was like somebody had opened the window and I could breathe again.'

Chris was not the only person in the industry who was relaxing about Coldplay's new ascendancy. Cynics, nay-sayers and other suspicious folk were realising that, as *Melody Maker*'s Emma Johnston observed, 'in the end Coldplay's sunny, non-angsty outlook feels genuine. It's not just an act to make you like them before they stab you in the throat and turn into Slipknot.'

Buoyed by recognition, Phil's next challenge was to steer Coldplay through some murky financial waters. BMG, Coldplay's publishing company, had called him to relay an offer of £100,000 from a financial services company that wanted to use 'Yellow' on the soundtrack of their TV advert. Phil responded with a resounding, 'No!' But afterwards he questioned this knee-jerk reaction, pondering his adamant (and expensive) refusal to sanction the use of any song for commercials.

Many artists had previously chosen to license their songs for commercial use; every single track on Moby's multi-platinum album *Play* would be recycled for film soundtracks or commercials. For this he suffered a serious backlash extending even outside the music press, damaging his credibility as a musician. John Robinson of *nme.com*'s reaction to the Moby album *We Are Made Of Stars* is a prime example: 'Mr Clothes Shop Music 2000 returns secure in the knowledge that now his *Play* album is piped into every fitting room in every retail outlet in every country, he can now do whatever the hell he likes.'

In the end, the band's consensus was that Coldplay's songs should never be sold to advertisers. The main reason for this lay in the group's own experience of hearing and experiencing classic songs. The band had a powerful vision of the way that music affected everyday life. So many songs had made Chris jump up and down in a dorm room, on the stairs, or in the launderette. Hearing Johnny Cash on the car CD player as he travelled towards another dull day in primary school led to Chris's discovery that his emotions could be expressed powerfully in music.

'We just wanted to make a record that gives as much enjoyment to people as records that people have given to us,' Guy told *Pausenplay* magazine. 'The way I see it, records are a way of documenting your life; if I hear something old, it'll trigger something in my brain, like "Oh, yeah, that reminds me of a certain time and place in my life."'

Coldplay's music had the potential to provide the score to the most precious, or heartbreaking, moments in the lives of their fans. Farming out their catalogue as drab work-donkeys for commercial products meant that people who identified with the songs would experience a kind of musical betrayal.

Beyond the fact that there were many products the band would never want to be linked with,

Chris in rapture at the 2001 V-Festival in Hylands Park.

SEVEN

NEVER STOP GOING 'TIL WE GET THERE

Will Champion lay paddling along on his surfboard, his skin the colour of a skeletal white whale under Australia's summer sun. He saw a promising wave rising and scrabbled toward it fast. But a bronzed local surfer cut him off, snarling, 'That one's mine, mate.' Will watched him ride it in to shore. Craig Tansley from *Massive* magazine, who was there on the beach interviewing Chris and Will, asked, 'Why didn't you tell him who you were?'

'Oh I'm sure he'd give me the wave then,' Will answered sarcastically. 'Yeah, I'm the drummer of some band you've probably never heard of, can you give me the wave?' Meanwhile there was Chris, looking like an updated Jesus surfing into the shore, shouting, 'Did you see that, mate, did you see that?'

It was January 2001, just after Coldplay's first Christmas as a famous UK band, and a week or so before February's Brit Awards, for which they were heavily nominated. The nominations were largely determined by an academy of over 1,000 members, with the exception of a few awards voted for by the public. *Parachutes* was nominated for best album alongside Craig David's *Born To Do It*, Radiohead's *Kid A,* David Gray's *Lost Songs* and Robbie Williams' *Swing When You're Winning*. Their nomination for Best British Newcomer was predictable, but Coldplay were also up for Best British Group against Radiohead – now thirtysomethings, their most recent album had met with massive critical acclaim and appropriately corresponding sales. (The other nominees were All Saints, Moloko and Toploader.) It was a contest between generations, between the musical sorcerers and their apprentices; between avant-garde originality and Coldplay's more subtly melodic accessibility.

There were other heartening signs that Coldplay's British detractors were getting used to the quartet, processing and assimilating them – as cyclically occurs when new bands appear – into an arbitrary scene. The print heads were now clustering bands together around Coldplay in the way they had once grouped them around Radiohead.

In early 2001, it seemed that quiet was the new loud. *NME* identified a 'New Acoustic Movement' that encompassed Coldplay, Travis, the Turin Brakes and Starsailor. When their debut single, 'Fever', reached number eighteen during February, the music paper called Starsailor 'the best new band in Britain'. John Aizlewood of *The Guardian* wrote a piece defining this swelling wave of acts that he claimed were as exciting as Oasis, The Clash and The Who had been in their time. Of the popular response to Coldplay, Aizlewood wrote, 'First hearings suggested Radiohead and, based on early live performances, an extra-smug Richard Thompson. Countless

What's the spatial difference between a tour bus and a laundry basket? Coldplay looking cheery before their Heineken Music Hall gig in Amsterdam, July 2002.

83

hearings later, *Parachutes* is still unfurling new charms and, as a frontman, Chris Martin has become as compelling an onstage figure as OMD's Andy McCluskey.'

In addition to scoring pub quiz points for remembering Orchestral Manoeuvres in the Dark (OMD), Aizlewood perceived the crucially distinct elements within Coldplay – their almost contradictory immediacy and evasive subtlety. It had taken only six months for critics to develop a richer appreciation of Coldplay as a band. But then, six months is a virtual eon in terms of British pop. Streams of UK acts rise and fall in the time that it takes one US idol to change hairstyle. Inevitably, British record companies were now trying to hoover up gently mannered 'new acoustic' acts from every pub venue.

Starsailor were even being asked by regular Coldplay interviewer Dave Simpson whether the association with them was a curse or a blessing – just as Coldplay had been asked about Travis. In truth, Starsailor were not Coldplay copyists, but their name derives from an album by Tim Buckley, similarly short-lived father to the tragic Jeff, thus identifying common influences. 'You have to be honest about who you're inspired by,' said their songwriter James Walsh. In what sounds like the perfect Chris-ism, he also claimed, 'My songs start off a lot more [Jeff] Buckley than they finish. I have so much respect, I'd never try to copy him.'

Following the series of rejuvenating sold-out European gigs during November and December, Coldplay had made a quick promotional sortie to appear at LA radio station KROQ's annual holiday show on 16 December. At this first ever US engagement, the foursome played for 6,000 fans on a revolving stage. 'For us it was the oddest seeing Los Angeles,' Chris told Mark Watt of *Hear/Say*. 'I suppose it's similar to an American visiting London and thinking they are going to see the Queen and Big Ben and then you realise it is a normal town with people going about. Since Los Angeles is the town with all of the films, we had a rather pre-conceived idea, which obviously was false.' KROQ's show was a 'fun hospitality Christmas night' with souvenir CD spin-offs.

Not everything about Hollywood was embraced with open arms. 'Yesterday I spoke to Sly Stallone on the phone because they want "Trouble" in a film,' Chris revealed. Coldplay politely turned down a request from Stallone to use the song in his new film, *Driven*, after he had phoned the boys personally to entreat them. 'It was very flattering,' said Will, 'but we turned him down because we just didn't think it was appropriate to the film. We have had quite a few offers but we haven't decided on one yet.' Before flying home for Christmas, the band recorded a live session for LA's KCRW on 20 December.

After an extended New Year break, Coldplay flew to New Zealand for the first leg of their Australasian tour. The 19 January show at the 38,000-capacity Ericsson Stadium in Auckland was the opening leg of the 2001 Big Day Out Festival, a roadshow that also took in Queensland's Gold Coast, Sydney, Melbourne, Adelaide and Perth.

Much of the Big Day Out bill was comprised of far heavier acts like Limp Bizkit (who pulled out after the Sydney show where a fan was tragically crushed to death during their set), Queens of the Stone Age, Rammstein and Placebo. Despite confessing to some nerves, Chris amused the Auckland press by donning a Fred Durst-style red baseball hat during the pre-show interviews. The frontman scored more sartorial brownie points by taking off his jumper to reveal an 'I Love NZ' t-shirt to the appreciative Kiwi crowd. Oddly, Guy opted for a cowboy hat.

Following the Queensland show, Coldplay arrived in Sydney. The morning after their arrival, Chris and Will dashed out to Sydney's Freshwater Beach with *Massive* magazine's Craig Tansley. Ever since a phone interview a month before, when Chris had discovered the journalist was a life-long surfer, he had bugged Tansley to take him out to 'get tubed' inside the curl of a big wave when he arrived Down Under. Will was equally up for the expedition, although definitely less familiar with a surfboard – 'I'm not afraid. *I'm bloody not,* I just can't figure out how to work this thing,' he insisted.

Jonny and Guy were on a different wave, blissfully sleeping off a 'night shift' out on the town and a tide of jetlag. They'd been out with the road crew and musicians from other Big Day Out bands, sampling the local nightlife and gigs.

'I'd love to come back really soon and do some smaller shows,' Chris told Tansley as they waited for some waves. 'Bands like Limp Bizkit have more immediacy on big tours like the Big Day Out. We just struggle to get atmosphere going. At a gig where it's your band and it's much smaller it's easier to get a connection with the crowd.' 'We've never been hugely convinced of the appropriateness of our set within a main stage, festival context but this time it feels pretty good,' declared Phil. As Chris waded deeper into the surf, he shouted to Tansley, 'That's why we're ditching acoustic guitars for our next record. We're going to get *loud*, man!' This may have been pure impulse speaking, of course. But, as an artist, Chris liked formulating 'anti-principles' for the sake of perversity. Could Loud be the New Quiet?

> **'My songs start off a lot more Buckley than they finish. I have so much respect, I'd never try to copy him.'** – James Walsh

Coldplay were always eager spectators in-between their festival slots, having received a good part of their musical education at such events during their youth. The band would grab a drink by the neck, then slalom eagerly through the backstage crowd like kids keeping pace with a parade, hungry to be stunned by some musical brute force. They were hugely excited by the mighty PJ Harvey, and Texan rockers At The Drive In, with their excellent songs 'Arc Arsenal', 'Quarantined' and 'Non Zero Possibility'.

Chris later acknowledged to the *A Beautiful World* site that Coldplay had entered into a slightly bizarre ritual pact with members of At The Drive In: 'We're kind of friends with them. I mean, they're amazing! . . . We did some sort of thing where we cut our own wrists and swore something together . . . can't tell you what it was.' Despite the inverted snobbery that Coldplay had been subjected to by elements of the UK music business, this was only one of a number of firm friendships they would establish with bands on the international live circuit. Later on, Guy and At The Drive In's Jim Ward would also make plans to collaborate on a new album under the spikily antithetical name of the London Country Rebels.

The band were also less than two weeks away from the most important campaign of their career thus far – the tour to crack the North American market. Breaking the USA remains a hazardous holy grail for many British bands, with little guarantee of success. Triumphant conquerors such as Led Zeppelin or U2 tend to be the exception rather than the norm. The history of rock is littered with casualties such as Slade, T. Rex and the Stone Roses who'd tried and failed. As teenagers, like most of their fans, the band had read enough music press obituaries that ended with a fatalistic 'couldn't crack America and then they did a tail-spin'. Now, with cameras flashing all around them, such a sorry scenario might have seemed dangerously imminent.

America would be a mountainous shitload of exhausting effort, fuelled by the adrenalin of performance. The first US tour was always a hellish rite of passage for any British band with big ambitions. Stateside success had eluded Blur during the heyday of Britpop, and more recently Travis and Embrace. 'I wish selling records was about being a genius,' Alex James of Blur told *The Observer*. 'But it's about being turfed out of a bus at 8am in Washington, being confronted with people you hate, doing something you don't want to do, and coming back here feeling confused.'

Helpfully, Coldplay's path to success was actually paved for them by another band. Travis's summer 2000 US tour, in support of their album, *The Man Who*, had not been terribly success-ful. But, although they were bogged down in their work schedule, Travis also took Coldplay's music along for the ride. Whenever they went on radio, they actually took copies of 'Yellow' and talked up the song's success in the UK. Chief among those paying attention to Travis's altruism was KCRW's Nic Harcourt, who immediately aired tracks from Coldplay on his daily show.

Ironically, Travis had promoted a band that had been tagged early on as copyists of their own style. Similarly, Radiohead were another giant upon whose shoulders Coldplay initially, and inad-vertently, stood. The Stateside success of their extraordinary landmark album, *OK Computer*, reawakened the American industry's interest in British acts. This momentum sent their later, more experimental album, *Kid A*, straight to Number One. Coldplay were honest enough to admit they hoped to get picked up and carried along in the wake of Radiohead's success. They even joked with journalists about calling their own second album *Child B*, and told *Select* that they thought the timing of their tour was good since *Kid A* had just hit the top of the *Billboard* chart.

Crucially for Coldplay, Radiohead's decision to go all-out experimental had given rise to a musical vacuum. In the US, Radiohead had created an appetite for the reflective soft rock of *OK Computer*, and then left fans hungry by, as John Aizlewood put it, 'deciding to alienate their audi-ence with the incomprehensible *Kid A*.' It was hoped that Coldplay's more accessible material would fill that gap in the market.

> **'I was pretty nervous when I arrived not only because it was all so alien, but also because I really don't know all that much yet about the US music industry.' – Phil Harvey**

While the band were still in Australia, *Select* ran a piece by Dorian Lynskey which captured them at their moment of optimistic bounce-back from fame's early traumas. The article praised the new unrecorded material – 'The brooding "Animals", in particular, is magnificent' – but sounded a more rueful note when reflecting on how the band believed they could manage and maintain a creative balance while in America. They wanted, they said, to debut new songs by playing under an alias in tiny venues. 'Most importantly,' noted Lynskey, 'they intend to take alternate fortnights off to write the next album and allay the paranoia that they won't be able to follow *Parachutes*.' Coldplay still believed their saturation schedule would allow space for songwriting and experimentation outside of the customary soundchecks, when they might bash out a reggae version of 'Yellow'.

However, the group's schedule would allow for little in the way of time off. 'Essentially, the secret to success in America is swallowing your pride,' commented *Bang*. The magazine was exam-ining Coldplay's US success which, as *The Guardian*'s Alexis Petridis observed, 'hangs heavy over the UK music industry' due to the doleful lack of any other new British acts making an impact there. *Bang* talked to an 'industry insider' who had worked with Oasis and Morrissey on their US tours. Speaking anonymously, he explained, 'Promotion would be every day on the tour, and very demanding. You'd fit in a day of radio interviews, and pre-recording late night shows like Jay Leno's or David Letterman's, with newspapers slotted in around them. It's very demanding, but if you want to break the market it's the only way. You've got to tour hard and play in venues a lot smaller than the ones you've been playing in the UK' – or, as Guy Berryman so crisply put it, you have to play 'the toilet circuit'.

When breaking America almost a decade ago, Radiohead had taken a less than accommodat-ing attitude to their 'meet and greet' obligations. Their documentary, *Meeting People Is Easy*, vividly captures the band being gradually engulfed by a corporate promotional nightmare. The massive network of American radio stations play a vital role in breaking (or breaking down) acts. Damon Albarn of Blur had to get a doctor's note in order to take a week off sick from an American tour, thereby opting out of some festivals that were to be broadcast live on radio. 'All hell broke loose,' he told *The Observer*'s Gary Mulholland. 'There are two conglomerates who basically own all the radio stations in America. The attitude – which is the worst side of America – was, right, you don't play our game, we're cutting you out entirely.'

The previous autumn, Phil Harvey travelled to Los Angeles on reconnaissance ahead of Coldplay's forthcoming tour. Whilst there, he encountered the Radiohead team working the American radio stations. 'They're all out here to do their first US shows since *Kid A* went straight in at Number One,' he wrote. 'From what I can gather, this is just about the first time they've really ever enjoyed their success.' It must have crossed Phil's mind that, if Coldplay achieved stateside success, he too might only be able to relax and enjoy it five to ten years down the line.

'I was pretty nervous when I arrived not only because it was all so alien, but also because I really don't know all that much yet about the US music industry,' Phil admitted. 'The past few days have, however, been an excellent introduction. On Tuesday I met all the staff at Capitol Records along with the inner team at Capitol affiliate label Nettwerk who will be most closely involved with the band during the early stages.'

'I'm not mandated to release *stuff*,' Nettwerk chief Terry McBride stressed forcefully to *Pollstar*. 'My mandate is to release music that I like and also music that I think by releasing it and working it, we can actually help.' It had already been decided that 'Yellow', rather than the earlier 'Shiver', would serve as Coldplay's introduction to the US. And with all their restless executive energy, Nettwerk didn't wait for the band's February tour to release it. By mid-October, *mtv.com* announced that Nettwerk had already express delivered the track to college and alternative radio stations throughout America. McBride also appointed the label's general manager, Dave Holmes to be responsible for the band in the USA. Effectively, Holmes was now Coldplay's American co-manager, mercifully reducing Phil Harvey's heroic workload.

Newsflashes from Phil, about the excellent reception *Parachutes* and 'Yellow' were receiving stateside, shored up the band's shaky confidence at exactly the time when they needed that support. And American radio needed an act like Coldplay at that very moment. At first, it may have seemed that America's fast-moving current of rap and nu-metal bands could whip Coldplay's fortunes off into oblivion. But in fact, as Steve Lamacq commented, 'Coldplay were an alternative when they first sprang onto the scene . . . One of the reasons American radio first played them was because programme controllers were becoming sick to the teeth of copycat rock bands. I know that because I spoke to someone at a pretty big, influential station in the States, and they couldn't wait for the Coldplay album.' *Los Angeles Times* music critic Robert Hillburn was in agreement with Lamacq's assessment: 'At a time when so much of US commercial rock is taken up with paint-by-number aggression, a band with its own voice and a down-to-earth approach is doubly rewarding.'

Released just ahead of the LP in November 2000, 'Yellow' became a huge airplay hit, with radio exposure stretched right across the nation within weeks. The song was receiving heavy rotation at the all-important KROQ-FM in Los Angeles, one of the most influential stations in the country. Within a month of 'Yellow''s release, ABC-TV noted its magnificence and rapidly exploited its appeal by licensing the song for use over the network's holiday season, which broadened its exposure immensely.

Jim DeRogatis, pop music critic of the *Chicago Sun-Times*, cited ABC TV's use of 'Yellow' as a fundamental reason why Coldplay were quickly building a buzz in America. But when he interviewed Chris by phone while the frontman was down in Australia for the Big Day Out shows, he noted, 'Martin didn't seem to understand quite what a boost this TV exposure had given the band.' Chris asked him, 'Is it an advert? I don't think we get paid for it or anything like that because we've always been extremely anti-advert . . . Oh, if it's just trailing programs I don't mind that. But we'd never, ever advertise Coke.' It was typical of Coldplay's good fortune – or shrewd US marketing – that this perfect opportunity arose for coast-to-coast saturation coverage without entirely compromising their principles.

Mtv.com's Corey Moss wrote a very long article showing that TV shows like *ER* – as much as radio and CDs – are now the dynamic medium for showcasing new songs to the national audience. After citing 35 artists who had broken a new song through TV shows – including Foo Fighters, Paula Cole, the Dandy Warhols, Sterophonics and god-rockers, POD, Moss observed, 'ABC received praise for its use of Coldplay's "Yellow" in advertising its entire roster last winter. The network also helped to break the song along the way.'

In an interview with *Pausenplay* Guy gave his view of the dynamics behind their airplay bonanza. 'It must be that time, where someone needed to make a decision up there, like the media, to start putting good songs on the radio before people become completely disillusioned with music.' As he saw it, 'I just can't believe that everyone in America listens to and enjoys listening to rap-metal and the manufactured boy bands. I personally don't get any musical pleasure from listening to that music. I think people are getting fed up with it all and they want something new.' Timing, he felt, played a large part in their acceptance. 'Maybe radio stations and the people just weren't ready to accept groups like Travis this time last year, whereas they are now.'

'Tour Sold Out In Advance!' the *Pollstar* website trumpeted, 'Coldplay has definitely proved that it affects people.' Driven by ABC's trails and the widening radio coverage, the demand for tickets for the group's ten-city North American tour ensured that venues in big cities like Los Angeles and Toronto were quickly upgraded to larger halls and theatres. 'We moved a lot of the venues from 1,000 seaters up to the 2,000 seaters,' Nettwerk's chief Terry McBride said, 'and the extra thousand tickets went in, like, one day.' For example, Coldplay's Chicago gig had to be moved by popular demand to the beautiful old 2,500-seater Riviera Theatre. Tours are usually a means of 'getting behind' an album, but clearly the first single was now promoting the tour.

Such enthusiastic response to 'Yellow' ensured that the band by-passed smaller venues in favour of legendary halls like the Fillmore, San Francisco, a building associated with the political and musical earthquakes of the 1960s, or the Irving Plaza, New York, where U2 had performed 'New York, New York' and the Ramones' 'I Remember You' at a free radio-broadcast concert two months earlier. With these dates sold out way in advance, Phil Harvey went into overdrive, liasing with Dave Holmes on a bigger follow-up odyssey across the States for May and June.

In *The Guardian*, Alexis Petridis claimed that Coldplay conformed to America's basic requirement of British bands: 'It seems America's notion of what a British rock band should be was codified in the early seventies, when Pink Floyd's *Dark Side Of The Moon* spent 741 weeks in the US album chart. With the exception of an early eighties blip, virtually every English rock act to gain US success has conformed to this stereotype. They are wistful, melancholy, big on epic, elegiac ballads and rather middle-class.'

It's a very seductive analysis, with Petridis tagging the band as 'four musical Hugh Grants, staring into rain.' But Hugh Grant, in *Four Weddings and a Funeral*, was a verbal bungler when it came to expressing love. Contrastingly, Chris uses his own verbal bungling as a powerful form of self-expression. Even the darker Pink Floyd stereotype seems inadequate, when one considers the joyous nature of 'Yellow'.

Although Nettwerk had given *Parachutes* a low-key release in November, the response from the American media was overwhelmingly positive. '*Parachutes* ultimately rises above its influences to become a work of real transcendence,' wrote *Rolling Stone* critic Matt Diehl. 'On songs like the unrepentantly romantic "Yellow", the band creates a hypnotic slo-mo otherworld where spirit rules supreme. When frontman Chris Martin moans about "Skin and bones/turning to something beautiful," he could very well be talking about his own band.' Equally enthusiastic were *mtv.com*: 'Coldplay's sublime pleasures tend to creep up on listeners, Martin's cheeriness lends levity to the British quartet's set, with its ethereal sound.'

Will Champion reflected on the critical perception of Coldplay in America to *The Daily Telegraph*. In the UK, he observed, 'we went from being seen as Radiohead-lite, to this corporate rock band. But in America we were seen as this cult-type band. That probably did us a bit of good.'

Coldplay's Australian dates had reached an end with a show on 4 February, and instead of flying to British Columbia ahead of their opening North American date in Vancouver four days later; the band opted to make a brief stopover in Britain to attend the 2001 *NME* Awards. At the ceremony, held in what the paper described as 'a large cellar' in London's Shoreditch, Chris appeared visibly jet-lagged. He seemed to have no problems accepting their first award for Radio One's *Evening Session* of the Year. But unknown to the gathered audience, he was rapidly unravelling. Partly it was returning out of the sunshine to gloomy Britain, but Chris also felt overwhelmed by the company around him. He confided later to *Real Groove* journalist James Oldham, 'I just felt like such a fake . . . Because I was sat near Noel Gallagher and Bono and all of them and I thought, "What the hell am I doing here?" . . . And then I had to get the awards and I was terrified.' So the near-teetotal, jetlagged, empty-stomached Chris had some champagne.

> ## 'We've always been extremely anti-advert . . . Oh, if it's just trailing programs I don't mind that. But we'd never, ever advertise Coke.' *– Chris Martin*

When he went up to collect the second award for Best New Artist, gripping both award and champagne bottle tightly, what came out of his mouth was a long-winded joke about Craig David's 'cauliflower hair'. Sections of the audience started to boo him. 'I don't know what that was about. I meant to say Brussels sprouts and it came out as cauliflower. Everything came out wrong,' he told *nme.com*. By now in a hyper-anxious state, he became convinced that he had also insulted Bono. Chris loped offstage, absolutely mortified, back to his seat.

As it happened, they won a third award, for Best Single – thankfully, Chris added, 'I was glad we won three, because it gave me a chance to patch up what I said.' After apologising on stage, Chris slipped off out of the reception hall, and escaped the whole event. After he snuck out, his girlfriend, Lily Sobhani, 'like a patient angel', tracked him down and found him walking around near Liverpool Street, in London's financial district.

Chris would shortly have the opportunity to make amends (or a mess) at another awards ceremony. In the 2001 Brit Awards, Coldplay had been nominated for Best British Group, Best British Newcomer and Best British Album. The Brits are the UK's equivalent of the Grammy Awards, and Coldplay's nominations received a lot of mainstream media coverage, which also had an impact in America.

The nominations were much on the mind of journalist Benjamin Nugent, who wrote a high-profile piece on the band for *Time*, America's most august national news digest magazine. 'Since Radiohead, the band infamously given to brooding, has emerged as the most prominent British rock export of the early '00s, the rise of a cute alternative has seemed almost inevitable,' posited Nugent. 'If Coldplay can steal just one Brit from Radiohead at the awards ceremony on 26

Chris hauled a young co-ed up to sing 'Yellow' when his voice gave out at Irving Plaza, NYC. He looked radiant but, minutes later, the gig collapsed.

February, it will confirm its claim as the cute Radiohead alternative, instead of just Radiohead Lite.'

Nugent implied that *Parachutes* indicated promise rather than delivering brilliance. 'Who says first records by bands smack out of college have to be lyrically complex or push the envelope musically?' The omniscient *Time Magazine* also didn't seem to know that the halls Coldplay were playing were very respectably sized. 'Chances are, the band members are playing venues considerably smaller than the ones they're used to. But the experience may be just what Coldplay needs to develop from British darlings to world-class rockers.'

The band had been knocked too much in their homeland to feel like 'British darlings'. Nugent was also unaware of how inexperienced Coldplay actually still were as live players. Until their recent UK autumn tour, they had mainly played small venues, so that many of the US gigs represented a large step up in scale and prestige. From crossing the Pennines to play Leeds Cockpit, they would soon be crossing the Rocky Mountains to play the Fillmore.

On 9 February, the first US gig of the tour began at the Seattle Showbox with . . . silence.

Out from the wings came Chris sporting a black Oxford shirt, black pants and a crew cut. He had the regulation appearance of a felon or a soldier. 'Get Sex Appeal' hollered the imperative visible on Guy's t-shirt as he took the stage. Jonny shouldered his guitar in his Mohawk-striped trainers, and Will's head poked out of his drum kit. Chris greeted the crowd not with a word or a wave, but with a snappy military salute from the microphone. His dumbness was a typically awkward form of eloquence. After all, if Quiet was the New Loud, it was surely conceivable that utter silence could be a roar.

After the fifth song of the night, Chris finally spoke to the auditorium: 'We just wanted to get the first few songs out of the way in case they were shit. But since they weren't now we can start talking.' At that moment, Coldplay truly landed in America. Chris introduced 'Sparks' with the wisecrack, 'This was originally written by Shania Twain, but I believe we really make it our own.'

It was a well-paced 65-minute set, delivered at a brisk clip. *Mtv.com*'s Chris Nelson commented that the brute energy of Will's intro to 'In My Place' opened the song with a bang, 'slamming out a Black Sabbath thud behind the band's melancholy melody and delicate guitar.'

Using his mic as a prop, Chris played at being David, and then Goliath – towering above it, singing down to it, bending and begging to it. He strummed busily through 'Shiver', where Nelson felt his static delivery missed out on dramatic possibilities: 'Each time he plopped his lanky frame behind a small centre-stage keyboard, he looked like a college student shoved behind a grammar-school desk.' The overall performance style was too introverted, Nelson opined, where Jonny's deft and delicate playing might best be described as Guitar Anti-Hero: he barely stepped into the spotlight when he riffed, and, during his vocal on 'High Speed', 'he threw out his lines with no more drama than someone humbly adding his two cents to a conversation.'

By the time of their Valentine's Day concert in Los Angeles, the band were putting on a much more passionate show. In *The Los Angeles Times,* Robert Hillburn gave their two Mayan Theatre shows a rave review. *The Chicago Tribune*'s Greg Kot wrote, 'Coldplay upped the rock ante not with bombast or overheated angst, but with a sublime mix of delicacy and carefully rationed aggression.' In terms of content, they gave the same show that they gave in Seattle, but this time, something about them soared.

Chris was enjoying the experience, 'It's very exciting to see the clubs we've heard so much about.' The young quartet was equally enthusiastic about the great American pastimes. 'We've been bowling a few times recently,' Will told *Hear/Say.* 'It's a fucking different cup of fish out here in the States. They have it on TV and the guys wear those big gloves and everything. In England, it's just something to do when you're drunk. Just throw the ball down the gutter.'

Coldplay's tour-bus soundtrack also matched the new landscape that opened up before them. Chris was listening to Bob Dylan as they journeyed. 'Most of our influences are from the US,' he explained. As well as Chris's affection for old Corncrake, Guy put on his headphones and made his brain a Willie Nelson sandwich. He had recently bought Nelson's *Shotgun Willie.* 'I love it. It has the Memphis Horns on there and it was amazingly produced,' he told *Pausenplay.*

For a couple of years, Guy had been reading about and listening to Amnerican folk and country rock. 'Right now though, my big passion is Gram Parsons and the Flying Burrito Brothers,' he enthused. 'I've got all his records. I love his whole story, about his family and his life; it's such a tragic story.'

In terms of the rigours of touring abroad, Chris observed, 'it's like being married, we don't sleep together, but being on the bus is about as close as you can get . . . Will is a nice bloke, but if you take his seat on the bus, you've had it.'

'Meet-and-greets, or "grip-and-grins" as many bands refer to them, can be the most soul-destroying part of a tour,' asserted *Bang* writers Adrian Grist and Emma Morgan. 'Beyond the relatively painless meetings with fans and competition winners, bands will be expected to press the flesh with countless record industry "suits": label, radio and retail honchos. Working the room, sharing jokes and anecdotes and displaying appropriate gratitude to VIPs becomes as important an element of promotion as interviews.'

'You don't go from playing 300 capacity venues in the UK to selling out the Hollywood Bowl two nights running, as Coldplay did this year, without a lot of hard work away from the studio and the stage,' the unnamed 'industry insider' told *Bang.* 'It's 50 per cent talent and 50 per cent commitment which brings success on this scale.' As the band travelled, mobile calls ran back and forth from Phil and Nettwerk to brief the band on their hospitality obligations. Here comes another hand outstretched, here comes another smile. Coldplay's good manners, direct gazes and low-key conversation appealed to suited middle management, and they could generally muster up some authentic pleasure in the encounter. *Observer* business correspondent Jamie Doward reported in a profile of Eric Nicoli,

EMI's executive chairman who was previously in the confectionary industry, that Chris Martin was something of a Nicoli fan. 'Not because Eric is head of EMI, but because he invented the Lion Bar.'

These folk never complained about Coldplay being 'too nice', like some of the British music media. 'They're not a bad-boy band . . . they're not trashing hotels. A lot has to do with how you treat the media. Oasis didn't show any respect – whenever they did interviews they were always rude – and once you piss off the media they are gonna jump on you,' said Tim Webster, 'Romeo on the Radio' DJ and assistant director of New York's Z100 station. 'When Liam Gallagher went on stage in the States and started spitting at everyone, people just thought it was pathetic. They thought, "Who is this thug and what's he doing here?"'

As the tour progressed, *Parachutes* finally climbed into the *Billboard* Top 100 at Number 68. And then, flu hit. Perhaps it was the exhaustion of the relentless promotional odyssey, jetting through climactic zones, flying with their peeling Australian sunburn through British drizzle and Vancouver rain, Seattle snow and LA smog, and finally to icy New York. On the day Coldplay reached the Big Apple, *Parachutes* rose to Number 57 in the US album chart. By late February, it would achieve gold status.

The sudden onset of shivering illness seemed to be an affirmation of general British band lore that America is a place where you wait for the disaster to strike. On 16 February, the day of the important gig at New York's Irving Plaza, the crisis halted everything. Earlier that day, Coldplay staggered through the taping of a performance of 'Yellow' for Conan O'Brien's TV show. Clearly, the usually radiantly healthy Chris was suddenly in bad shape. His voice began to crack. His nervous hand strummed forcefully down on his acoustic guitar and then – snap! A string broke and he lost the mid-range notes in a series of gap-toothed chords. 'Heartbreaking' was the verdict of *Hear/Say*'s Mark Watt, 'especially for those fans who didn't have a chance to download live tracks off Napster and instead had their first "live" experience with the band on that show.'

Later that night, Coldplay heroically attempted to struggle through the Irving Plaza concert. They felt their resolve go hot and cold, their nostrils flared like a tortoise's. They were so sensitised they could feel the cold coming off the hospitality ice bucket. Chris was the first to falter. He wrestled with the first song, 'Trouble', and then simply had no voice left to sing with. Desperately, he improvised by hauling a Connecticut co-ed up from the audience who, star-struck, warbled her way inexpertly through 'Yellow'. Then the band had to back off their mics and abandon the performance. Jonny succumbed the following day, his body still weak from recent glandular fever, and that night's Boston gig was called off.

24 hours later, Guy joined the sick list. Phil, Dave Holmes and Nettwerk announced a make-up date for the New York gig in April, to be held in the Roseland Ballroom, three times larger than Irving Plaza.

After Chris's shredded voice had a weekend of rest, the band decided they should try their utmost to get through the all-important Chicago concert on Monday. 'With the equipment already set up in the venue, it was felt that this gig could be done as a final push,' Phil Harvey recalled. After looking at the tour schedule and trying to prioritise, Toronto and Miami were sacrificed. But Chicago is the Manchester of America – a crucial mid-West sales territory for the band. However, it was no certainty that the stricken trio of Chris, Guy and Jonny would make it through the set.

On 19 February, as fans fought the evening chill beneath Chicago Riviera's marquee, a rumour began to creep around that the band had cancelled the rest of the tour, and the guys probably wouldn't make it through the show that night. The anxiously expectant masses filed into the old theatre as the opening band, Australia's Powderfinger, laboured to create a thaw.

Coldplay came onstage to a roar of acknowledgement, but Chris's pallor could be seen from the audience. 'This should be an interesting show for us. We're all just about dead.' He also announced that the band had cancelled the final two shows of the tour. Then it was time to see how much they had left to give. Driven by the desire to ensure that their last US performance would be special, Coldplay dug deep – and really rocked out, giving a truly Chicago-sized show. But illness had forced some of the charisma out of the performance, with Chris slugging down water between songs and breaking several guitar strings. The snapped strings mirrored the damage to Chris's voice, but he swung his hands behind his back and compelled himself to sing on.

The others could be seen deteriorating as the balls-out set drove forward. 'Don't you shiver,' sung pleadingly by Chris, had fresh meaning here. The band sprang along through the majority of *Parachutes*, with 'In My Place', 'Animals', and their surprise Bond cover 'You Only Live Twice'. His old fever resuscitated, Jonny's face was melting into an ever-sweatier mask as he wrung clear, icy notes from his Telecaster. Guy's head jerked repeatedly over the bass, as if he were trudging toward collapse. Empty-handed Chris stomped out to the edge of the stage for some Jagger-style hand clapping that scored a big roar from the crowd. It was a powerful show, 'doused in inspiration and emotional power . . . steeped in devotion.' *Hear/Say* magazine's Mark Watt noted. 'Martin shuffled out onto the stage one last time,' observed *Glorious Noise*. 'And after playing a brand new song, "never played before, anywhere, honest," the lone blue spotlight followed him as he made one more guitar-to-keyboard transfer. Standing up, Martin slowly sang, "what the world . . . needs now . . . is love . . . sweet love . . ." and with that . . . he waved and was gone.'

The boys had played their asses off, there was a sense of victory, and they were still willing to do an interview with a *Hear/Say* journalist. Guy, sat alone on a sofa, unable to talk. Jonny's hands kept trying to prop up his feverish face like a guitar on its stand. Chris's voice was destroyed. Will, as so often, carried the interview with his vehement words: 'We *want* to do all of this . . . You don't get another chance to do these kinds of things. You don't get to record another debut album. It might all end within the next week. That's proof of all these things I've thought about, thinking about my mum and all that. You realise that it can end so quickly and you can't take things for granted. You've got to do everything to the full and you have to enjoy things as much as you can.'

Will had resolved to take his music as far as it would go, not just in memory of his mother, but mindful of how quickly and completely she disappeared. Cut down in its own prime, Coldplay's first American tour was still a great success, with sell-out shows. But, just as suddenly, the tour was over. Phil quickly reassured fans that the band was planning an extensive North American tour to take place in May and June.

Success wise, everything over the past year had worked out with an almost incredible ease. Coldplay had conquered England in a few weeks. Their first single in America broke them with a similar rapidity, and they'd played major US venues without the muck and sweat of a journeyman slog. Now returned to London, Coldplay – a band who basically wanted to *earn* things – were made uneasy by ease. But still, they were faced with a genuine disaster that might finish them for good – Chris's voice was as dead as a shorted amp, and they had to cancel a whole European tour. A statement was issued: 'Chris has been advised by his doctor that attempting the April schedule as it stands would result in total voice loss and could cause permanent damage.'

Total voice loss, permanent damage. Chris was expected to recover in time for the American dates scheduled to redeem the aborted US tour. Doubtless it was initially feared that his voice might develop some intermittent instability or, knowing the worrisome Chris, stay forever – breaking up his beloved band.

In terms of media coverage, it was back to the embedded British parochial preoccupations. The press was still marvelling that Coldplay had been to university and yet were actually musical (as if they were equating them with old-style progressive rock bands like Genesis). On 20 February, *The Guardian* published a league table for universities scored according to their number of rock-star graduates. Lee Elliot Major's article had been prompted by UCL's Head of Media Relations, Patrick Edwardes, who mentioned on the university website that famous graduates Coldplay were just about to clean up at the imminent Brit Awards.

With these nominations, Coldplay were again placed in direct competition with their supposed progenitors, Radiohead. The results were never going to please everybody, and *The Guardian*'s Caroline Sullivan was quick to declare her dissatisfaction. 'Compared with the Grammy awards, which proved that rock warhorses were still alive by handing Steely Dan a best album statuette at last week's ceremony, the Brits should have been a relative oasis of coolness . . . Where were the industry bigwigs when nineteen-year-old Craig David became the most acclaimed British singer of last year, selling 1.5m copies of his debut album and teaching even over-thirties to associate the word "garage" with dance music rather than cars?'

Sullivan gave a broad perspective on the 2001 Brits, which were televised for the nation on 26 February. What clouded that year's awards was not that Coldplay won recognition – but that other artists who deserved it were apparently unfairly left out. The fact that R & B star Craig David lost out to the boy band A1 for Best Newcomer, and to the overrated Robbie Williams (who won three) fuelled a sense of injustice that encouraged Sullivan to brand Coldplay 'young fogeys'. Once again, an awards ceremony had served to cast the band in the role of whipping boys.

As for Phil Harvey, he was so ill he hardly knew he was attending the Brits. There is a conventional wisdom that, in order to be all-powerful, managers or film producers need a 'visual hook' – a ponytail, a fat Cohiba cigar, or (as in Alan McGee's case) an attitude capable of stripping paint at 30 yards. Phil's hook was his purity. Even when he slouched a little, a part of his nature stayed upright like a gently burning candle. Phil was feeling like death when he should have been on top of the world. The stricken manager could at least draw some consolation from his band bagging two Brit awards. 'It was two days later that my doctor phoned to say she was worried I might be about to slip into a coma,' recalled Phil.

Phil was not going to recover quickly. He told the Coldplay e-zine, 'My body finally decided enough was enough in early 2001 . . . I certainly thought about giving up then. It crossed my mind that I simply wasn't tough enough. It was only later that I discovered most international bands have huge teams and organisations supporting them, not just one bloke in a shithole office.'

Phil had worried constantly that, despite his best efforts, some aspect of his naivety would damage the band's chances. But he'd damaged his own health instead. He'd had his head down, occasionally schmoozing with other managers without taking the time to study the way they did things. He simply didn't notice how he was operating in unprecedented isolation. Beyond the pressure of circumstances, what stopped Phil dead was his inability to stop.

Recovering from exhaustion is not a simple matter. If you try to get well by spending two weeks in bed without moving, you won't rise from that bed re-charged. But neither will a condition that arises from constant physical and mental effort allow itself to be healed by yet more exertion. The recovery process is frustratingly gradual.

Chris's silenced voice, Phil's exhaustion, Johnny and Guy's illnesses – everything felt like it was going wrong for the band. 'We were fucking desperate,' said Chris. 'We had to decide whether we were a bunch of students who got lucky or were we going to admit that we are really fucking good? Actually it was me. Was I going to admit we are one of the best bands in the world?' A solution to this psychological impasse came from an unlikely source – singing lessons, arranged to diagnose Chris's voice problems and, crucially, to protect against their return.

It must have felt strange, to come off of a rock 'n' roll tour and stand reflected in the black lacquered piano beside internationally renowned voice coach Mary Hammond. To have her listen to his voice and take it apart, when he could hardly eject a note. To be made to go back to an absolute beginning, a beginning he never really began at. To start with simple breaths, in and out, not using the vocal chords at all. Simple little two-note exercises. How on earth would *that* help him to play a 70-minute set at Wembley Arena?

But Chris would be taught to sing with his mind so that he could sing with his whole body.

To be taught to hit a note correctly by *imagining* he was hitting it correctly, with the sound as an interface between mind, soul and matter. Although Chris still stretches his neck up very high and tense for a singer: a voice coach would teach him to feel his neck resting on his feet, feel the connection to the floor. But, in full song, Chris's Adam's apple is like a painful second chin.

On 3 March 2001, Chris celebrated his 24th birthday. His family, all hailing from the village of Whitestone, Devon, had obviously been delighted by Coldplay's growing fame, but were always on hand to offer a healthy range of advice and observation. His uncle once took him aside and said, 'Listen son, you may be rich and famous, but your lyrics are crap.' Likewise, Anthony Martin once looked at a smiling picture of his son on the cover of *Q* and boomed, 'I bet you're glad you had those teeth fixed, boy.' After the band wowed Glastonbury, Chris came home to a ticking off from his mum, Alison, because he'd left the milk out of the fridge.

Something inside Chris and Coldplay was beginning to heal. In *Esquire*, Martin credited the change in attitude to Mary Hammond. 'She is amazing. She's like a psychologist as well as a singing teacher. She really sorted me out . . . gave me a lot more confidence. I love feeling like I know what I'm doing. Being in control.'

> **'You realise that it can end so quickly and you can't take things for granted. You've got to do everything to the full and you have to enjoy things as much as you can.'** – *Will Champion*

It was dawning on Chris that Coldplay might actually be *good*, rather than just lucky: 'I thought, I might die at any moment and I've been given this amazing opportunity with my friends. And at that point we were doing ridiculous things – hanging out with U2 – and I thought, I wouldn't want to be in U2, I am actually already in one of the best bands in the world! Once we'd decided we had the chance of a lifetime we worked harder than we ever have in our lives.'

The workaholic Phil ended up having to take several months off work to regain his health. When he came back, he had the much-needed help of an assistant manager, Estelle Wilkinson. He'd finally learned to move beyond his early days of buying batteries for Jonny's pedals, trying to hunt down music industry types at the venue's bar, or arguing over £10 on the fee. 'Now my assistant manager Estelle hires planes and tour buses months in advance; Jonny's guitar pedals have to be hooked up to the national grid; I don't go to the bar so much because the dressing room is stuffed with vodka and champagne; I'm more likely to be desperately avoiding music industry types at gigs; I leave the arguing to our tour manager Jeff who is much better at it than me.'

Within a month of the aborted February tour, a return visit to America was arranged. Brisk ticket sales were an indication of the band's increasing popularity. This meant that they'd be playing halls that were anything up to twice the size of the 2,000 capacity venues that had been booked last time around. Undaunted by this, Jonny told *Pollstar* 'I'm not really nervous at all. I tend to get nervous if we haven't sold very many tickets. But we've done alright.' He added practically, 'Not too many people go to gigs who hate the bands.'

With sales of *Parachutes* having already passed the 350,000 mark in the States, it was decided that Coldplay would release their second US single, 'Shiver', in April. They had already made a simple, studio-based promotional video with director Grant Gee, who also filmed the Radiohead tour documentary, *Meeting People Is Easy*. Despite Coldplay's relaxed attitude to business schmoozing in the US, they deliberately chose the director of a documentary that satirically conveyed the agony of that same 'grip and grin' process.

'Shiver' was released to radio in early April. Several days beforehand, the band flew in and played *Saturday Night Live*, with actor Alec Baldwin as their fellow guest. This was a significant landmark for any UK band hoping for success in the USA. They were further distinguished by being allow time for two songs, 'David Gray and Nelly Furtado (the only other 'new' artists to guest this year) only got one each,' observed *Saturday-Night-Live.com*'s Mark Polishuk. Rather than promote 'Shiver', Coldplay opted to play 'Yellow' and 'Don't Panic'. 'I was in the MOMENT!' howled *Vh1.com*'s Bob Lefsetz, who had not been a fan of the band until this live, un-mimed performance. 'You could hear the drummer slap out the beat. The lead singer's acoustic, warm but with backbone . . . but the lead guitarist. He was playing a Fender JAGUAR!'

As well as the *Saturday Night Live* appearance, the purpose of the visit was also to play a one-off show at New York's Roseland Ballroom, to compensate fans for the Irving Plaza gig that had been abandoned two months earlier. The Roseland was twice the size of Irving Plaza and the additional tickets sold out almost instantly.

With all personnel now fit and well, the Coldplay tour machine swung back into action. Returning to Europe, the band played a week-long string of dates in Germany, Italy and France. This was immediately followed by a six-date mini-tour of Britain – which took in Aberdeen and Edinburgh, and was followed by a pair of two night stints at the Manchester Apollo, and South London's Brixton Academy.

After a short break, the band arrived in Boston on 24 May, to play another show that made up for a cancelled gig at the Paradise Rock Club back in February. Coldplay had also lined up similar compensatory gigs in Chicago and Toronto. The Avalon in Boston was a big, black box of a venue; the starting point for the management team who went on to found the sperm-soaked Studio 54 in New York. Within the black box, the rig lights hung like upside down bats. During 'Yellow', the squared walls and ceiling became a dizzy dome of concentric circles of razor-sharp yellow light, a mirror-ball effect through which Jonny and Will flexed their rhythmic muscles.

'Sorry we're a bit later than expected, like three months or something,' Chris told the crammed venue. 'But it gives you a build-up.' Chris pulled out a little voice-spray from his pocket and sprayed a chemical down his throat. 'I should say this is cocaine just to spice things up a bit.'

But as an unidentified member of the Coldplay crew (who'd started adding to the band's website diary) observed, 'no amount of friendly or latterly slightly more aggressive banter from a worried frontman was going to save their sorry selves . . . Day One was painful . . . Whilst their own gig was alright they were creaky and the set was "a bit wrong". But it was not bad (and I have seen some of their shockers).' That the band seemed perfectly happy to allow insiders to make very straight, even critical, public observations was indicative of Coldplay's continuing emphasis on brutally honest self-assessment.

These opinions were shared by *mtv.com*'s Paul Robicheau, whose piece was headlined, 'Coldplay Tour Opener Inspires Delayed Reaction'. Although he found much to praise in an 80-minute set he described as 'floating, chiming, ethereal, delicate, exquisitely harmonious,' Robicheau was unconvinced by 'a group supporting a solitary CD', a record that that lacked immediate impact and whose 'sublime pleasures tend to creep up on listeners'. He felt that the set peaked in the middle with 'Everything's Not Lost', where Chris, positioned at the piano, sang exquisitely in harmony with Jonny's stratospheric guitar. After that the set became too subdued, and when Chris closed the show with a solo 'See You Soon', the song 'seemed well-placed only in terms of sentiment.' Robicheau also interviewed an unnamed fan from Cambridge, MA who told him that he enjoyed the show for Coldplay's 'vibe and talent', but added, 'I think they're one of those bands where you're almost as well off sitting at home with a bottle of red wine at one in the morning.'

When Coldplay are on good form, they burn to the extent that no one thinks to question either the staging of the show as static, or the band's ensemble charisma. When they have an off night, their

Straight off their first US tour, Coldplay win the Brit Awards for Best British Group and Best British Album, 2001.

vibe and talent just about hack their way through to the audience. It's clear they aim to embody a kind of subtle musical fundamentalism, the absolute reliance on the songs to sing themselves. They were *not* going to contrive some baroque Spinal Tap live experience.

As the mystery crewmember intimated on the website diary, the band were aware that the Boston set was below par, 'but they philosophised, and went to Washington full of drive.' On such journeys, what really buoyed Chris up was snatching some time to work on fresh material. 'Whenever we have a break all I do is sit and try and get new songs. I think there are about sixteen good ones (out of about 50, but since I was twelve there were always more thrown away than kept) and the rest of the band have worked their magic on about seven of them and these are the best.'

The band arrived in Washington on 27 May to take part in the radio-sponsored HFStival. As Will pointed out, the band had some misgivings about appearing in Washington alongside so many other acts that once again offered a far heavier sound than theirs – nu-metal acts including Linkin Park and Limp Bizkit, and punk-lite popsters Blink-182. 'It seems as though the organisers of these events are convinced that a band such as ourselves will fit nicely into an afternoon's entertainment where the least heavy band apart from us was The Cult.' Will encapsulated Coldplay's dilemma as performing 'back to back on a revolving stage with The Disturbed'.

'We were this acousticy band and everyone was waiting for Staind and Blink 182,' Chris told the website. The anonymous road crew member elaborated: 'What was bad was the next three days, when the soft rockers Coldplay found themselves playing under Maryln [sic] Manson, and other acts of that genre, in front of crowds who were less than patient . . .' But Chris had roused the band to the task. They went in there, as Will put it, with the attitude, 'let's show these people how they don't have to bleed and vomit to enjoy a concert.'

This tactic was not wholly successful, and Coldplay were pelted with bottles and CDs by the crowd. Imagine the ignominy of being decapitated by a Linkin Park CD hurled like a razor-sharp weapon from a martial arts film. The band's attitude, 'Let's show these people,' was, according to

97

Will, soon transformed into, 'let's make sure we play our best for the people who have come to see us, and let's be nimble and quick on our toes in order to avoid the countless projectiles that are hurled towards us.'

With their form of musical self-expression drawing lethal fire, the band may have longed to be back in Britain, where the worst they faced was being called bedwetters. The quartet had never been physically threatened on stage before and it came as a huge shock. As usual, Coldplay collected a fraternity of bands around them, not a circle of rivals, and this support dragged them up from the depths. As Will stressed, 'What was great was the reaction to our music from the heavier bands on the bill; bands who we honestly thought would hate our music made a point of coming up to us to tell us how much they like the album.'

As Chris told *Real Groove*'s James Oldham, 'We came off stage in Washington and I thought we either stop now and let everyone who doesn't like us get on top of us, or we just go bollocks to all of you because there's a few million who do like us. I guess it just suddenly struck me, I'm me and we're as good as anyone ever. There's no need to worry about anybody else, because we're all just little creatures running around. Everyone from Nelson Mandela to Myra Hindley is a person whose been given life and it's what you make of it. Suddenly I just stopped being afraid of anyone.'

With Chris drawing Nietzschean strength from the Washington fracas, the band travelled south to Atlanta for a gig at The Tabernacle, an old church. Inside, the venue was beautifully galleried, the stage was incredibly wide, the auditorium extremely shallow. Imagine you are playing on a stage that takes up the whole starboard side of a boat; You are facing the galleried audience who stretch along the whole port side, and the gap between your face and theirs is quite shallow.

'Atlanta was possibly the most surprisingly great reaction we've ever had,' Will enthused. 'Having never ventured near the South we were unsure of the reception awaiting us, but we were left with no doubts that all involved had a great night.' Two years later, Chris was to tell another Atlanta audience, 'We almost gave up on finishing the dates here in the US until we came across you guys.'

Atlanta was the turning point where their luck changed on the May/June 2001 tour. Whereas the Washington crowd had been both bored and boring, looking for predictable violence, the Atlanta crowd simply wanted to be entertained. There was a great cultural harmony between the band and its audience: shared interests in folk, country, the spiritual and the protest song. It all crystallised in gentle power and humour, combining to create a sweet show that really worked.

As the tour passed through Philadelphia, Detroit, Chicago, Dallas and Austin, the band were continually startled to look out over ecstatic seas of uplifted faces that joyously sung Coldplay's lyrics back at them. 'You start a song on your own in a room, and then you take it to Jon or Will or Guy, and they do something with it, and then a bit of time later and 3,000 Texans are there telling you what was or wasn't yellow,' beamed Chris.

Behind all the promotional mania, this endless year of travel had left them no time to write and experiment – the sound-checks being the only real oasis of spontaneous new jamming.

It may have seemed like a marvellous life, since the band were hanging with musicians they really admired, but Chris was firmly in the grip of his compulsive urge to create. 'It makes me want to improve everything no end, so nobody has to waste their ear-time on shit when they listen to or see us,' he proclaimed. 'Life is short and I don't want to waste peoples' time, and hence feel highly driven. When you see the Flaming Lips live, or hear *The Boatman's Call* by Nick Cave, or watch *Life is Beautiful* by Roberto Begnini, it is pure undiluted quality time, and that is what we must be.'

As well as the American dates, the Coldplay roadshow also made a two-concert visit to Canada, so the band headed for the border by bus. In contrast to the American South, Canada is a virtuous country, but it is also a little on the smug side. Smug that it is fairly multicultural; smug that it never created a Vietnam war; smug that it has had many more Catholic power figures than WASP America's assassinated Kennedy.

On the Windsor-Detroit border between the States and Canada, the band were given a chunk of 'pure, undiluted quality time' from the Canadian customs officials. As road crew member John Besley put it, 'We were in Canada for a bit, although three hours less than we would have been if we hadn't been stopped at customs for so long.' The expert Canadian customs officers could not distinguish Coldplay crew member Hoppy's dead, weedless roll-up from a spliff, and to help make up their minds decided to search the whole bus from top to bottom.

About six weeks later, Canadian Customs created a stir by confiscating 150 CDs by the Frogs that the US indie band were bringing with them to sell at their gig in Toronto – CDs they'd had to buy themselves from their record company. The satirical albums *Racially Yours and Bananimals,* whose tone had something in common with Eminem's, were deemed by customs officers to be unfit to enter the country. Clearly, Canada didn't want the American 'Eminem culture' to contaminate their dominion, but its native pop press complained that this repressive act would generally discourage indie bands from visiting Canada. As for the Frogs' reaction on their website, it ran, 'That's absolute bullshit about Canada, fuck Canada, we should go to war and put that rediculus [sic] country out of its misery!'

> **'Once we'd decided we had the chance of a lifetime we worked harder than we ever have in our lives.'** – *Chris Martin*

Chris and Jonny later complained that, while they were held and treated as criminals on the slender suspicion that their bus might contain a joint's worth of pot, a middle-aged macho man toting two rifles cleared customs in minutes. It seems Canada has more in common with gun-toting America than it's prepared to admit. As crew member Besley pithily put it, 'It is futile (and probably over dramatic) to point out that you would have a hard time killing an elk with the end of a cigarette. But still, there we were, each individually searched by mean-faced uniforms.'

It seems customs didn't know of Coldplay's clean-living, innocent reputation. The very next day they did, however, allow Californian support act Granddaddy to whiz straight through the border on the grounds that Coldplay had been given such a thorough going-over the day before.

Such touring experiences, as Besley saw it, were having a distinct educational impact on the band: 'often accused of being a little starry eyed and innocent, [they] strike me as becoming a little more politically aware, and certainly less tolerant of things with which they disagree.' On 27 June, when Coldplay gave a pristine, dramatic performance of 'Trouble' on *The David Letterman Show*, Chris took the opportunity to signal one of his personal convictions by appearing in a 'Stop Handgun Violence' t-shirt.

The following night, the American leg of Coldplay's world domination roadshow climaxed with their biggest gig yet at New York's Radio City Music Hall. Radio City's curving, Art-Deco stage frame made the venue look like an indoor Hollywood Bowl. The historic venue, which has hosted legends such as Frank Sinatra, Ella Fitzgerald and B. B. King, had sold out instantly, and the lucky ticket holders gave Coldplay an overwhelming end-of-tour response. 'It's so hard to believe that the tour is over, yet it seems years since we left England,' remarked Will. 'The overriding thought we have all been having is that roughly three and a half years ago, we four were sat in Jonny's bedroom writing songs and putting towels over the drum kit so as not to annoy the neighbours, now we've just completed a US tour, played at Radio City, and played on national television in front of millions of people.'

ON A RUSH

EIGHT

From their tour bus, Coldplay had viewed endless foreign vistas, punctuated by shopping malls and gas stations. Now back in the UK, they faced a leaden London sky, but were comforted by the familiar: Camden High Street, cups of tea, and their own beds.

'When Jonny lies in bed at night he doesn't think, "I'm going to buy a speedboat tomorrow." He's thinking about guitar sounds,' commented Chris, in an interview with Scott Wilson of *Pitch.com*. *Esquire* asked Jonny if he had nightmares whilst on the road, 'If I'm on the bus, yes absolutely,' he replied. 'Mainly claustrophobic dreams. I had this mad dream before Glastonbury where everyone was on stage in a tent that I couldn't get on. No one turned up to watch us. All I had to wear was a brown suit and gold waistcoat!'

After returning from the US, the band's non-stop schedule had taken them to Norway for the Quart Festival, alongside pop-rockers Ash and the Dandy Warhols. Coldplay then headed south to Kinross for a return visit to T In The Park on 8 July – where they were scheduled to appear on the main stage, sandwiched between Beck and Toploader. The remainder of the month provided welcome relief from the rigours of touring. Such respite was merely temporary, as a second Australian tour was scheduled for the start of August.

Four days before the Australian dates, Coldplay joined Travis for a co-headlining performance at the 12,000-capacity Kallang Indoor Stadium, Singapore. After a long flight and an exhilarating gig, Chris crumpled into a plush couch in the Four Seasons hotel foyer. He attempted to finish an interview but, wracked by jetlag and insomnia, was practically talking in his sleep. The band had showcased a new song, 'Idiot', which prompted *Lime* magazine's Chelsia Toon to ask if it was about anybody in particular.

'What's it about?' Chris wearily replied. 'Well, it's about being an idiot. It's about me. But it's kinda also the way I feel about everything. Half the time you feel really stupid and the other half you feel everything is good. I don't know.'

Coldplay then flew on to Australia, arriving in the breeze-blessed western city of Perth to begin a week-long trek. Once there, thousands of miles away from home, the group were astonished to encounter a classic British band.

Echo and the Bunnymen were on the second night of their own week-long Australian tour when Coldplay and their crew caught the re-formed indie giants at the same Metropolis nightclub they were due to play two nights later.

The acoustic-strumming descendant of Jeff Buckley plays T In The Park, 2001.

At the very start of the 1980s, Echo and the Bunnymen had become established as part of the UK's post-punk soundscape by flinging forth epic guitar lines and powerful ballads. Coldplay and their road crew, who had bopped, hooted and sung their way through the Bunnymen concert, were well aware of the difference between McCulloch's performance and their own. A *Redbackrock* review of a Coldplay concert at the Hordern, Sydney on 8 August pointed out, 'When you buy a ticket to see Coldplay, the first thing that goes through your head is the thought that this probably won't be the most active concert you've ever gone to. And you would be right.'

But, the implicit suggestion was, you'd still buy your ticket. 'What they lack in up-tempo, get-you-up and pogoing tunes, they more than make up for with a selection of melodic, well-rehearsed songs, which are a delight to hear live. Audience participation was good, especially during "Yellow". But one could not help but think that in a smaller venue, this band, with its intimate and personal selections of songs, would have made an even bigger impact,' *Redbackrock* declared. The short tour finished at Brisbane's Festival Hall on 10 August. Coldplay then headed back to the UK via a one-off show at Auckland's St James Theatre.

> **'We were desperate to go in and prove ourselves again. We wanted to get back into the studio and prove to people we were as good as they were saying we were.'** – *Guy Berryman*

Now the band was taking huge festivals in their stride. In August, they played the V-Festival, where rain poured but didn't stop play. Coldplay's presence on the main stage, third on the bill behind Texas and the Charlatans, annoyed *Playlouder*'s Adam Alphabet into giving a jaded view of Coldplay's set and Chris's stage patter: 'the only time he shuts up during Coldplay's damp set is when they play "Yellow", and he encourages the audience to fill in. A few of them do, but most of them are busy watching their drool mingle with the pouring rain.'

On 25 August, Coldplay supported U2 before an 80,000 strong crowd at Ireland's premier festival venue, Slane Castle. The concert was the culminating gig of U2's *Elevation* tour, and the twentieth anniversary of their first ever appearance there supporting Thin Lizzy. To be invited to play was thus an enormous endorsement from Coldplay's heroes. Other acts on the all-day bill included the Red Hot Chili Peppers, Kelis, and JJ72.

It was also a momentous gig for Chris, who overcame his usual timidity with women to pluck up the nerve to invite along Natalie Imbruglia – or 'Beth from *Neighbours*', as he still thought of her. Jumping the gun just a little, *Q*'s Michael Odell declared, 'it augured well for love.' Coldplay received a rapturous reception and then, in the middle of U2's set, Bono segued into a few tribute bars of 'Yellow'. The Irish roared. Admiring eyes turned Martin's way. 'Fame is bullshit,' Chris told Odell. 'But that was a moment where even I thought, "You lucky bastard. Enjoy it!"'

Chris declined to say how the relationship developed afterwards. From his rueful downward glance and his observation to Odell, 'Actually, I behaved like a twat,' it wasn't all it might have been.

Regardless of Chris's twatism, Coldplay's growing popularity, intense media attention and a ceaseless work schedule, their record company was in the frontline of an industry-wide crisis. 'The music industry is undergoing one of the most fundamental shifts in its history – and EMI, the biggest and best-known of Britain's record groups, is suffering badly,' wrote John Casey in *The Guardian*. 'A dire global market for record sales, growing piracy and the thorny issue of internet distribution has got the five "majors" – Universal, Warner Records, Sony, EMI and BMG – in a spin.'

During this period, it felt as if the most permanent company personnel were the star-struck temporary secretaries. In the autumn of 2001, EMI's Head of Recorded Music left with a £6 million pay-off. Troubled superstar diva Mariah Carey quickly became EMI's highest profile artistic casualty. The climate of desperation was such that, after just one disappointing album, the company found it financially imperative to pay her off with £38 million.

Coldplay were often cited as one of EMI's strongest assets in the business pages of the day. However, Mariah Carey's 'downsizing' showed that a successful band's label relations could be as solid as melting snow. It was a tall order to expect such a relatively young band to play a key role in the salvage of their record company's fortunes.

'We had only done one album, and in the grand scheme of things, that's not a lot of work,' Guy reflected, his thin, concave face reflecting his worries. By now, *Parachutes*, with its concise, melodic pop, had passed the five million sales mark, a fact that both reassured and challenged the band.

'We were desperate to go in and prove ourselves again,' Jonny admitted to *Vervegirl.com*. 'We were getting all this praise and acclaim and we were getting annoyed by it,' explained Guy. 'We wanted to get back into the studio and prove to people we were as good as they were saying we were.'

Like the assassination of John F Kennedy, almost everybody that was around at the time remembers exactly where they were, who they were with, and what they were doing, when the news of the World Trade Centre atrocity filtered through from New York on 11 September 2001. When the towers fell, thousands of record collections became ghost towns. The memories that also evaporated then were a trillion favourite phrases of music, lyrics, light-shows, down-loads, t-shirts, and pictures of music icons from Elvis to Eminem.

Coldplay had just returned to London after recording an acoustic radio session in Paris for the Europe 2 station and were preparing to fly out to New York for the 21st annual CMJ Music Marathon, due to take place on 13-16 September. Writing in the band's online diary, Will found a sense of determination. 'Whatever the outcome of the next few weeks, be certain that these events have changed the modern world forever, and the ease with which they were able to take place is perhaps the most scary thought of all. It has made it clear in my mind that all it takes is a few people to create such massive destruction and pain and suffering, and that life is far too short and unexpected to hold things back, to procrastinate or to not live every day like it could be your last.'

This would not be the band's sole response to 9/11. At this time, a new Coldplay song, 'Politik', began to crystallise around the catastrophic event. Chris had begun to compose the song within a few days of the disaster. His lyric, 'Love, tell me your own politik' was a powerful invitation. A tiny group of men had just shown us *their* politik – in so doing, they killed thousands of people and forced history to undergo a sudden detour.

Speaking to *Rolling Stone*, who were gauging reactions to the attack, Chris provided some much-needed perspective. 'It made us feel incredibly blessed that the biggest thing in our lives to worry about is whether our bass drum is too loud or something. We really live inside of an amazing little bubble where we can be obsessed with records. We're not exploited by anyone and we're not trampled on by anyone . . . So on the one hand it made us feel incredibly blessed, and on the other hand it gives us an added sense of urgency, because you never know what's going to happen.'

The 9/11 holocaust had the effect of propelling the band into the studios sooner than they expected. As Jonny explained, 'We had to cancel a tour to America, and none of our equipment could be moved. We had to reschedule the tour, so we went in to record slightly earlier.'

Coldplay booked into Sir George Martin's state-of-the-art Air Studios in Hampstead. Now they could live at home in Camden and walk up the hill to work. To get to Air, you head up Haverstock Hill where a right turn will take you down Pond Street. Make a left instead, and you find yourself among Victorian manors that once had their spiritual needs administered to by a large church complex. Sir George, whose extraordinary musical career encompasses over 50 years of studio experience, has since converted the complex into an audio utopia. His credits are end-less; legendary for his groundbreaking work with the Beatles, in 1999 he became one of a select group of producers to be inducted into the Rock and Roll Hall of Fame.

The first task before a studio stint is to sus out the local pub, then the newsagent's for reading matter to occupy you while your bandmates fight endlessly over a drum loop. For Coldplay, it was probably better not to buy the trade rags, with their blood-clot inducing headlines about 'Difficult Second Album Syndrome'.

'Every now and then, a second album is treated as if it were far more important than a mere bunch of songs. Managers scurry back and forth across the Atlantic with advance copies hand-cuffed to their wrists. Critics are required to sign contracts that make them promise they will not so much as hum the contents. The music press acts as if the world is about to witness the most significant release since the Big Bang.

'Previous examples include the Stone Roses' *Second Coming* and Oasis's third LP *Be Here Now*,' wrote *The Guardian*'s Dorian Lynskey. 'One of the stranger sights in Britpop documentary *Live Forever* is that of fans slavering clutching copies of *Be Here Now* as if they were fragments of the Berlin Wall. Then they went home and played the accursed thing, and second hand shops nationwide braced themselves for the deluge.'

Lynskey listed follow-up albums that led to disaster, the kind of pop trivia that's a specialty of Will's: apart from the Stone Roses, there was Elastica's *The Menace*, Guns N' Roses' *Use Your Illusions 1 & 2*, and The Clash's *Give 'Em Enough Rope*. So would Coldplay join the roll call of artistic failure?

Chris was already mulling over these same issues. As Ted Kessler noted on *nme.com*, he had been 'asking difficult questions of himself and his craft. He wondered whether Coldplay had the depth to improve on the concise, melodic pop of their first set.' In particular, would they be able 'to achieve the artistic step-up their forefathers Radiohead and U2 had made at a comparable crossroads?'

Entering Air Studios is like stepping into a peculiarly English seat of excellence. Space shuttle consoles and esoteric technical gadgets are always at your elbow. The place has massive acoustic canopies for huge orchestras and choirs, but also caters for the smallest of projects. Most delectable of all is the legendary Air 'Toy Box', a cupboard that stores a staggering array of gadgets and effects.

It's not known whether Chris once again pinned up signs calling for 'Energy!', 'Passion!' and 'Emotion!' – but he barked out some forceful wisdom inherited from his grandfather, successful businessman John Besley Martin, who always told him, 'Do it *now*.'

'That's me,' Chris cried to Ted Kessler. 'Urgent, urgency. It's the word that sums me up. When human life ends, what will it all mean? Who'll listen to all the great records, read all the great books, watch the great movies? So do it *now!* Chris and Kessler were walking through St James's Park doing an *Observer Magazine* interview when suddenly Chris weirded Ted out by grabbing his arm and staring deeply into his eyes. 'Now, now, now,' he implored. 'Don't put anything off!'

During their creative brainstorming sessions, the other band members declared their enthusiasm for recording 'Warning Sign'. Chris didn't approve of the way this song had turned out. As far as Chris was concerned, it was old news, inspired by his breakup with Lily Sobhani. The others argued against him and ultimately prevailed.

Certainly the finished track makes you feel a disturbed compassion for the singer. Its rotating, sawing arrangement of strings and guitars brings you into the very central stillness of self-knowledge. The line, 'I started looking for a warning sign,' indicates that he was actively searching for an omen that his relationship would break up. But, in the refrain, his ambivalent feelings move painfully around full circle again to cry out, 'When the truth is, I miss you.'

Chris has said that falling in love with Lily hit him 'like a ton of bricks'. It was a first-time experience for the frontman, who had basically been rejected by every girl he'd asked out since the age of thirteen. When Lily met Chris, she didn't look at his emotional baggage, this person full of emotional pain. Aged 22, he'd found a lovely girlfriend who was his supportive 'patient angel'. After he'd made a fool of himself at the Brit Awards, she'd come looking for him. In Australia six months previously, Chris had stressed importantly to *Massive* magazine's Craig Tansley, 'We don't look around – we have girlfriends.'

Chris had even contemplated buying a ring and proposing to Lily. He had grown up in the glow of a very happy marriage, and was going through a period of being horny for marriage. However, the course of true love does not always run smooth; In February, he told *Time*'s Benjamin Nugent that he was reading *Men Are From Mars, Women Are From Venus* because his first long-term relationship was proving difficult. Coldplay had been away on tour for much of the seven months or so that Chris and Lily had been together, which made the relationship hard to sustain. Subsequently, it broke down. 'Warning Sign' was a song of deep remorse about the break-up – but, according to Chris, he barely deserved the opportunity to express it.

'Romantically, I'm a complete cunt,' he later told Ted Kessler in an interview for *The Observer*. 'Absolutely. I'm a complete loser and failure in all things romantically.' As Kessler concluded, 'The reason for this is the obstacle hogging his one-track mind: Coldplay. He's obsessed with the band, and for a hopeless romantic, that's pretty hard to balance.'

> 'When it comes to girls, I just behave like an idiot . . . I'm very good at maintaining my relationship with Jonny, though.' – *Chris Martin*

Chris's romantic inclinations came a poor second to his musical passion. He identified his lack of attention as a cause of his romantic failings. 'The problem with me and romance is that I've watched too many films – too many Woody Allen films, specifically,' he explained. 'There's always the big build-up to people getting together, then they get together and you never see what happens next. I'm obsessed with that build-up, with the moment when the violins are playing and it's soft focus and unusual. I'm ashamed to say that after that I lose interest.'

Although Chris was at a stage where he hated himself for his failure to maintain the relationship with Lily, he hadn't lost his sense of irony: 'For some reason, I'm convinced that the main relationship that I was destined to be in was with Jonny. When it comes to girls, I just behave like an idiot . . . I'm very good at maintaining my relationship with Jonny, though. If we had sex, though, it would ruin everything,' he quipped to *Pulse*.

When Coldplay started work on the new album, *Lime* magazine asked Chris if it was true they were going to be 'ditching acoustic guitars for a seriously loud sound'. While agreeing in part, the band didn't yet know what the relative proportion of electric to acoustic sound would be, 'just seeing what sounds best' in the studio. But they were very certain about other features. 'More up-tempo songs with drums as a driving force,' said Jonny, citing Joy Division, New Order and Echo and the Bunnymen as influences for their new direction. Will's improved drumming had further expanded Coldplay's aural palette. 'Will has got so good that we use him as a central force, whereas it used to be driven by acoustic guitar,' explained Chris.

'Coldplay's allure stems also from a precise, pulsating rhythm section, drummer Will Champion and bass player Guy Berryman,' commented Scott Wilson of *Pitch.com*. 'Martin's piano lines – part of the Coldplay formula that most distinguishes the group from U2 and Radiohead – often stutter along beside Champion and Berryman rather than hum with

Buckland's guitar.' Will emphasised that their bigger and bolder sound 'wasn't a methodical, kind of clinical contrived difference, it was the result of playing live a lot . . . just being together as a band and travelling the world for two years.'

As Guy explained to *Hear/Say*'s Mark Watt, 'we were on the road for almost two years of touring and we didn't really expect that we'd have to do it that long. So I think when we made the second album, we were a bit more clued up. We knew . . . we'd have to go out and tour behind it for a long time. In the studio, I think we subconsciously wanted to write more upbeat tracks because they seem to come across better live. Also I think that since the first album did quite well, the second time around we weren't afraid to be a bit more bold and daring with trying out different types of songs.'

Initial leaks about 'Politik' created rumours that Coldplay's new album was entirely written around the events of 9/11. In the *NME*, Chris firmly denied any talk of the band taking a wholly politicised direction: 'All I said was, "How could anyone not be affected by something big like that?" The song "Politik" . . . comes out of us thinking, "Fuck! We're all going to die!" That's what most of the album's about. There's a theme running through the album which is, "This could be your last meal – so make it a nice meal."'

> ## 'We're passionate about music and very critical about the music that we listen to.' – *Will Champion*

'It's turned into our loudest, bashiest song,' Chris exulted. 'I've gone from thinking it's just me in my bedroom to thinking it's four of us in front of millions of different people, and it brings out a different kind of song.' Incredibly, the band kept 'Politik' under wraps for eight months until its debut at the Meltdown Festival in June 2002.

The sessions at Air Studios were often stalled by the group's compulsive perfectionism. 'To this day, Coldplay remain a far more fractious group than you'd expect,' *Q* emphasised. 'They're clearly close – but they're frank about the battles over the new album. Champion has been ever harder to please when it comes to new material.'

'If you come in with a shit song, Guy and Will, they just won't want to play on it,' Chris told *Pulse*. With the rhythm section taking charge of quality control, Chris was finding Will a tough creative nemesis. 'Will's the only one I have to please. If he goes, "Ugh," then I have to acknowledge it's no good. That's one of my great hobbies in life . . . trying to convince Will that my songs are any good,' laughed Chris. 'Sometimes I write incredibly shit lines and it's Will's job to tell me so,' he told *Chart* magazine.

'We're passionate about music and very critical about the music that we listen to,' Will explained. 'When you write something it has to hit the level that you accept as being good.' Will's critical approach contains an element of poetic justice, given how Chris harried him in their earliest, sweltering recording sessions down at the Elephant and Castle. 'I think we should be enlisting in UN peacekeeping forces,' Will joked. 'We're getting good at conflict resolution. There's always some conflict that needs resolving. Whether it's over a drum loop or a bass drum pattern.' 'The famous bone of contention on most songs,' said Jonny, laughing.

Subsequently, the band would have to spend eight months and a thousand studio hours to get everything exactly right. But at that point, speeding through the sessions, they already had a long list of tracks underway: 'A Ghost', 'Your Guess Is As Good As Mine', 'Politik', 'Deserter', 'Fingers

Crossed', 'Amsterdam', 'Murder', 'This Hollow Frame', 'In My Place', 'Animals' and 'In Isolation'. Despite the pressure of living up to *Parachutes*, they were making rapid progress.

Two summers ago, down at Orinoco Studios, their first producer Chris Allison had viewed Chris as extremely talented, but surprisingly limited in his knowledge of popular music. Since then, the band had gained a whole new reservoir of experience by touring. *Lime* magazine later reminded Chris that he had once said of Limp Bizkit, 'I'm not interested in meeting people that I don't think are very good.' 'I take that back!' cut in Chris. 'We went on tour with them in Australia and I think they're good . . . I think "My Way" and "Rollin'" are good songs.'

On the silent afternoons of the American tour, Coldplay had driven through the kind of boiling fields where Johnny Cash picked cotton all day as a dirt-poor ten-year-old. Beside the direct sense they gained of this side of America, they developed what some journalists found to be a strange musical affinity with Cash. 'It's hard to imagine Coldplay listening to the Man in Black,' *Pulse*'s journalist commented to Chris.

'For a long time, I always felt slightly afraid of listening to things I thought were too different to what I was supposed to like,' Chris replied. 'Then suddenly I realised that's absolute nonsense. And you can listen to anything.'

Chris was assimilating new influences rapidly. 'You hear something you like, learn how to do it and steal it. It's like stealing cars and welding them together. We've stolen the Bunnymen's cars, the Cure's car, the Stones' car . . . Everyone!' he testified. 'It all just goes in your head, and we were really, really desperate to do something different.'

The group's musical development was now catalysed by a vast range of positive stimuli. 'The last two years of touring had been just like a cultural sponge,' Chris told *Pulse*. 'So much new music, new places, new people, and we just wanted to sort of spew some of that out, you know?' 'Just yesterday we were watching The Coral when they did *Top of the Pops* and the two guitarists are amazing,' enthused Jonny. 'It really makes you want to be better.'

The seasoned toughness and musical maturity of the many bands whose work they gobbled up could have cowed Coldplay, completely destroying their confidence. Luckily, they were brought up by strong mothers like Sara, Alison and Joy, who absolutely demanded that their sons work on their positive outlook. Such preparations didn't always stop the insecurities experienced by their sons, but they definitely limited them.

The song that would become the next single, 'In My Place', would provide the musical key to the next album. 'It was a bitch. The hardest song we've ever had to record,' Chris attested. In their efforts to nail the definitive cut of the track, the band recorded around a hundred different takes, none of them satisfactory. 'We almost dumped it because we were struggling,' Chris said, 'but Jonny's guitar riff is just gorgeous, my favourite riff of his ever, so we kept at it.' And at it, and at it . . . The powerful potential of the song haunted the playbacks, but never quite synchronised with what they actually recorded.

Another song under construction during this period, 'A Rush Of Blood To The Head', perfectly expresses the extent to which Coldplay's writing had moved on. It creates a perfect unity of musical mood with its brooding lyrics, words that gracefully manage the difficult feat of being aggressive, devotional and ironically passive all at once. The open guitar strum at the beginning immediately triggers an association with protest songs. The singer states he is going to start a war, 'if you can tell me something worth fighting for.' It's a protest song that asks, what should we protest *against*?

'Certain songs when you're recording get much more attention than others,' Chris commented to *Shakenstir*. 'Because they're more troublesome or they're more exciting, because they're new or whatever.' An exception to this rule was, he explained, 'Amsterdam': 'that's pretty much live and it was just done and we did it very quickly and just left it . . . and it was really quick and I think it's a nice song. It's the only song I can think of where the verse and the chorus were [written] over a thousand miles apart.'

Guy found that another new number, 'God Put A Smile Upon Your Face', proved particularly troublesome. The band had been playing the song live on the road as a no-holds-barred free-for-all, with a noticeable PJ Harvey influence. But, initially, they couldn't get the bass part right. As Guy remembered, 'when we came to record it in the studio, we struggled because there was something not quite right about it. I wasn't happy about where we'd left it . . .'

Frustrations erupted frequently. Arguments broke out. There were verbal fouls. 'Being in this band is like being in a relationship,' Chris joked to *mtv.com*'s Jon Weiderhorn. 'Every time you have a big argument you walk out and slam the door. And then as soon as you slam it you think, "Oh, why did I do that?" Then you walk back in and have sex.'

The first cracks began to show by the mixing stage in late autumn. 'It's panic stations at the moment,' Guy admitted to *Rolling Stone*, 'because we've got a deadline we're trying to meet, and I don't think we're going to meet it. We've got a lot of pressure on us.' The pressure was not just from the record company, but from the band's workload, their fatigue – and, most of all, from their own mercilessly high expectations of themselves. As Guy put it, 'The only pressure we feel is the pressure we put on ourselves. We're our harshest critics.'

Some relief from an autumn of intense studio work arrived in mid-December, when Coldplay flew back to America for a series of important radio shows. First, they took part in the Los Angeles KROQ Acoustic Christmas Show, following it up with shows in San Francisco, Boston, New York, Washington and Philadelphia, before wrapping up the jaunt with a return visit to David Letterman's *The Late Show*.

> **'I've gone from thinking it's just me in my bedroom to thinking it's four of us in front of millions of different people, and it brings out a different kind of song.'** – *Chris Martin*

After the Christmas and New Year break, the band got together and listened with fresh ears to the material they had recorded during the autumn. The hard realisation then was that the album they had produced was rather mediocre and bland, and didn't show a great deal of musical development from *Parachutes*. 'It was just sounding a bit like a band who had loads of money and could afford to make an expensive record, but it didn't have any passion or soul,' recalled Chris. Guy put it bluntly: 'Some of the songs just didn't mean anything.' 'I think we day-jobbed it,' agreed the frontman.

As Chris subsequently explained to *nme.com*, 'What we'd done sounded okay, but I thought it was an opportunity to do something mega.' In order to achieve this, Coldplay were not prepared to be swayed by industry praise or marketing deadlines. Long-term artistic self-preservation was at stake. Two years before, Dan Keeling had rushed down to Wales to tell the quartet that their first go at recording 'Shiver' lacked their hallmark passion. Then they had presented a united front against him. Now, Jonny, Will, Guy and Chris would once again present a united front to Dan and their record company to insist that a whole album's worth of material – all eleven tracks – lacked passion and vitality. Tens of thousands of pounds' worth of studio time had been spent creating them, but they simply weren't good enough.

It is a measure of EMI's faith that Coldplay once again got their way. Work diaries were

Supporting U2 at Slane Castle, August 2001. Chris's voice duets with Jonny's riffs.

revised and time was freed up until the summer of 2002. 'We want to make the most passionate, moving, melodic, uplifting and sad record of all time,' Chris insisted. 'There's no point in trying to do anything less, and if we get maybe one-tenth of the way there, that will be better than no part of the way there.'

After the exhaustion of two years' solid touring and intensive recording, Coldplay had decided to go back to the start. Their decision to jettison everything – an album in the can, a succession of release dates around the globe – was a characteristic display of artistic wilfulness. As *mtv.com*'s Jon Weiderhorn wrote, 'understanding Martin's work ethic is essential to grasping why Coldplay struggled through agonised songwriting and crushing self-doubt during the creation of their second record . . . For Martin, perfection isn't just something to strive for. He'll accept no substitute.'

The band's next move was to quit London and its distractions, and go back to Parr Street Studios, where so much of *Parachutes* was written and recorded. Parr Street's very basic equipment was the antithesis of Air Studios. 'You have to rely on the tunes and the emotions, rather than the heavy technology,' Chris later explained to *Rolling Stone*. 'It's a really cheap studio, so there was no pressure . . . We just went to this tiny room where we did a lot of the first record and which seems to be a really good room for us.'

The band made an almost masochistic resolution 'to do it the excruciating way we did it before.' They retreated with Ken and Mark to create a 'Fortress Coldplay' mentality. No thoughts about magazine covers, radio sessions, tours, large gigs, or visits to distant territories. Tracks from the Air sessions had to be sorted through and discarded. 'We threw away about ten songs that didn't have any resonance,' Guy later recalled. 'Other songs were scrapped in the process because they sounded as if they could have been on *Parachutes*.'

'It's no good for anyone if we make *Parachutes Mark II* because it's not interesting for us,' Chris emphasised to *mtv.com*. 'It would have shown that we're happy to sit back on what we'd done, and we're not. For us it was important to progress and try to improve upon our abilities as musicians.' Some of the songs abandoned were 'I Ran Away', 'Murder', 'Idiot', and finally 'Animals'. This last track was a firm live favourite, so the decision to ditch it was particularly courageous.

'I'm glad because now we'll have something we'll be happy to tour with for two years,' said Jonny. 'The good ones got kept,' Chris explained to *Yahoo News UK*. 'Like "In My Place", "A Rush Of Blood To The Head", "God Put A Smile Upon Your Face", "A Warning Sign", "Amsterdam" and a song called "Politik".'

'When we first started this record, the five songs that we now think are the best songs on the album didn't exist,' Chris revealed. 'It was the same on the first album too, and for that I'm eternally grateful. We had no idea where they came from, they just sort of arrived.'

Songs like 'A Whisper', 'Daylight' and 'The Scientist' were now recorded in a frenzy of creativity. Will recalled, 'We'd be working on something and Chris would go in the other room and just bash something out on the piano and say, "Guys, I've got this. What do you think?" And we'd put [the track we were recording] down and start working on it right away, so it was really spontaneous.' After the frontman plucked an original lyric, melody or riff from the ether, Guy, Jonny and Will got to work.

This swift momentum created the gorgeous piano ballad, 'The Scientist' – 'the only song we've ever written and recorded on the same day,' Chris noted, 'It doesn't mention the periodic table, but it is about when you start analysing things too much and it doesn't do you any good.'

'The Scientist' was 'a real turning point for our record,' Chris revealed to *mtv.com*, 'It was really the first song we had which was not in the original plan, and it just came out of nowhere.' As Chris explained to *Crud*'s Will Jenkins, the inspiration of the track came from listening to George Harrison's album *All Things Must Pass*. 'I was sitting at this battered old piano that was completely out of tune and I'd just heard . . . 'Isn't It A Pity' with this circular chord sequence. And this is all very anal but I felt I would like a chord sequence that went around and around, and where you don't know where it begins or ends.'

Chris fooled around, trying to capture the song's ambience on the clanging piano. Out sprang a beautiful sequence of chords, and he and Jonny knew they were hearing something very special. Chris explained to *Shakenstir*, 'I thought it was really lovely. And then the whole song just came out and so we recorded it then and there, and the piano and vocal was from the day it was written. And the best moment of the entire record for me was when we came back three weeks later . . . I just heard through a wall this riff and that's what [Jonny] does at the end, and that's my favourite bit on the record.' 'That's the song that really turned it around for us,' Jonny told rock critic Matt Diehl. 'Suddenly "The Scientist" came out of nowhere . . . We thought it was the best thing we'd ever written.'

This sense of creative achievement was reinforced by some moral support from a most conspicuous quarter. As Lorraine Carpenter of the *Montreal Mirror* commented, 'Some people hire shrinks, gurus or personal trainers to get their minds and bodies up to snuff but, while re-inventing themselves for their sophomore album, Coldplay had the help of a certain British music legend, entirely by accident and free of charge.'

With Teenage Fanclub and Embrace recording in the studios next to Coldplay, Parr Street was crowded with notables. But one face stood out and grabbed Coldplay's attention: a guy in a full raincoat and sunglasses, with his hair in a truncated mare's nest. So vibrant was his aura that he made everyone else in the cafeteria queue look like a grey-toned publicity photo.

It was Ian McCulloch, tall and wiry, queuing for his food and drink. Coldplay had seen him give a sterling performance with Echo and the Bunnymen in Perth, five months ago – and had never heard a mention of him in Britain since. McCulloch is from Liverpool, and shared a manager with

Ken Nelson, working from the Parr Street building.

As *ChartAttack* observed of Ian McCulloch, 'There are advantages to never having sold out a football stadium: you can still retain an aura of cool,' unlike his peers and disciples from Bono to Liam Gallagher. McCulloch was obscure and cultish all over the world, while Coldplay had only managed to secure cult credibility in America. 'He's a proper rock star, you know, the kind of man who controls a room when he's in it,' an awestruck Chris marveled.

Chris went over to him, and nervously proposed to buy the flamboyant McCulloch some refreshment. Some people send over drinks as a means of saying hello. What would be more natural for the quaintly semi-teetotal Chris than to offer to buy one of his musical heroes a bowl of soup?

Unfortunately, this strategy did not work right away as the awestruck Chris struggled to make an impression on his ice-cool idol. 'With Mac because he's so infamous and he's so as you expect when you meet him, all cigarettes and sunglasses you're shit scared for a bit, but then you realise that what's driving him is the same as what's driving you and your band,' Chris explained. 'Mac sometimes has a drink and he's harder to talk to then.'

'The Bunnymen's career was just littered with fuckin' half-baked shit, and we should have been massive,' McCulloch insisted in an interview with Canadian webzine, *Chartattack*. 'We are the Van Goghs of rock, which is not a bad thing to be.'

> **'The only pressure we feel is the pressure we put on ourselves.**
> **We're our harshest critics.'** – *Guy Berryman*

Eventually Chris was able to communicate his genuine admiration to Mac, a man who first hit the charts before any of Coldplay had entered primary school. 'We struck up a bizarre friendship. He gave us a lot of confidence, and some songwriting advice,' Chris acknowledged. Indeed, it was an unlikely friendship, with Chris bounding around enthusiastically, and Mac spraying out caustic witticisms over his fag end.

'He's got it,' said McCulloch, who was talking to *Q* about Chris, adding the candid admission that Coldplay were the band he would most like to be in today. 'I want to hate them but they're so good. He's too much of a perfectionist. He should relax. I never enjoyed that level of success and I think they should just try and enjoy it.'

The bunker of isolation and intensity that had been Coldplay's studio opened up to McCulloch. Will remembers his talismanic entrances: 'He'd come in, drink wine and listen to us play and stuff. He's an amazing storyteller and raconteur. He can captivate a room. Completely hold court over everything. There's no chance of anyone else being the centre of attention in the room.'

Chris later defined Mac's input to *Rolling Stone*: 'he wasn't there telling us what to do, but it was nice to have him around, sometimes as a voicing board. We took loads and loads from the Bunnymen certainly in terms of being inspired, so you know, we'd already stolen all his ideas.'

In particular, Mac showed Chris the value of supreme self-confidence. He was one of those whom Chris identified to *mtv.com* as 'various people who've made me more and more at peace with what I do musically with my friends . . . What I love about Ian . . . he's not scared of anyone. He certainly doesn't show it anyway. Whereas I'd say, "I've met David Bowie," he'd say, "No, no, no. It's David Bowie met me." I thought, "Right, yeah."'

However, Coldplay were still uncertain about some aspects of their musical identity, and their perceived duty to be wild, charismatic personalities. With Ian around, they could delegate the tiring role of Rock Star, and at the same time, learn the tools of cool by observation. Although Mac is never short of confidence, when invited to sing on the final recording of 'In My Place', he refused. 'We came up with this really nice melody, and he's got such an amazing voice, but he was quite tense about singing in front of us. He'd also had a few, so he just ended up telling jokes into the mic,' Chris told *Q*'s Michael Odell.

Mac wasn't the only nervous one during the band's final attempt to clinch this elusive track. Chris was on edge about getting the vocal exactly right. To bolster his confidence, he turned to the Bunnyman for support. 'I did the vocals to "In My Place" wearing Mac's coat and with him sitting next to me in the booth. He was sat there, really pissed on red wine. He just kept saying, "Go on, son. Go on."'

'In My Place' represented a land bridge from the old album to the new, reprising the old longing of a broken soul: 'Please, please, please/Come back, come back and sing to me . . .' But despite the song's retrospective essence, Will appreciated the new aspects of its theme and delivery. 'It's a lot more confident, I think, than anything on *Parachutes*. Even songs like "Yellow" that were apparently "up" songs and big songs had a bit of fragility, I think, and to my mind, "In My Place" was the first step toward the whole album . . . it kind of was the first coming out of our shell a bit, and a bit more bold, more confident.'

> **'For us it was important to progress and try to improve upon our abilities as musicians.'** – *Chris Martin*

For 'Daylight', Coldplay recorded the piano and vocal first. The interesting sound at the start is a twelve-string guitar with a slide *à la* George Harrison. There was a mysterious kind of drone on the recording, Chris recounted to *Shakenstir*, 'because it's very hard to play. So there's these amazing little noises on it and we still don't know why they were in there.'

Being able to record a lot of the material as soon as it was composed was very fortunate, 'because you spend most of your life trying to recreate the first moments that you wrote. With "Daylight" we were all sat in a room and there was the piano track and the singing going.' The whole band played along over the top of that, and afterwards embellished the rousing performance, with Mac's baritone backing vocals. 'We just recorded all of it with Mark [Phythian] who does all the computer stuff with us. And then just chopped bits of it and there's quite a lot of samples or loops in it.'

When *Shakenstir* asked him if 'Green Eyes' was the most personal song on the album, Chris joked, 'When Pete Waterman sent it to us we just thought what a great song, what a great track. Just add a few sleigh bells on it and we've got a Christmas Number One.'

A new element of jagged menace in 'A Whisper' further put the old *Parachutes* sound to rest. The track originated with a question from Mac: 'He asked, "Chris have you got a 3/4 song on there?" And I thought shit, we haven't! So we quickly wrote "A Whisper".' This track contains a striking duel between the voice and the guitar. As a composer Chris revels in a friendly rivalry with Jonny, creator of the melodies that help define Coldplay's music. 'When I come in with something, he always then comes up with the best melody. It's always better than the singing melody. That's why we have so many rest bits. He's like Johnny Marr or something in my head. If you think the singer's good, wait till you hear the guitarist sort of thing.'

Guy's dissatisfaction finally rescued the almost discarded 'God Put A Smile Upon My Face'. 'It was a really nice day when I was trying to record bass at the time, and me and Chris were sitting down trying to brainstorm it to find what was wrong. And so I just started to do some bass lines and between the two of us we came up with this kind of groove which stays on the same note as opposed to changing,' he told *Crud*'s Will Jenkins.

As for 'Warning Sign', Chris eventually conceded to the opinions of the rest of the quartet. Similarly, 'Amsterdam' was another of the songs from the first recording session that made it though to the final album. After essentially forgetting about the track for four months, the band simply remixed it.

All was going according to schedule. However, at the last minute the innovative 'Clocks' emerged and was duly included on the album. It's now impossible to imagine the record without it. 'We already had ten songs for the album, and then Chris came in late one night and wrote it on piano,' Ken Nelson told *VH1*. 'It just arrived; it wasn't planned on at all,' Chris told the *Cleveland Plain Dealer*. 'The riff just came out, and I showed it to Jonny . . . and he picked up his guitar (a sure sign that he likes a song) and played these brilliant chords, and then Guy came in and added a bass line and it sparked something else. It was like a chemical reaction process.'

It is the disc's most technically accomplished and original sounding track, though the band initially left it off the album listing. It seemed to them to be the next stage in their musical development, better suited as a springboard for the third album just as 'In My Place' had been for the second. They didn't have time to finish the recording, so the band made a demo CD marked, 'Songs for #3', ready for their third album.

As the album's June release date approached, the band still had to mix all the tracks to their satisfaction. As Chris remembers, 'We were just about to hand the record in but it was sounding rubbish but we thought we had to do it because we wanted to release it then. Some of our record company guys came in and basically everyone decided that we had to put the record back to take the pressure off.'

Parlophone's original release date had been planned to take full promotional advantage of the band headlining on the Pyramid Stage at Glastonbury on 28 June 2002. There was a sense of *déjà vu* in the timing, for it was after a powerful Glastonbury performance that *Parachutes* had first charted at Number One. But then it was announced that the album would be postponed until the end of August, with the complete promotional schedule for the UK and the US altered accordingly.

This further delay created a great opportunity to record 'Clocks' properly. Chris says it was Phil Harvey who convinced him to record the track right away. 'He heard it and said, "No, you must do that song now 'cause you're going on [in the lyrics] about urgency, and you're talking about keeping this song back. That doesn't make sense."'

The sense of urgency in the song came from Coldplay's ceaseless travelling. The band were afraid of becoming Buddy Holly die-alikes, particularly Chris: 'There's a death obsession in the band at the moment – we've been travelling in so many planes we feel we've got to do everything right now just in case we crash. This is the tune the next record could have been written around, but we did it now because we might be struck down at any point.'

The final production process for 'Clocks' began by recording Chris's sparse, melodic foundation. Then Jonny added his guitar chords, and Guy his bass line, creating the rhythm of a speeding, staccato, Morse code – intermittently punctuated by Will's drums. This 'odd, trotting rhythm which seems so simple . . . is incredibly ingenious, alternating a 6/8 with a half time signature every other bar,' the Dutch *Progressive Rock* website meticulously observed.

'Clocks' is not so much Coldplay as we have known them, but Coldplay as they may become. The track's atmospheric synth line, bubbling guitar, unusual rhythm and decaying cymbals are also strangely reminiscent of the early, Chris Allison-produced track 'High Speed'.

As for the overall themes of the album, Guy's comments to *Rolling Stone* at the time now seem particularly myopic: 'I don't think we've been influenced massively by our success and by our travels. The lyrics [Chris] writes are more basic than that . . . emotional ideas rather than experiences.'

Poster boy for good behaviour at Glastonbury – despite staring like a child from the movie Village of the Damned.

For the four young former students, most of their experience of life since graduation had consisted of rushing around to meet promotional duties, speeding along in buses, vans and planes. The album's themes of urgency and *carpe diem* transience are universal, but it was Coldplay's overwhelming experiences that inspired them.

In the midst of all this fraught musical activity, Coldplay received an unusual approach from the Oxfam charity. Would the band be prepared to use their public position to highlight a campaign for international fair trade? Oxfam were determined to lobby to change global trade rules, so as to save the world's most vulnerable countries from destruction. To this end, they were organising a fact-finding trip to show observers the appalling effects that Western protectionist trade rules were having.

In responding to this, Coldplay followed the good example set by their altruistic predecessors. Chris confessed, 'We only got into it because of people like Radiohead, U2 and Blur. We saw what they were trying to do and thought it was a good idea.' As Chris pointed out to *The Telegraph*'s Craig MacLean, rock 'n' roll should have room for a variety of different roles: 'I'm not rock 'n' roll like Bobby Gillespie is, and Bobby Gillespie isn't rock 'n' roll like I am . . . If I started pretending to do that sort of stuff, I'd look stupid. The most rock 'n' roll thing we've done is get involved in all this Fair Trade thing.'

'Coldplay have clearly taken a page out of Bono's guidebook to being rock stars who care,' *Maxim Blender* commented. But they also had principles of their own to enforce. In the previous year, Coldplay had rejected offers of £4 million for the use of their songs in TV advertising. Diet Coke and Gap wanted to use 'Trouble' and 'Don't Panic', while the American soft drink company that made Gatorade wanted to use 'Yellow'. 'The sad thing about American TV is that you can't escape consumerism,' asserted Chris. 'America has so much amazing culture, and it's buried in fifteen-minute segments between ten minutes of ads.' *Q* reported that Coldplay had asked Phil Harvey not to tell them about such offers, in case 'a discussion might lead to compromise'. Instead, the band had donated songs for use in Red Cross ad campaigns.

So Coldplay had their own set of commercial principles, but international trade was a mystery to them. Chris told *The Guardian*, 'When they said: "Do you want to get involved in this Fair Trade Campaign?", they may as well have been speaking Japanese. We did not know what they meant.' Jonny agreed. 'To us, "trade" just meant figures on the stock market.' Oxfam's preliminary briefing would change their view forever. As Chris said, 'Someone comes in and tells you that the problems with trade are one of the three biggest causes of poverty in the world. I think everybody agrees with the idea of fair trade; it's just that no-one really knows about it . . . If you say to anybody: "Do you think that a man who grows something and does some work should be rewarded fairly?" then 99 out of 100 people would say yes. And yet most of us aren't really aware that that doesn't go on.'

It was agreed that Chris should go along on Oxfam's fact-finding trip to Haiti and the Dominican Republic, to study the effects of unfair trade on rice and coffee farmers. He would be accompanied by Phil Harvey, 'to make sure that I don't turn into a wannabe Mother Teresa with a microphone,' Chris quipped. Also on the trip would be Emily Eavis, the daughter of Glastonbury Festival founder Michael Eavis, who aimed to represent the festival and help link the issue of world poverty to popular music. As for Chris, another of his roles would be to write a diary of the trip – a journal that would be quite different from the band's tour diary that he intermittently contributed to.

Meanwhile, the resoundingly positive response to *Parachutes* continued with a 2002 Grammy nomination for Best Alternative Music Album. The other nominees were Icelandic indie pixie Bjork's *Vespertine,* Tori Amos (*Strange Little Girls*), Fatboy Slim (*Halfway Between The Gutter And The Stars*) and Radiohead for *Amnesiac.* In the *Time* article a year earlier, Radiohead and Coldplay had been stereotyped as a 'nasty' English band and a 'cute' English band. Beating Radiohead to a Grammy might even diminish the weary assertion that Coldplay were little more than Radiohead copyists. However, the February ceremony would coincide with the Oxfam trip, so Chris decided to opt out in favour of his important charity commitments.

Chris had been so frantically busy making the new album that he didn't really think about the Oxfam trip until he turned up at the airport at five a.m. for the flight. 'I was petrified,' he wrote in his diary. 'I also didn't feel I knew enough to act as a spokesman for an aid organisation . . . When we finally got there I felt like a fourth-rate Bono. Later on I felt like a third-rate Bono, and hopefully it's going to escalate until I feel like a full-on Bono.'

First stop was the Dominican Republic. The Oxfam party set out across country in a convoy, and at first Chris had a sense of detachment from the mission. He seemed to stand outside and observe others making their own observations. 'It felt like those Comic Relief trips you see on TV – Land Rovers, mud lanes, lots of red-faced Brits trying to look important.' Chris visited one of the co-operatives that oversee and assist the small coffee farms in the Dominican Republic, enabling them to avoid selling to middlemen who buy their coffee at rip-off prices. 'Even with the co-ops they are struggling,' Chris reported. 'World coffee prices have plummeted in the past decade, with farmers often selling their coffee for less than it costs them to grow it. Yet the price in the supermarkets at home hasn't dropped.'

During an interview at a local radio station Chris discovered that Coldplay had had a number one hit in the Dominican Republic: 'Though no-one could confirm which single! I guess this is why I am here – because I have access to the media, and I'd rather talk about Oxfam in interviews than the colour of my socks.'

The second leg of the tour involved flying on to Haiti in a primitive aircraft. Chris was flying into a region whose people had experienced ecological, agricultural and economic disaster on a catastrophic scale. Although Haiti is a world away from life in London or Los Angeles, when these poor farmers lose, we all lose. 'Everyone said we'd be shocked by Haiti – and I was,' Chris wrote. 'It looked like a war zone, except people were just getting on with their daily lives. Everything was so beaten down – and we hadn't even seen the real slums.' Chris played 'Yellow' on his guitar at a radio station, and visited a TV station where the staff had no idea who he was, or what he was doing there. Such incidents reaffirmed Chris's belief in the transient nature of fame, and lent a helpful perspective on his extraordinary recent experiences.

On Day Three, a two-and-a half-hour dawn drive over jarring terrain shook off any sense of the trip as a docu-dream replay of Comic Relief. On this edge of the world, any path covered with broken rocks was considered a main road. The group saw coffee being water-processed, and the difference that Oxfam's support had made to the venture. Next day, at another co-op, the party was told that local people couldn't afford basic health care or education. Such hardship increased Chris's humane sense of despair. 'Keep looking for the hope,' Yolette Etienne, Haitian head of Oxfam told him. 'We've just got to do things bit by bit.' Chris found it hard. 'At lunchtime I said to one guy that I didn't have any solution to these problems, and he said, "Of course you don't. You're a singer." And I thought, You're right, what the hell am I doing here in a bandana trying to look like Axl Rose?' Chris felt lost. Back in his hotel room, he sought refuge in his headphones and Echo and the Bunnymen.

The bleakest day of the whole trip was Day Six. Eight hours of bumpy driving brought Chris and the Oxfam crew to the desolation of St-Marc, a settlement where all the trees had been cut down by former French colonists or, later, by the newly independent Haitians, so that the soil had completely eroded. The whole region looked like a barren lunar landscape.

> **'We only got into [the Fair Trade campaign] because of people like Radiohead, U2 and Blur. We saw what they were trying to do and thought it was a good idea.'** — *Chris Martin*

Chris's final day with the expedition focused on the desperate Haitian rice industry, almost destroyed by the influx of cheap American rice. The economic independence of Haiti has been severely damaged, Chris stressed. 'Haiti has been forced to drop all restrictions on imports, making it one of the freest markets in the world. So it's flooded with surplus rice grown by heavily subsidised farmers in the US, and many of its own rice farmers are now moving to the already overcrowded slums in the cities in search of work.'

With these disturbing experiences fresh in his mind, Chris returned to Parr Street Studios with an expanded view of the world. The Fair Trade trip had left a huge impression on him, so much so that the news from America that Coldplay had won the Best Alternative Album Grammy for *Parachutes* seemed almost irrelevant. 'After that, the concept of an awards ceremony was the most farcical thing in the world,' he told *Maxim Blender*. 'Because you see poverty, and no one gives a shit who J-Lo is. It's like a big slap in the face: "Don't get too pleased with yourself, idiot, because you've had a lot of opportunities other people haven't had." It's a reminder not to be a twat.' Realising that the band's effective involvement with Fair Trade was underpinned by their continuing success, Chris observed, 'We've got to be good because now we've got more responsibility than just our own careers.'

A full report of Chris's Oxfam sojourn was published in an issue of *Q* magazine, timed to publicise the Fair Trade Campaign launch on 11 April 2002. Chris ended his account by urging music lovers and Coldplay fans to help 'by buying Fair Trade products and pressuring politicians to change this insanity, to make trade fair.'

Coldplay's first practical act of support for the campaign meant returning to the same spot where they signed their record contract, Trafalgar Square, where Oxfam were publicising the campaign. The band also decided that their new album and their future releases would advertise the Make Trade Fair website address. 'That's so uncool but that's something we really, really believe in,' Chris told *The Telegraph*. 'I thought it was rock 'n' roll to put all those website addresses on the back of our record sleeve.' Coldplay have been excellent campaigners ever since: talking about the subject in interviews, wearing Make Trade Fair t-shirts, and promoting the campaign at their concerts. Chris always writes 'Make Trade Fair.com' on his photo-friendly hand for gigs, photos and TV performances. Coldplay are the Mobys of the Fair Trade campaign. They will sell themselves shamelessly for it.

At Glastonbury, the band promoted WaterAid. The sombre message was that during the 72 hours of the festival, 43,200 people in the developing world would die from lack of safe drinking water and adequate sanitation. Coldplay got festival-goers to help them build a statue representing world poverty, drawing attention to the desperate global issue, while WaterAid built African pit latrines at the festival to show just how cheaply effective sanitation could be provided.

Finally, after eight months, the band's second album was ready for its 26 August release. The mixing had been completed between New York and Air Studios, with Chris sleeping in a hotel across the street between sessions. The title, *A Rush Of Blood To The Head*, reflected Chris, Will, Jonny and Guy's emphasis upon immediacy. 'We all thought it just seemed to fit with everything,' Chris explained. 'It seemed to pull everything together. It's about impulsiveness, it's about doing things now.'

The cover of *Parachutes* had featured the warm-coloured globe glowing hazily out of the darkness – a strictly 'analogue'-style photographic image. The cover of *A Rush . . .* is a shocking contrast: monochromatic and sharply focused, though equally mysterious, the digitally-inspired design shows a detached head, or sculpted bust, severed in mid-section above a pair of full, sensual lips. The image is complex and sophisticated, mirroring the band's development. The only ambiguous part of the image is what seems to be a small Pharaoh's beard growing from the chin.

Flanges that stream out behind the head suggest the image is moving at great speed. The final sense is of a moment of intense impact, an image that conveys all the satisfying and destructive effects that are possible in a single moment in time.

Coldplay marked the release of *A Rush . . .* by paying to plant a forest of 10,000 mango trees in India, at a cost of £10 per tree. As it's calculated that producing a single CD creates 2.5 lbs. of carbon dioxide, to counteract this Coldplay created an oxygen-producing forest with the help of Future Forests, a company who create these ecological plantations worldwide. Thanks to Future Forests' initiative, over 50 million CDs are now 'carbon neutral' – that is, the forests have created oxygen to restore equilibrium to the earth's atmosphere that was damaged by the CD's carbon dioxide emissions. Coldplay also chose to plant mango trees because they provide an enormous harvest, food and saleable goods for the people of Bangalore. Dan Morrell, founder of Future Forests, explained that Coldplay fans can also add to the band's efforts by buying a tree in their forest: 'You get a certificate and a map showing where your tree is.'

With artistic and ecological concerns duly addressed, Coldplay breathed a collective sigh of relief. 'We're empty again now. Drained of ideas. Who knows if we'll do it again?' Chris told *Q*. Jonny agreed, 'I honestly can't tell you where another [album] would come from.' Inseparable from their exhaustion was the reassuring feeling that they'd given their all. 'If someone said, "You've got to start a new album tomorrow," I'd say, "I don't think we can do better than this." We'll only do a new album if we think it'll be better. I don't really care about the whole fifteen album thing,' Chris told *nme.com*.

At this time, Guy told Mike Doherty of *Chart* magazine, 'You're interviewing us in a strange transitional period in our lives. We haven't really relaxed from recording the album and we haven't really geared up [for] going out, touring and all this promotional mentality . . .' Doherty had come to interview the band at the north London rehearsal space where they were preparing for Glastonbury. 'It would be terrifying if we just kind of turned up there under-prepared.' Chris told Doherty that he had started taking singing lessons again. 'My teacher told me this morning that I was basically shit. I said, "You're right."' However, despite such typical self-deprecation, Mary Hammond's voice work with Chris had paid off abundantly. It was immediately apparent that his vocal range had broadened significantly. But none of Chris's intense efforts had robbed him of his genius for goofy behaviour, Doherty was relieved to note. In rehearsal, the band launched slam-bang into the introduction to 'In My Place'. Then suddenly, Chris dashed across to Doherty and hollered in his ear, 'We're playing to a backing track because we can't afford strings!' – and then ran back just in time to croon his first line.

Meantime, the much-delayed financial rewards of rock success had finally filtered through. 'The money doesn't come through in a steady drip,' explained Joy Buckland, adding that with the band's intense touring schedule, they 'barely had time to touch base, let alone spend money.' Nonetheless, Chris found a moment to buy a house in Belsize Park and moved there from Camden, where he and Jonny had lived since their early days in Ramsey Hall. Jonny also bought a house in Camden that he still shares with a very old school friend from Wales, John Hilton. 'He's staying round his old student haunts . . . He still lives like a student, really,' said Joy.

Chris was enjoying his house, a few streets down from Finley Quaye and Travis's Dougie Payne. With his all-consuming obsession, *The Telegraph* later commented, 'it's hard to imagine him doing anything . . . other than practice old songs and write new ones.' Indeed, when *Q* visited him one Saturday, the house rocked with the Bunnymen's 'Nothing Ever Lasts Forever'. Chris was practising the vocals in order to back Mac at a Finsbury Park gig the following day. It was a happy way of returning all Mac's support. 'I felt like the little boy at the school disco not knowing what to do. I mean, you can't try and upstage him, can you?'

Another source of enjoyment for Chris was hanging out with Tim Wheeler of Ash. The duo had great fun that spring playing an acoustic set at a lock-in session at Islington's rock-star pub, Filthy McNasty's. Wheeler was a friend who, Chris said, helped him to feel at ease about Coldplay's place in the music world. Tim also broadened Chris's outlook by getting him to watch the Sex Pistols documentary, *The Filth and the Fury*. 'I'd have a hard time convincing you Coldplay are the direct descendants of the Sex Pistols,' Chris advised *The Observer*. 'Johnny Rotten had so much compassion. He said he didn't do the things he did because he hated the British people but because he loved them and thought they were being sold short. That's exactly why we do what we do! We want to make music with heart and soul because culturally people are sold short in this country. We just want to prove that you can be a massive group and have some meaning, some feeling.'

Just as the promotional push for *A Rush . . .* was getting underway, a storm-in-a-tea-cup erupted when *nme*.com quoted Chris as saying, 'As far as I'm concerned this will be the last one we ever make. But I hope that some day we have more songs, you know?' This off-the-cuff comment gave rise to intense speculation that the band would quit after the album was released. Shortly afterwards, when an interview the band did with *Q* posed the question, 'What is the one thing you wish Chris wouldn't say or do?' Guy replied, 'Say, "We're not making another album."'

Promoting *Parachutes* had been a media ordeal, with criticism taking the rookie band by surprise. But this time around, Chris maintained his mercurial persona, alternating high-strung elation with diffidence, wariness with a wish to entertain. 'We're not Travis, OK? We've just been doing horse off a hooker's back,' he told *Q* journalist Michael Odell, winking. Chris brimmed with utter delight that eight months' agonising work was finally ready for release. Odell described the effervescent frontman as 'fizzing like a child on food additives.'

'The danger was we'd make a half-arsed, shitty, bargain-bin, average follow-up record with songs now half as good as "Yellow",' cried Chris. 'I'm not interested in, "Here are some off-cuts of the first album and I've got loads of money and coke and I'm in *OK!* magazine." That's bullshit.'

'Yeah, that's our next album,' said Jonny, looking up from his evening paper.

'Ironically, Chris Martin is less optimistic about the band's second outing. He told the BBC that the band is expecting a backlash and will probably be getting more criticism than praise,' *coldplaying.com* reported. 'It might not happen' became a pervasive theme of Chris's interviews where he defensively downplayed the album's chances.

Will wanted to reassure fans that the most valuable qualities of the first record would remain consistent in the second. 'We write and Chris sings about stuff we have all experienced. The only way you can be honest with your music is by singing things you know about. At the end of the day you can only write what you know. It's just our lives and stuff like that.'

It was time to get out on the road to promote the album, and prevent Chris from brooding. He still had difficulty making any sense of the band's success, as he told *Q*: 'I think, is it chance? How did I have the luck to be born here and meet Jonny and get signed and get success? I reckon there must be something higher. It feels like it was given to me and that's why I get scared I'll die before we make the most of it.'

As a warm up for Glastonbury, Coldplay played a 'secret' gig at Liverpool University on 2 June, a fitting thank-you to a city that had always served so well as their muse. *Shakenstir*'s review commented that the band had 'once again recorded huge chunks of their new album right here in Liverpool and it shows . . . one part Beatles, one part Bunnymen, and for the most part Coldplay.' Fittingly, Ian McCulloch appeared as support, telling *ChartAttack*, 'Chris said to me, "Mac, just remember: you're the best. You've got the best voice in the world." And I went, "I know. Remember you might have the second."'

> **'We've got to be good because now we've got more responsibility than just our own careers.'** – *Chris Martin*

After the show, dazzled by the enthusiastic reaction, Chris announced, 'We now want to go on to justify the coverage, justify earning this amount of money, justify people paying money to come and watch us – by becoming the biggest band ever.' Jonny's view of world conquest was more idiosyncratic. He told *The Pitch*, 'We don't want to be the biggest coconuts on the tree – just the hairiest.'

The band's next appearance, at the Royal Festival Hall's annual Meltdown Festival, was surrounded by some mild controversy. As that year's artistic director, David Bowie was responsible for choosing the acts that would appear across several nights. Bowie was dogged by criticism that his selection of acts – Coldplay, Suede, the Divine Comedy and the Dandy Warhols – was very middle of the road. His choices showed, argued *The Guardian*'s Alexis Petridis, that the former 'decadent gay saxophone-playing cokehead alien pierrot with an interest in fascism and the occult' was now simply 'a multimillionaire father of two'. Bowie subsequently replied, stating stiffly, 'My choice of billing reflects both my populist and fringe tastes in music.'

When Will hinted in a pre-gig interview that they might feature a 'surprise mystery guest', some people made a general assumption that Bowie would join them on stage. (The band had rehearsed a version of his 'Heroes' with Meltdown in mind.) When Coldplay struck up 'Yellow' and fans stampeded toward the stage, a figure leapt from the audience and grabbed the mic from Chris. However, rather than the Thin White Duke, the crowd were treated to a completely drunk 26-year-old from Birmingham whose rationale had been, 'Bollocks to it, I'm getting up on stage, man!' Chris motioned to security to let the interloper have his fun; and the Brummie sang the entire number before plunging anonymously back into the crowd.

Although Bowie never did show up, the most significant aspect of the evening's performance was the debut of 'Politik'. Confident in its worth, the band opened their set with the song. 'Two minutes into 'Politik' and it becomes clear that Coldplay's new stuff pisses all over everything else from an extremely great height,' enthused *virtualfestivals.com*'s Andrew Future.

Chris's intense focus on live performances had developed to the extent that, when the band played London gigs, he often stayed in a hotel the night before. 'He likes to feel as if he's on tour before a show even if he's not,' revealed Ted Kessler. 'He loves that sense of adventure, that sense of heading off to make camp with your friends.' Kessler asked Chris if he felt that such behaviour was a little odd. 'Well I am odd, I suppose,' Chris told him. 'You know, I'm in a rock 'n' roll band and people think it's weird because I don't do anything remotely rock 'n' roll besides playing it . . . but for me, rock 'n' roll is all about doing whatever you want. It's about defying convention and being who you are. And that's me.'

On Friday 28 June, Coldplay walked out onto the Pyramid Stage at Glastonbury to headline the festival. The sun shone upon the enormous crowd, stretched like a giant tarpaulin across the landscape. 'It may always rain on Fran Healy, but Coldplay have no such problems,' cracked *Chart* scribe Mike Doherty. Chris told the audience they'd been preparing for this for 25 years. Headlining this massive event, before a 100,000-strong throng, confirmed that Coldplay were now Britain's biggest band.

> **'We'll only do a new album if we think it'll be better. I don't really care about the whole fifteen album thing.'** – *Chris Martin*

Once again they opened with 'Politik'. The crowd's ferocious and euphoric response came as a huge shock, 'as if the band were playing their biggest hit instead of a completely unknown new number,' recounted Alexis Petridis. Such enthusiasm was quickly established as the norm, as each successive song got an epic reaction. 'Occasionally artists triumph at Glastonbury because they somehow manage to encapsulate the experience of being at the festival in their music,' Petridis continued, 'partly because they are at the peak of their powers as a live band, partly because their music is simultaneously grandly ambitious and warmly inclusive.'

The reason for the instant applause, Petridis argued, was because it created 'a bizarre sense of instant familiarity' with the second album's songs. 'You feel you already know and like these songs the first time you hear them. The last band to pull off this remarkable feat was Oasis.'

Chris was even beginning to relax over the prospect of giving interviews – although this wasn't always immediately obvious. His mercurial nature was much in evidence as he bounded into a hotel bar to meet *The Observer*'s Ted Kessler, and immediately asked, 'Why are you doing this, you've always hated us.' When Kessler, much surprised, replied to the contrary, Chris said at once, 'Sorry, it's just me, I do worry.'

Despite Coldplay's defiant ripostes of the previous year, Chris confessed to Kessler that, originally, he had feared sometimes that Alan McGee's criticisms might be right. But now, 'He'd love to ask him what it was all about and tell him how helpful the flak was, personally,' explained Petridis. 'It stopped us from making our very own *Attack of the Clones*,' commented Chris, referring to the much anticipated but largely disappointing *Star Wars* film.

In early August, three weeks before the release of *A Rush . . .*, Coldplay travelled to America for a short club tour to debut their new material. 'Feeling terribly worried about how this album was going to be received,' Will revealed to the *Coldplay e-zine*, 'we were bursting to play the new songs but knew full well that people wouldn't know them and might be disappointed. We played them anyway and thankfully they went down ok.'

The tour opened on 2 August at Chicago's Vic Theatre. *Hear/Say*'s Mark Watt observed that Coldplay 'displayed an elevated sense of stage presence with Martin commanding the show like a young Michael Stipe or Bono.' Despite the raging performance Coldplay had given on their last visit to Chicago, Watt noticed there was 'obviously something different in the band's approach. Namely, they rocked harder than before,' with 'an arsenal of strong, fresh material.'

During the tour, Chris enjoyed playing the mischievous front man role. 'This song's dedicated to anyone who's been in a car accident,' he announced at New York's Bowery Ballroom. In the crowd was Noel Gallagher, still recovering from a recent taxi crash in Minneapolis. Oasis were touring the States, and their New York gig gave Coldplay an opportunity to get to know them better. At the end of the show Chris sprang a surprise on the Oasis party by performing 'Songbird', written by Liam Gallagher for his wife, Nicole Appleton.

The previous day, Coldplay had been to see Oasis play at the Roseland Ballroom. In an *après-gig* interview for *Rolling Stone*, Noel Gallagher told of a chance encounter with Ian Brown of the Stone Roses. 'He said, "I pass you the torch," and now, we're passin' it to them,' he said, in tribute to Coldplay. Later the *Coldplay e-zine* reported, 'the New York shows have attracted more attention as there have been celebrities in attendance including Oasis' Gallagher brothers and Hollywood actress Gwyneth Paltrow.' There were more practising thespians present at the Los Angeles show eight days later, as Jack Nicholson, Minnie Driver and other Hollywood stars attended the final date of the tour. When Chris started up 'Everything's Not Lost', dedicating it 'to all the actors and actresses in the house', he also altered one line to 'And if you haven't won an Oscar, and you think that all is lost.'

Despite Gallagher's 'passing of the torch', *mtv.com* reported that Chris seemed 'a jumble of nervous energy' when he and Jonny recorded an acoustic session for LA radio station KCRW on 20 August. In the middle of 'In My Place', Will, who was listening in, accidentally knocked over a guitar case, and Chris stopped abruptly. "What the fuck was that!" he snapped, shifting moods within seconds. Throughout the session Chris was terribly self-critical, *VH1's* Jon Weiderhorn reported: 'Even after he sang a flawless, emotive version of "The Scientist", he scrunched up his face and exclaimed, "That sounded shite. Let's do it again."'

'Not a single night goes past where I don't wake up sweating and thinking no one will like this record,' Chris told Weiderhorn, acknowledging his neurosis. 'We poured every ounce of soul, emotion and love into it, and now we can only wait and see.'

Meanwhile, there was great news from Britain – Phil Harvey phoned to say that 'In My Place' was receiving blanket airplay. By the time Coldplay returned home again at the end of August, it had debuted at Number Two in the UK charts – their highest singles chart entry to date. Chris got off the plane, went straight into BBC Radio One for an interview with their old ally Steve Lamacq, and announced a one-off gig to be played in less than a week at the Kentish Town Forum. Two hours later, all the tickets were gone.

'Playing at the Kentish Town Forum was a real relief,' Will later explained, 'for the first time we didn't have to apologise for playing new songs, and we certainly felt more relaxed and played the best we had for ages.' The gig was 'dead sweaty and heaving', *Playlouder* reported. The mighty vocal power of the 2,000-strong crowd provoked Chris to roar, 'We've finally made it to stadium rock!'

The coolest guest at the Forum gig was Dave Grohl of the Foo Fighters, who, having consoled them at that rotten Washington DC radio festival on their US debut tour, now saw them on top form. There was also something of a tributary touch to the set list. Ash's 'Shining Light' and Echo and the Bunnymen's 'Lips Like Sugar' were given the full-blown Coldplay treatment.

They also played Westlife's 'Flying Without Wings' – an odd choice, seeing as Chris had insisted that the song made him 'feel physically sick' in an *NME* interview two years earlier. The show reached a joyous finale as everyone bellowed out 'Happy Birthday' to Phil Harvey.

Once the release date for *A Rush . . .* finally arrived, Chris was besieged by the press. He revealed to *The Sun* that 'Warning Sign' had been written about his break-up with Lily Sobhani. He was ready again for a relationship, he told them, but very annoyed by tabloid rumours about his love life. 'It's really mad, fame,' he commented on one paper's gossip about Natalie Imbruglia. 'Another said Gwyneth Paltrow – should I sue them? I was really pissed off with them because it's not true. The only person I've ever been pictured embracing in public was Mo Mowlam [former Secretary of State for Northern Ireland] and I'm fine with that.'

Talking about 'The Scientist' and 'Warning Sign' to *The Telegraph*, Chris stressed their ambivalence. 'They're not entirely break-up songs, they're almost break-up songs. You save [the love] at the last minute. Which is weird, because that's not me at all.'

To mark the album's release, *Top of the Pops* featured Coldplay in a live performance of 'Daylight' – a real distinction, since the show has always focused on chart singles. 'Well, the waiting is over,' Will wrote in the website diary. 'Now there really is nothing we can do about it. That's the danger of listening to one's own records, there's always something that should have been done differently. I stopped listening to it when I knew there was no way of changing it any more, which was about two and a half months ago. The period of waiting that occurred between the finishing of this album and its release was probably one of the weirdest times we've had for a while.'

On 1 September, *A Rush . . .* blasted into the UK album chart at Number One with first-week sales of a quarter of a million copies. 'Coldplay Are Flippin' Wonderful – say several squillion people with taste' ran *Playlouder*'s headline. It amounted to five times the first week's sales of *Parachutes* and was the highest record sales so far that year, outdoing both Eminem and Oasis.

In its first two months, *A Rush . . .* sold 2.6 million copies in Britain alone. Since *Parachutes* had sold less than two million copies in total in the UK, this was indicative of the band reaching a new popular plateau. In the all-important US, the album had 140,000 sales in its first week and hit *Billboard*'s Number Five position. After all their work, Coldplay were now serious transatlantic players.

'Company Joy for EMI' ran *The Guardian*'s 6 September headline. The great increase in internet piracy had been blamed for a decline in the legitimate record market, but EMI had tried to downplay this by forecasting that global music sales would fall by no more than four per cent. The actual drop in sales was greater, challenging EMI's claim that it could avoid a serious fall in revenues, despite losing market share in both the US and Europe. Now, *The Guardian*'s John Casey wrote, 'the success of albums like Coldplay's . . . should enable it to hit its target for the financial year.'

In terms of reviews, the album 'exceeded everyone's expectations by a country mile,' said *The Guardian*'s Dorian Lynskey. 'A rare case of a British band who, seeing an open goal, didn't panic and hoof the ball over the crossbar.' *CMJ.com* were equally positive: 'Paranoid, epic, mysterious and full of heart and soul, it's a record with a firm sense of its own greatness.' *A Rush . . .* made many 'Best Albums of the Year' lists, including those of *Rolling Stone*, *Mojo*, *Q*, *Uncut* and *Spin*. *NME* called it 'an album of outstanding natural beauty, an organic, wholesome work.'

The Daily Mirror zoomed in on the decided change in the band's attitude: 'where there was once mealy-mouthed indecision, there is now steely determination. The result is an album that puts Coldplay in the premier league of home grown bands.' For once *The Sun* agreed with its competitor, stating that the LP 'proves the band can take on the mighty Radiohead and U2 to make it big in the US . . . Memo to Coldplay: book your table at the Brit Awards *now*.'

Rolling Stone called *A Rush . . .* 'a nervier, edgier, thoroughly surprising album . . . the band has figured out how to let loose and rock out . . . first-rate guitar rock with some real emotional protein on its bones.' *Q* raved, 'this is pretty much the apotheosis of post-Radiohead guitar-rock, a collection of vastly moving songs that will render stadiums as intimate as bedrooms.' *Uncut* opted for 'the best British rock album since *OK Computer* . . . accomplished, original and majestic.' *Mojo* called attention to the 'fragile love songs with a hint of the metaphysic,' adding, 'Coldplay still sound like they care about what they're doing.' They had certainly cared enough to ditch an entire album's worth of earlier recordings.

Hear/Say revisited the Radiohead comparisons: 'This is not exactly *Kid A* experimentation and, in Coldplay's case, that's a good thing. While Radiohead has, for the moment, cornered itself with a desire to venture further and further from traditional tuneliness [sic], Coldplay remains, at its core, a disciple of melody . . . Coldplay has a knack for writing songs that seem instantly familiar but somehow, fresh. Like some of the best bands in rock, its influences are obvious but the result is something fresh and exciting.' Conversely, *CMJ.com* argued, 'it's an album good enough to wipe away most urges for comparison.'

Maxim Blender were among those who appreciated the bigger, bolder themes flooding into Coldplay's music: 'a considerably wiser and more sophisticated record than its predecessor . . . Songs like the taut opener, "Politik", written in the week after September 11 . . . suggest that Coldplay have larger issues to tackle this time out.'

> **'I'm in a rock 'n' roll band and people think it's weird because I don't do anything remotely rock 'n' roll besides playing it . . . but for me, rock 'n' roll is all about doing whatever you want. It's about defying convention and being who you are. And that's me.'** *– Chris Martin*

Coldplay had indeed created a global vision of the current political darkness and sounded an outcry against it. *Pulse* described 'Politik' as 'a song that states its intentions clearly . . . Unlike the cosy, "We live in a beautiful world" lyrical sentiments of *Parachutes'* opener "Don't Panic", "Politik" is dark and ominous, suited for a world that, at the moment, doesn't look so beautiful.'

Overall, the critics agreed that the album's central theme of urgency was articulately expressed. *The Guardian*'s Ted Kessler talked about the 'hunger for the immediate on songs like the opening "Politik" where, over a blast of discordant keyboards and guitars that power forward like a warming jet, Chris demands that he be given "life over death" or on "Clocks", where he details missed opportunities flashing by through a piano's frenetic whirl.' In the innovative 'Clocks', the critic noted a second distinct stage in Coldplay's musical maturity. 'Like most songs on *A Rush*, "Clocks" is about love gone awry. But the self-pitying is far from cliché, and right before the chorus, vocalist Chris Martin sings the tune's most pointed line, "Come out upon my seas, curse missed opportunities/Am I part of the cure, or am I part of the disease?"'

Of this last lyric, Chris told *MTV News*, 'I reckon everybody questions whether they're useful to the world or not. Some people think they're doing marvellous things. Hitler thought he was doing great things for the world, and yet we'd all say, "No, no, no, he was doing terrible things."'

'We're not making it to be listened to in stadiums. We're making it so you can listen to it and feel like it's yours,' Chris stressed. 'I want some kid in Nebraska who liked our first record and took a lot of shit for it in the playground to walk around with this one and say, "See I told you!"' 'There was an aspect of "We'll show you," definitely,' Will agreed. 'More to the people who liked us than the people who were giving us [grief] – "We'll make you proud of us."'

WORLD DOMINATION

In the summer of 2002, for the first time in 40 years, there wasn't one British act in the US Top 100 singles chart. The British government were concerned that 'Cool Britannia' was proving as fleeting as New Labour's interest in socialism, and rapidly called together music business executives and ministers for an emergency brainstorming session. It was an unprecedented attempt to reverse a drastic downward trend in British music sales in America, which had been labelled 'Britflop'. A report commissioned by the Department for Culture, Media and Sport revealed that the British market share of US record sales had plunged from 32 per cent in 1986 to 0.2 per cent in 2002. With a kind of desperate whimsy, the report recommended opening a 'British music embassy' in New York to help new acts break through.

This was the wildly uncertain financial climate into which Coldplay released the second album they hoped would reach the epic rock heights of Radiohead's *The Bends* and U2's *The Unforgettable Fire*. Indeed, *The Observer*'s Ted Kessler noted that 'Parlophone . . . is pretty certain that by the end of this campaign Coldplay will be as big as these two acts: they've nominated them as their worldwide priority this year. Coldplay's much-coveted slot on the stadium circuit looks assured.'

A Rush of Blood to the Head hadn't yet been released when Kessler made his prediction. Parlophone was clearly certain that the album would be a success and, in the US, Nettwerk Records had set up a vast strategic campaign to promote the disc. The campaign with its expensive in-store promotion, was described by *NME* as 'the kind of marketing investment that sees teaser advertising in Sunday newspapers. And Coldplay billboards are racked up next to BBMak and Ozzfest banners across America's Tower Records stores.'

If the band had found the worldwide campaign to break *Parachutes* exhausting, this new push would stretch their endurance to an untested degree. 'It just seems like a monumental mountain to try and climb,' Will told *NME* journalist Johnny Davis. 'You know, U2 do it. But U2 have their own jet. And I don't imagine Bono has to do too many phone interviews with Brazilian journalists and stuff.' 'I feel surprised and very, very lucky,' added Guy. 'What we're doing is crazily ambitious.'

'I do worry that we come across as being boring,' fretted Guy. 'Because we're absolutely not boring people.' Chris observed that the 'boring' tag was ascribed to the band partly on account of their unwillingness to start media-friendly feuds: 'We've got a policy of not slagging off other

A Rush of Blood to the Head *won Best Album at the NME Awards, February 2003. Guy celebrated by wearing this extraordinary scarf.*

125

bands. And that's where all the fun is.' As Chris later told *Spin* magazine's Tracy Pepper, 'If some-one says you're boring because you don't do lots of coke or shag groupies – first of all, doing loads of coke makes you write shit music, and having sex with groupies is probably a) unfulfilling and b) I'm not sure how cool it is . . . I am boring,' he continued, 'But I also wrote "Clocks." So I'm not that unhappy. I'd rather have written "Clocks" and be boring than not have written "Clocks" and be in rehab. If I'd have written "Clocks" and been in rehab, everybody would be happy.' Chris's unruffled response to the 'boredom' issue was an aspect of the band's new confidence that had intensified during their fiery recent performances. 'Chris has become a truly engaging front-man. They're vastly improved live,' Pepper enthused. 'The music industry here is excited because they are one of the only non-rap/metal "rock" bands to have a bona fide hit.'

> **'We weren't as close when we started as we are now. It takes a long time to get to know Guy and Will. That's why often people think [Coldplay] is just me.'** – *Chris Martin*

An extended series of arena tours in Britain and the US were the natural next step for a band that was not yet on a par with Oasis in terms of playing the UK's biggest venues. In *The Observer Magazine*, Ted Kessler insisted that Oasis still set the standards for British bands: 'Their records stick to the Top Ten longer than any of those of other Brit groups, they sell out bigger gigs than the likes of Coldplay and do so very quickly and to a far younger audience – despite themselves being older.' When asked by *Q*'s Toby Manning how it felt to be turning into a stadium band, Chris's reply evinced a mixture of diffidence and expectation. 'I don't think we'll ever be as applicable to stadiums as Bon Jovi and U2. But there's nothing wrong with trying to reach as many people as possible. I get more and more excited the more people there are.' 'You're play-ing electric guitar now, too. Are Coldplay going rock?' Manning asked. 'We're working on a very Status Quo-esque number,' smiled Chris. 'We've got to move on. Life is about being as un-Coldplay as possible.'

Before flying out to the US, the band had one tiny, secret, spur-of-the-moment gig at the Shepherd's Pub in Highgate, north London. Proceeds from the show went to the Whittington Hospital, birthplace of a guitarist who had changed all of his band mates' lives – Jonny Buckland.

Coldplay's North American arena tour began on 4 September in Seattle. Following a show at the Hollywood Hills' Greek Theatre, the band hit Vegas for a smaller gig at The Joint, which is inside the Hard Rock Hotel. Despite Will and Guy's profitable visit to the blackjack table, the band found the whole tacky, celebrity-shrine environment slightly disconcerting. 'I'd dread to be relegated to the American casino circuit,' mused Chris. 'I won't mind the British seaside circuit. Butlin's is much cooler than Vegas. Vegas is all so fake. I think it affected us. I don't think we played very well tonight.'

The Joint concert gave Manning the chance to see Coldplay's expanded show in its develop-mental stage, with plenty of difficulties still to be ironed out. These simple but powerful innova-tions consisted of a dramatic, elaborately cued light show with lasers, and huge video screens that projected close-ups of the quartet. The screens, which were later to become such an effective com-ponent of the new set, remained stubbornly fixed upon Chris: 'Martin is caught in almost per-manent close-up . . . as far as the screens are concerned, the others barely exist.'

After the gig, Manning directly asked the others how they felt about the general focus on Chris, and Guy replied, 'It's frustrating. We'll all do interviews and then the only person who's quoted will be Chris.' But Manning felt that on stage at least, 'the other three' did little to wrest the limelight from their front man: 'Drummer Will Champion does add some spot-on backing vocals to a stunning "The Scientist", but black-clad bassist Guy Berryman simply melts into his Marshall stack. When Martin brings over Jonny Buckland for "that special moment between singer and guitarist" on "Green Eyes", Buckland manages the rare feat of disappearing under a spotlight . . . If the others can step up behind Martin, perhaps that Make Trade Fair t-shirt will end up behind glass in the Hard Rock Hotel yet.'

Despite the teething problems, the band could take heart from *Guardian* journalist Alexis Petridis's assessment of the new album's music as extremely arena-friendly. Even the experimental 'Clocks', he asserted, 'didn't lose sight of the back of the stadium . . . The lyrics, too, are usefully designed to be sung en masse by arena audiences. "Give me heart and give me soul." "Nobody said it was easy, nobody said it would be this hard." These are so oblique that they are universally applicable: anybody could find meaning in them.'

Coldplay's live whirlwind breezed through San Diego and LA and straight into the grip of Typhoon Hanna, which was menacing Atlanta. The typhoon had passed over their venue, the Masquerade Music Park, drenching it and threatening to short out the monumental sound equipment if it were switched on. The howling winds were oblivious to the carefully orchestrated tour schedule and the special affection that Coldplay held for the city. The Atlanta show was blown away.

Fans were told that the concert was off only minutes before doors were due to open – but the venue's management told them that 'the band wanted to do something special' to leave those that had braved the typhoon with some positive memory of the day. Davey Morgan, a devoted fan, raced round to the front of the venue and found, to his amazement, that Chris and Jonny were actually standing out there in the car park, playing an acoustic version of 'Yellow'. A crowd of about 50 people were happily 'singing along in harmony'. Chris, strumming and thoroughly enjoying himself, signalled to Will to come over and join in – but security actually held Will back at first, not recognising him. Chris asked for requests, but the absence of a piano limited the choice. Playing two expensive and unfamiliar guitars, he, Jonny and Will performed 'Green Eyes', 'In My Place' and 'Don't Panic'. Then Chris introduced 'The Scientist' as the band's current favourite of all their new songs, making the crowd hush to hear it properly. Although it may seem that the band were doing disappointed fans a favour, from Chris's view, these kind of impromptu sessions were giving him the life he had always dreamed of.

'I dream all the time,' Chris told *Esquire*, 'Every night lasts a long time for me. I think I've got a weak bladder. Don't print that. Well do, I don't care,' he laughed. 'I get up every two hours.' During the US tour he told *The Telegraph*, 'I know I'm supposed to be a cool rock star, but I am fucking blessed. I woke up the other night and I remembered being a little nine-year-old kid, dreaming of things. Then I thought, this is what we do now! And I just couldn't believe it!'

As might be expected from a musician that was living out his dreams, Chris was becoming more comfortable with each concert. 'On stage he's good at coming across as very confident, which he didn't used to be,' Will told *The Telegraph*. Equally positive, Chris remarked upon the growing unity within the quartet. 'We weren't as close when we started as we are now. It takes a long time to get to know Guy and Will. That's why often people think [Coldplay] is just me. If you sit with us for half an hour, I'm the only one you'll get an impression of because I'm a loudmouth idiot. They're my best friends really.' Who would he trust to tell him if he was acting a bit off? 'You can't fool the rest of your band,' Chris said at once. 'I can walk into a room now and be Chris from Coldplay . . . But Will's seen me running round in my pants backstage, doing an impression of Frank Spencer.'

On 19 September, Coldplay played their largest headline gig so far, at the Jones Beach

Amphitheatre on Long Island. Galvanised by a typically irrational fear of playing before a mostly empty 12,000-capacity arena, Chris spent the day promoting the show on local radio. He needn't have worried, on the night there were few spaces, and the band put in a show that was described by *Pressplay* magazine's Derek White as, 'creating a sensory texture that jabbed straight into the spinal cord.'

After a flying visit for a pair of shows in Toronto, Coldplay wrapped up the tour with a concert at the UIC Pavilion in Chicago on 24 September. The band had less than a week to complete work on a video for ' The Scientist' before heading out on a tour of Britain and Ireland's largest venues.

The promo video for 'The Scientist' was to be directed by Jamie Thraves, who had previously worked for Radiohead, Blur, the Verve and Travis. 'I wanted to do a story that's tragic but starts off happy,' explained Thraves to *mtv.com*'s Corey Moss. 'And the video is about rewinding to that happy ending.' Like most rock videos, there was something derivative about it: Spike Jonze had used the reverse narrative idea in Pharcyde's video for 'Drop', as long ago as 1996. But Thraves wanted a particular twist to it: the viewer would suddenly understand the story at the video's very end – even though it had been shown in rewind mode.

Thraves and the band came up with the storyline together: Chris would be seen walking backward into the scene of a horrifying car crash that – the viewer would suddenly see – had killed his on-screen girlfriend. Moving back through the crash itself, he would be seen happily in the car with her. Then, as the story rewound to its germinating moment, it would become tragically clear that she died because she loosened her seat belt for a second. Throughout all this, though the song would be heard in its natural forward mode on the soundtrack, during the filming Chris would have to sing the song backwards.

'The original idea was a straight narrative without the lead singer in the video,' said Thraves. 'But Chris wanted to be in the video and he was really excited to learn how to sing the song backward. He got a tape of the song recorded backward and he listened to it over and over. He's a very passionate guy, so he got really into it,' said Thraves. 'It makes you sound like you're from Pluto or something,' Chris told *mtv.com*. 'This was by no means a straightforward backward task,' Thraves pointed out. 'What [Chris] learned later on is about the problems with phonetics, because you have to be very careful with the lip movement so that when you end on a sound your mouth is formed in the right way.' So for each word he learnt, Chris also had to learn the position that his lips had to finish up in at the end of its pronunciation.

On the very October day that filming wrapped on 'The Scientist' video, Coldplay's only UK tour of 2002 began in Glasgow. The eleven sold-out shows were to culminate with two nights at London's Wembley Arena. Backing Coldplay on some of these dates was Ian McCulloch – or, as Mac told *Crud* magazine, he was magnanimously taking Coldplay on 'his' tour.

Despite the support of a rock personality of McCulloch's magnitude, bigger stages hardly served to make the band immune from the kind of sniping they had become accustomed to. In his review of a show at the Birmingham National Indoor Arena, *Dot Music.com*'s John Mulvey identified Coldplay's appeal as 'the elusive talent to turn gigs into group hugs'. Interpreting Chris's early tour enthusiasm as a cynical ploy, Mulvey accused him of 'working very hard at pretending he's some kind of ingénue who just woke up in a stadium rock band.' His spontaneity 'seems a bit forced', as did 'the snatches of cover versions he interpolates into his own songs once or twice too often.' But Mulvey concluded positively, 'It's nice – and nice is precisely the right world – that Oasis' successors in British rock are their opposites. A band who present themselves as humane rather than arrogant, who embrace rather than boorishly confront.'

While sections of the media chose to pigeonhole the band as 'nice' and, as an occasional afterthought, 'brilliant', such shorthand dismissal was by no means universal. Writing in the

NME, Steve Sutherland declared that Chris's love of today's pop music 'radiates through the band's set . . . All the little references to other songs, snatches of stolen melodies and scraps of cover versions are delivered free from irony, a feelgood reminder . . . there is a reason to celebrate the NOW!'

On the morning of 21 October, Chris awoke early. He demolished a hill of cereal to steady his nerves, in preparation for a big day. Not only were Coldplay scheduled to play the second of their two Wembley gigs that night, but in the afternoon he and Jonny were to attend the *Q* Awards, where the band were nominated for Best Act in the World Today – the other nominees being Radiohead, Oasis, Stereophonics, and U2. Coldplay were also up for Best Album, along with the Doves for *The Last Broadcast*, Beth Orton for *Daybreaker*, the Red Hot Chili Peppers for *By The Way*, and the Vines for *Highly Evolved*. The majority of the awards had been voted for by the listening public. The Coldplay team also had several other nominations: the team of Ken Nelson and Mark Phythian were in the running for the Best Producer award, but lost out to Moby. Also, Ian McCulloch's Echo and the Bunnymen were to be given a special *Q* Inspiration Award, 'for inspiring Coldplay to write the very Echo-like "A Rush Of Blood To The Head".'

> **'I can walk into a room now and be Chris from Coldplay . . . But Will's seen me running around in my pants backstage, doing an impression of Frank Spencer.'** *– Chris Martin*

To McCulloch, the award was a strange compliment, 'for a band that's generally only ever got three stars in *Q*.' The British music press still virtually ignored the Bunnymen, he told *CDWow.com*. 'I think we have re-established ourselves, more so with the Coldplay connection and Chris Martin talking about us in every interview. Luckily for us Chris Martin did. It meant we bypassed every journalist to become the firmly established band. Having Chris sing your praises is not a bad thing.'

Elsewhere at the ceremony, Radiohead were voted Best Act in the World Today – leaving Coldplay to aspire to that accolade in years to come. Then, beating off that year's extremely stiff competition, *A Rush . . .* picked up the Best Album Award. Chris opened his speech with, 'I've got a notorious reputation for being a dickhead at these things. So I won't slag off Craig David, he's wicked.'

When asked at the reception who was present that he rated, Chris cited Electric Soft Parade and Miss Dynamite. Happily, just over a week later, Jonny and Chris performed duets with her. This was at the all-acoustic Fairplay Concert at The Astoria, London. The event had been organised by Glastonbury's Emily Eavis to raise awareness of Oxfam's Fair Trade campaign and the ill treatment of the world's poorest coffee farmers. She explained, 'Coming from a farming family myself I was particularly struck by the injustice of this. As consumers we can change the system.' Emily's hope was to raise £40,000 for coffee farmers in Haiti. Chris offered his full support, wise-cracking to a journalist the event would be 'bigger than Live Aid. It should be bigger than Live Aid anyway . . .' Also due to appear were Idlewild, South, Lamb and Noel Gallagher.

The Fairplay gig's stripped-down, acoustic ambience created a sense of intimacy between the singers and the sung-to. 'Shorn from the bluster and pomp, stripped of bullshit and artifice, we get a string of bands cranking out their gems as if they were in their living room,' wrote *Drowned in Sound* critic Mark Reed. Chris and Jonny – or 'our stadium indie REM-in-waiting' as Reed called them – played 'In My Place,' 'The Scientist' and a cover of Jimmy Cliff's 'Many Rivers To Cross'. Chris joked, 'We've got fifteen hours till dawn and we've only got two hits.' At those words, on stormed Ms Dynamite to join them for a cover of the Bob Marley classic, 'Three Little Birds'. She continued with 'It Takes More' and 'Dy-Na-Mi-Tee,' with Chris and Jonny providing accompaniment. Their version of her theme song, 'stripped of its traditional backing and rendered on nothing more than two acoustic guitars, was irresistible,' commented Reed.

When Noel Gallagher teamed up with Coldplay, there was 'joy everywhere for everyone,' Reed observed. 'There was the marvellous "Yellow", a woefully under-rehearsed but sweet cover of the Smiths' "Stop Me If You've Heard This One Before", and finally a celebratory "Live Forever".' At the end of a spectacular sold-out evening, Reed pointed out, the challenge was not to feel a warm glow.

> **'We'd all like to meet the right person one day, but in one sense of my life, I've already met the right people.'** *– Chris Martin*

Coldplay's first ever Wembley Arena gigs were a glorious success. 'Wembley Arena is an easy place to be dwarfed in, but it took just four men to fill it comfortably,' declared Michael Osborn on the *Musiccomh* site. The band's evident confidence may have been encouraged by a special pre-show drinks party that was attended by family and friends, including Hollywood actress Gwyneth Paltrow. Indeed, the party continued after the gig at the Cobden Club, turning into a post ceremony celebration, and attended by such diverse Coldplay supporters as Alan Rickman and James Nesbitt from the TV series *Cold Feet.*

From the moment the Wembley concert started, and a blackout turned suddenly into blinding strobe lighting as Coldplay thrashed straight into 'Politik', the mood was 'magically epic', according to the *Virtual Festivals* correspondent Andrew Future. 'The combination of Chris Martin's Vaseline falsetto, the tingling perfection of the perfect chord changes, and the orchestral unison . . . leave an indelible spine chill of immeasurable pleasure.' The teething problems that had hampered their set in Las Vegas had been banished. Now, there was a newfound intensity in the performance of early songs like 'Spies' which, along with 'Shiver', 'Daylight' and 'Trouble', were now so powerful that *411mania.com*'s Phil McCann found them 'absolutely incredible to hear live'.

Two days later, speaking to London's *XFM* radio station, the usually caustic Ian McCulloch confessed that, with the exception of a Neil Diamond gig a few years ago, the Coldplay show marked the first time he had been nearly brought to tears by a concert for as long as he could remember.

The band's debut at Wembley featured a personal first for Chris. He habitually makes many song dedications from the stage – some of them in-jokes, some of them mischievous. This time, he chose to dedicate a song to Gwyneth Paltrow, who was in London filming *Sylvia,* a film recounting the dark relationship between poets Sylvia Plath and Ted Hughes.

Two months earlier, Chris had confessed to *Rolling Stone* contributing editor Touré, 'We'd all like to meet the right person one day, but in one sense of my life, I've already met the right people.' But, at the Wembley concert, he had noticed another 'right person' – Gwyneth Paltrow.

The song he chose to dedicate to her was the penultimate in their set, 'In My Place'. To any women sitting in the Wembley audience, wondering if they found Chris Martin attractive, his many songs about longing and lost love would not necessarily present a hopeful scenario for an angst-free romance. On the other hand, *The Telegraph*'s Joe Muggs implied that Coldplay had taught kiddiepunk boy-band Busted the 'vital lesson from indie bands: presenting girls as unattainable and mysterious might make you look wet, but it doesn't half flatter the girls themselves.'

Apparently, Gwyneth was not put off by the seemingly hopeless yearning in Chris's lyrics – six days later she accompanied him to the band's second gig at the Point Theatre in Dublin. 'Gwyneth makes judgments about someone very quickly, very instinctively and decides whether she likes or dislikes them,' revealed *Sylvia* producer Alison Owen. 'She's very instinctive about who she places her trust in, and once she makes up her mind, it's difficult for her to change it.' Owen, a close friend of Paltrow's from before her success, has remained close because Gwyneth 'is the same girl she was when I first met her.'

Those who view Coldplay as miserablists – since Chris is very capable of writing the saddest songs – will regard him as perfectly matched with an actress who sobbed with genuine anguish when she received a Best Actress Oscar for *Shakespeare In Love*. Gwyneth was known in the industry for her lively, good-natured humour. During the filming of *A View from the Top*, she ruined 50 takes by cracking up at co-star Mike Myers' impersonations.

Gwyneth's Oscar win coincided with a time of great personal trauma. Her grandfather, Buster Paltrow, was seriously ill and not expected to survive. To make matters worse, her father, Bruce, had recently been diagnosed with throat cancer.

The beautiful Gwyneth had also endured a string of failed romances. She was briefly engaged to actor Donovan Leitch in the early nineties. After this relationship ended, she then fell deeply in love with film star Brad Pitt after they starred together in the 1995 thriller *Se7en*. The romance raised her media profile, with the disadvantage that she was perceived as a star's girlfriend, not as a talent in her own right. The romance ended after a six-month engagement in 1997.

Gwyneth felt she had messed up this perfect love affair – she later told *Primetime* interviewer Diane Sawyer that she had been 'the architect of her own misery'. In 2004, Gwyneth told *Ms London* magazine that the reason for the break-up was that the couple felt they could not pursue their busy careers and at the same time maintain a happy marriage. Gwyneth also admitted she didn't get over Pitt for at least five years.

In 1997 she began a relationship with another handsome film star, Ben Affleck, one of her co-stars in *Shakespeare in Love*, but this finished after a year. After another briefer romance with Luke Wilson, who acted with her in *The Royal Tennenbaums*, for a short time she dated ketchup heir Chris Heinz, stepson of Senator John Kerry. It seemed that, among her ever-multiplying, ever-presentable acquaintances, there was nobody that was exactly right.

Gwyneth had also endured a surfeit of media attention, shooting movies non-stop and having her complicated love life charted in the media like a share price. 'I sensed that people have no real understanding of who I am,' she complained in a piece in *Scotland on Sunday*. 'If you sit up straight, chew with your mouth closed and have good manners, you're a snob.' Immediately after the Oscars, Gwyneth set about changing her life completely. In an attempt to attain some inner calm, she'd taken up yoga and arranged some time off. Afterwards, she struggled to achieve some sense of peace and emotional security while trapped in an endless cycle of film sets, photo shoots, trailers and interviews. Life went on, with infinite repetition and no special romantic encounter.

Two weeks before Coldplay's Wembley concert, tragedy hit. Bruce Paltrow, Gwyneth's father, had taken her to Venice specifically to celebrate her birthday. Such holidays were a tradition within the family. Bruce had taken Gwyneth to Paris as a girl because he wanted her to see the city for the first time accompanied by a man who would love her forever. This time, the venue was to be Venice. But, tragically, death was to intervene. 'I had the most incredible birthday weekend until my dad died,' she said. Bruce Paltrow died from a sudden attack of pneumonia, caused by a recurrence of throat cancer. 'He was the one person in your life that you always think: "I'm safe because they're there, and they're so smart, and they know everything, and I can always go to them." And then they evaporate,' she said.

Only a fortnight after her father's death, Gwyneth had to travel to London to begin shooting *Sylvia*. 'I don't know how I got through it,' she told Donna Freydkin of the *Journal News*. 'It's been, in many ways, the worst year of my life and will continue to be.' In this mood, she took herself out to Coldplay's Wembley concert.

Ever since Gwyneth had attended Coldplay's Bowery Ballroom gig in New York the previous summer, tabloids had speculated about a romance between her and Chris. In an interview with *The Sun*'s Dominic Mohan on Virgin Radio a few nights after the Wembley gig, Chris denied everything: 'It's all bollocks,' he said. 'She just likes the band. I like *Shakespeare In Love* but it doesn't mean I'm dating her.'

However, just two weeks later, press suspicions were confirmed when *The Sun* ran pictures of the pair out together. Chris subsequently had little option but to confirm he had been on a date with Gwyneth. 'I'm proud to be with someone who's very nice and very beautiful but she's not my girlfriend at the moment', he explained. 'I feel out of my depth with all this. I met her for the first time at our gig at Wembley two weeks ago. It's early days. I got her number, rang her and asked if she wanted to meet. We went out at the weekend and we seem to get on. This is still very weird because she's a big Hollywood star and I'm just the bloke from Coldplay.'

Chris was subject to recurrent inner conflicts whenever he was confronted by the prospect of romance. He felt hopeless with women, compounded by the self-knowledge that he would always put his band first. 'If I was good with women I'd go and enjoy it. But also I'm obsessed with the band, so I refuse to commit to a relationship . . . I'm an ambitious little tosser,' he told *Q*'s Michael Odell. 'One thing about girls is that I get scared. I get scared of my feelings being in the hands of another person. I know that feeling of waiting for a girl to call. That's scary.'

Although Chris found dating a world-famous actress 'weird', the couple quickly discovered that they were well matched. What Chris and Gwyneth had in common, besides vitality and talent, was a lively and stoical sense of humour that carried them along – and that helped them through their unsuccessful quests for love. They had also both been bullied at private school during their teens. At New York's fashionable and expensive Spence School for Girls, Gwyneth was alternately shunned and picked on. 'I had braces, I was skinny and I had a bad haircut,' she recalled. 'At fourteen, things changed. I got better.'

Now she was the sophisticated A-lister but, nonetheless, still needed to meet someone as above and outside the norm as herself – someone like Chris, who'd grown up outside of her social sphere.

Unluckily for Chris and Gwyneth, new developments in the world of magazine publishing, were to greatly affect their courtship. Canadian-born editor Bonnie Fuller had transformed *US* magazine, blazing a trail that other celebrity gossip-sheets would be quick to follow. Previously, such publications had mainly run 'shock' photos of celebrity drunkenness, fighting or snogging, but now Fuller introduced a campaign of saturation photography of the stars, slavishly capturing every dull moment of their lives – sipping coffee in sidewalk cafés, or getting into taxis. North American newsstand sales increased significantly and copycat weeklies such as *In Touch* took off. 'They want volume, and they don't mind banality,' observed Toronto's *Globe and Mail*.

Gwyneth had been immediately affected by this editorial shift. 'It used to be that your fame was proportional to your work life. If you were in a movie that everybody saw, or if you went to a lot of parties and premieres, you were famous for a while. But then the movie went away and people backed off.' Now that this was no longer the case, Gwyneth was finding such intrusive journalism immensely distasteful – when asked about Bonnie Fuller, she was angry enough to tell the *Globe and Mail,* 'She is the devil.'

'What people don't know is the ugly aggressiveness that goes into getting a picture for a weekly celebrity magazine,' Gwyneth told *Teen Hollywood* magazine. 'The paparazzi stop at nothing. You appeal to their sense of humanity, but they don't care. They'll shout stuff at you, try to run you off the road, anything to get a picture.'

However, with Coldplay embarking on a major European tour that would occupy most of November, any lurking pressmen hoping to catch a glimpse of the couple together would have to wait. The itinerary kicked off with dates in Brussels, Rotterdam, Paris and Cologne. These were followed by shows in Munich and Montpelier, between which, on 11 November, 'The Scientist' was released as a single in Britain.

Next came gigs in Madrid and then Barcelona, where Coldplay picked up the prize for Best UK & Ireland Act at the MTV Europe Music Awards. At the event, R&B star P Diddy was full of praise for Coldplay: 'The whole melancholy, emotional vibe of *Parachutes . . .* It's unmanlike, it's so strong.' Another surprising reaction came when super-producer Timbaland admitted to *mtv.com* that he was hugely impressed with the band: 'Hip-hop is the same ol', same ol' . . . The only [act] I'd like to do a song with is Coldplay. That's the only one I really want to work with now.'

> **'If I was good with women I'd go and enjoy it. But also I'm obsessed with the band, so I refuse to commit to a relationship . . . I'm an ambitious little tosser.'** – *Chris Martin*

Teen-pop icon Justin Timberlake was also outspoken in his desire to work with the group. Although Chris was politely non-committal about the possibility of any collaboration, his response was positive. 'Funnily enough, I don't have a problem with Justin Timberlake. I think he's pretty good. I think he's very good at what he does; I think he's really a talented guy. I just don't want to admit it because I'm not a thirteen-year-old girl.'

Such populist tastes were indicative of Chris's quest 'to get passionate music into mainstream'. He explained this ideal to Steve Ciabattini of *CMJ New Music Monthly.* 'That's why I'm so pleased to see Springsteen and even Dave Matthews out there . . . And Eminem. I mean Eminem is as good as Springsteen. They're all doing passionate stuff and that's great, I just want to be part of that.'

After the MTV bash, Coldplay jetted off to fulfill the remainder of their European engagements, playing dates in Milan, Berlin, Copenhagen, Stockholm and Oslo. 'We're touring until alien invasions occur and prevent the world from existing any longer,' Chris joked to *mtv.com* – indicating the band's sense of resignation toward the endless thrust of touring that would continue right through into 2003.

Such extended absences from their loved ones explained Coldplay's habit of requesting stamped postcards as part of their on-the-road rider. 'Yes, we get homesick,' Will told *Australian Musician.* ' I phone home every day, we e-mail, when possible we fly our family over so we can spend time with them.' Will also mentioned that he'd found a novel way of occupying himself on tour. 'I've started to compile my own travel guide for each city. So when I come back, I know the best restaurants, the best bars and the best record stores.'

Many relationships stand or fall by practical details – with regard to Chris's touring commit-

The MTV Europe Music Awards in Barcelona, November 2002. Despite four nominations, Coldplay's only victory was Best UK and Ireland Act.

ments, Gwyneth had an immediate practical advantage over Lily Sobhani. The flexible working rhythm of her film career gave her a relatively adaptable schedule, with the ability (and financial freedom) to travel at will to see Chris, wherever either of them might be at the time. The power of distance to break up the love affair was diminished. It was helpful to Gwyneth's understanding of Chris that she had some empathy with his mode of performing. She had performed vocals on her friend Sheryl Crow's record, 'C'mon, C'mon', and even had a Number One single with Huey Lewis, with whom she'd recorded a cover of Smokey Robinson's 'Cruisin', for the film *Duets*. In January 2001 it hit the top of the Australian charts. Critics were very surprised by Gwyneth's voice, which was praised as 'smooth, wonderful' and 'fantastic'.

Of course, all the advantages in love were quickly countered by the increasingly ferocious pursuit of the tabloid paparazzi. Here, one crucial difference between Gwyneth and Chris became clear. While Chris had experienced a typically low-key upbringing, Gwyneth grew up at the very core of American show business. Her mother, Blythe Danner, had also been an actress, appearing in films such as *Meet the Parents*, *Prince of Tides* and *The Great Santini*. Similarly, Bruce Paltrow had produced such TV hits as *St Elsewhere*. When first married, Blythe and Bruce had lived on a Californian beach with a group of aspiring-but-impoverished peers – one of whom was Steven Spielberg.

The relationships established back then endured, and much later on, when many of the group had become famous and influential, another old friend, Michael Douglas, used his influence at his old *alma mater* to help Gwyneth to be accepted as an art history major at the University of

California. Since then, Gwyneth had adapted to the public world of influential media players, with poise, grace and groomed beauty.

As she made her way through the rarefied celebrity stratosphere, Gwyneth had a sense of stability provided by parents who put family first. Blythe Danner turned down many roles that would have made her a superstar in order to give her kids full attention. This was something else that she and Chris had in common – the support of a stable family environment that provided a powerful template for both their future lives. As Chris had revealed to *The Observer*'s Ted Kessler, if he saw a girl he fancied, the fantasy could quickly turn to one of marriage. Gwyneth, too had initially viewed marriage as an ultimate ideal.

But now Chris was in a similar position to that which the young Gwyneth had been in with Brad Pitt – abruptly thrust into the global limelight by dating another star. The press interest was extreme and unexpected, even to a rock star who was used to a degree of intrusion.

Toward the end of Coldplay's European tour, the *NME*'s Johnny Davis caught up with the band in Stockholm, and wrote a fun interview for the paper's Christmas issue. Summarising Chris's amazing year, Davis enquired, 'So Chris: start of this year – can't get a girlfriend. End of the year – you and Gwyneth Paltrow in *The Sun*.' 'I got into a fight with a cabbie over that,' replied Chris. 'I got out of a taxi with my friend at my house and the taxi driver pulled out a fucking camera. And I'd tipped him! I'd given him fifteen quid. I bet he made a fortune selling that.' Half an hour later, Chris came out with Gwyneth to find another observer parked outside. 'I said "What are you doing?" and he said, "Oh, my mate phoned up and told me." The taxi driver had gone and tipped him off.' Chris found the entire incident incomprehensible. 'Why am I in a tabloid?' he asked. 'We haven't done anything to court that.'

What Coldplay *had* been courting, with all their attendant promotional efforts, was a second successful album and coast-to-coast success in America. The effects of their campaign in reviving the UK's music industry began to be seen by late autumn. According to BPI figures, total UK music sales had grown by 3.5 per cent of that year, while album sales climbed by nine per cent in volume terms and five per cent in value. The three positive sales dynamics behind this were, researchers claimed, sales of Oasis and Coldplay records plus the 'perennially reliable' *Now . . .* compilation series. 'The figures are likely to be good news for EMI, which has seen a sharp fall in its share price this year,' John Casey reported in *The Guardian*.

As Christmas approached, Chris got to be a music fan himself all over again. Asked about a story that he had given Gwyneth a signed David Gray album, he clarified, 'That's a melange of about fifteen stories. I bought a David Gray CD and bought my friend Gwyneth a Sigur Ros CD . . . I didn't give a signed David Gray CD to my "wife" Gwyneth Paltrow', declaimed Chris, comically. As a promotional gimmick, Gray's album *A New Day At Midnight* was released at midnight. 'There was a queue outside HMV at about five to twelve and I went to have a pint of Guinness, and by the time we came back the shop had shut and I thought "fuck" . . . so I went up to the window and this guy recognised me and let me in. It was like being Michael Jackson or something.'

Sloping around Oxford Street at midnight like a student: this was the kind of novel experience that Chris had to offer Gwyneth. As *People* magazine reported, 'He has been a great strength and support system. There is a really nice ease between them.' He also encouraged her to partake of a less rarefied lifestyle, that included pub lunches with friends. Gwyneth had her first Devon Christmas that year and went along with Chris's family to see his eleven-year-old sister in a pantomime, where the pair signed autographs for local fans.

In keeping with the spirit of the season, Coldplay contributed to the *Maybe This Christmas* album that Nettwerk Records released in America, with some proceeds going to the Toys For Tots charity. The twelve-track disc provided a pleasant opportunity for the likes of Phantom Planet,

Vanessa Carlton, Bright Eyes, Jimmy Eat World, Semisonic singer Dan Wilson and Coldplay to power their way through time-honoured holiday songs, or to showcase new material. Coldplay contributed their interpretation of Chris singing 'Have Yourself a Merry Little Christmas' – a track that they had first recorded as a gift to their fan club members. The song highlighted the marked improvement in Chris's voice, following his work with Mary Hammond.

Maintaining a seasonal tradition begun the previous year, Coldplay also performed at the KROQ FM Almost Acoustic Christmas show. This time around, it had expanded to a two-day festival featuring some twenty acts. The near-acoustic slant of the sold-out show affirmed the ascendant popularity of more subtle forms of rock music. Along with variations of 'Yellow', and 'Trouble', Chris sang 'Have Yourselves a Merry Little Christmas' at the piano. 'If [Chris Martin] needed any assurance, he got it when Coldplay stole the show,' affirmed Corey Moss's report for *VH1.com*. He also took part in a funny, all-star performance of Band Aid's 'Do They Know It's Christmas?' Others in the chorus included Dashboard Confessional's Chris Carrabba, and the apparently tone-deaf actress Juliette Lewis.

When asked to join in, Chris found that he just couldn't say no to Beck and the Flaming Lips, who had organised the half-satirical number. Singing with other bands was an experience that Chris generally viewed with ambivalence. 'Doing collaborations is kind of like how I imagine it is when you sleep with someone else's wife. I mean they're fun, but I'll always regret them in the morning, not that I've slept with someone else's wife,' he rattled on to *mtv.com*. 'If you do a collaboration and you're really good, you think, "Well, I wish I'd done that with our band." And then if you do a collaboration and you're really bad, you think, "Oh, I shouldn't have ever done that."' But the audience loved the yuletide collaborations, to the extent that afterwards, when the show's headliners, Creed, came on, they encountered much booing and a rapidly emptying venue.

Coldplay further repaid US radio stations who had supported their music by performing at WBCN's Boston show, and at the WHFS Radio show in Washington DC. The warm reception accorded the band was indicative of their growing US popularity. Speaking about the Boston gig, Will told *Herald.com*, 'We were a lot more confident about it than we were last year. Also, we were headlining this year, so we knew if there was anyone left in the arena, they would be here to see us.' The next stop on what was becoming a typically hectic tour saw the band quickly fly to Iceland for a late December gig, where they honoured local stars Sigur Ros by covering one of their songs, 'Svefn-g-englar'.

At Christmas, *NME*'s Johnny Davis asked the band, 'This year, you've become proper pop stars, hanging out with P Diddy, Jennifer Aniston, Mos Def and Ms Dynamite. Have any of them made it to your Christmas card list?' 'We don't know where any of them live,' replied Jonny. 'Maybe Bono,' Chris cut in gleefully. 'We went to Ireland and Bono invited Will and Guy over for lunch. He said, "Just jump in a taxi and say 'Bono's house', and it worked! So we might send him a card: "Bono, Ireland."'

Johnny Davis was also able to break some good Christmas news to the band – *A Rush . . .* had been voted *NME*'s Album of the Year for 2002. Chris was surprised and delighted. 'There's a lot of people coming out of the woodwork who hate us. That's what's mad about *NME* giving us album of the year. I thought by now they'd have hated us. Where's the backlash?'

Will, in particular, was looking forward to the holiday. 'Our presents to each other will be not seeing each other for a couple of weeks,' he declared, 'A bit of time off.' 'I'm sure we'll speak to each other on Christmas Day,' Guy countered, 'it'll get to about seven o'clock in the evening and I'll go, "Oh, I suppose I'd better ring them up."'

Once the yuletide season was over, the band and their newly expanded, 30-strong crew returned to the road for a fourteen-date US tour, beginning in Florida on 21 January and scheduled to end in Arizona on 9 February. The tour focused particularly on blitzing medium-sized cities of the south. There were also some shows in cities that were often overlooked by touring bands: Birmingham, Alabama, New Orleans, Kansas City and Phoenix.

This time, some alterations to the band's travel arrangements had been made. For the trek across the Southern states, two tour buses had been booked: one for Chris and Gwyneth, and one for the other band members. Chris explained the reason to *Esquire*: 'It's a smoking thing; they smoke, I don't. They drink, I don't. I hate drinking. I hate it. But we're best friends.' Was this physical separation the first sign of a rift between band members? 'Absolutely not,' insisted Kevin Westerberg, an *NME* photographer who was covering the tour. He insisted, 'They really are four super-close friends who are focused on the music. That's the first priority in their lives.'

Clearly, by arranging a separate tour bus, Chris and Gwyneth showed that they wanted to invest a lot of time and attention to their relationship. However simple, practical, arrangements like these encouraged press gossip. For instance, the false rumour that Gwyneth was going to sing on the next Coldplay album. Such nonsense was clearly an attempt to cast Gwyneth as a controlling Yoko Ono figure, who wouldn't let Chris leave home without a macrobiotic lunch. Will found such unfounded tittle-tattle highly amusing: 'my favourite was Gwyneth banning us from drinking and smoking on our tour bus,' he told *Esquire*. 'Another one was that Chris and Gwyneth insist on having their own room backstage, which is also nonsense,' Will revealed to *Australian Musician*.

> '**Eminen is as good as Springsteen. They're all doing passionate stuff and that's great, I just want to be part of that.**' – *Chris Martin*

Since most of the gigs were in the Southern States, where the winters are mild, the band were far less likely to catch 'flu than on their previous American tour. Kevin Westerberg had a great time capturing the ambience of that part of the US: places like the Grady Cole Centre in North Carolina, which 'had a bit of a David Lynch feel'. There, the lone sign advertising Coldplay's gig stood against a barren *Last Picture Show* background of spare power lines. As for the gig hall, Westerberg remarked, 'it was one of those classic gyms where you had a row of wooden bleachers on either side – they obviously play basketball there.' With his lens focused on the crowd, Westerberg noted their composition: 'The audiences are fifteen to 50, a real mix. I think that's why they're doing well in America, because they're not appealing to just one age group.'

In Houston, the photographer ran onto the stage at the concert's end and jumped up on an amp to catch 'a nice moment where they're acknowledging the crowd and everyone's going nuts.' He was struck by the singular euphoria of the band after the gigs – so different from their mood on their first US tour: 'Afterwards they're all really happy. There's a fair amount of drinking, a fair amount of laughing. They're not really party animals at all, but they have fun with it. Nobody's po-faced on the whole tour.'

At the tour's opening show in Orlando the band was greeted by a huge cheer from the massed throng. It prompted Chris to declare that Florida had given them one of their grandest welcomes ever. Within moments, the crowd were singing along to 'Politik' with unstoppable fervour: Chris went silent, briefly, to make audible the audience's word-perfect singing. As was usual, the band began some of their familiar songs by improvising new material during the introductions, teasing the audience until the arrangements eventually became familiar.

Coldplay briefly stopped the tour – and traffic – by travelling to Los Angeles for the day of the US Superbowl Final, which was being televised right across the continent. Traffic was closed off on Hollywood Boulevard for an unusual open-air gig by the band. Fans waited there from very early morning, until finally the audience became 10,000 strong and the entire street was closed for much of the night. The set of five songs included 'High Speed', 'In My Place', 'Clocks' and 'Yellow' – the last two songs broadcast live right across America during the Superbowl.

After performing a gig, Coldplay would travel on their buses from around midnight until the early hours of the morning. The rest of their time was occupied by radio or TV promotions and endless signing sessions. 'They're totally fine with it,' observed Westerberg, 'they understand that that's a huge part of the reason why it's going well for them. So they're working all the time.' Firing a note of caution, he added, 'I'm not sure how much longer they'll be able to do it at that pace.'

The band would customarily do an hour's soundcheck during the daytime – often trying out new songs, some of which they'd be playing for the first time that night. For a touring band, soundchecks are their own distinct little time capsules, assimilating rehearsals, experiments among the stencilled equipment cases, and a chance for the music to take on an identity beyond the album they're currently promoting.

> **'Doing collaborations is kind of like how I imagine it is when you sleep with someone else's wife. I mean they're fun, but I'll always regret them in the morning.'** *– Chris Martin*

In St Louis, when the haunting and familiar strains of 'Trouble' started up, the audience stood up as one, singing, cheering and leaping. Observing the unified mass, Chris stopped for a moment and implored the audience to burst out into song: 'This could be the greatest English-meets-American collaboration since Fleetwood Mac!' Chris and the crowd roared their way through the rest of the number. Without warning, the front man then burst into the lyric of 'Dilemma', in tribute to St. Louis's homeboy rapper Nelly. Before the audience could assimilate the diversion, he crooned his way back into Coldplay's haunting song.

After such a rapturous response, Chris ran onto the stage again with his mic in one hand, and a cellphone clasped in the other. 'I need a favour from you,' he told the crowd, 'and it might be corny in a Mariah Carey sort of way.' He wanted them all to sing happy birthday to Gwyneth's mum, Blythe Danner, who was turning 60 that day. The crowd duly obliged, and Chris held up the cellphone so that Blythe could hear. Such innocent thoughtfulness served to cheer up his recently bereaved girlfriend and her mother. In the darkness at the concert's end, the crowd stayed noisily put, encouraged by the fact that the house lights weren't going up. Sure enough, the band bounded back on stage to introduce a new song, the passionate 'Ladder To The Sun': 'Cause if you want me then you can have me/you're not just anyone; you're a ladder to the sun.'

The press remarked very early on in the tour that the quartet were attempting some surprising new covers. 'If you catch Coldplay in concert and happen to hear something resembling Justin Timberlake's "Like I Love You", don't let your jaw drop too far and don't strain your neck looking for the eclipse,' *mtv.com* advised. The band had also been working some parts of Destiny's Child's 'Independent Women, Pt. 1.' into their repertoire.

Another aspect of Chris's inclusive enthusiasm involved lavishing public praise on songs that he particularly liked. One example of this was his hyperbolic eulogy of Liam Gallagher's 'Songbird' during a Radio One interview. The music and tabloid press distorted his comments to provide some rather ridiculous headlines. 'Chris Martin has revealed that he thinks Liam Gallagher is like Beethoven,' trumpeted the *NME*. What Chris actually said was, 'Liam Gallagher always gets some awful stuff [i.e. press] but it's like that film about Beethoven . . . anyone who can write "Songbird" is basically alright by me.'

Noticeably, Coldplay used the US tour to try out a clutch of new songs such as 'The Water Flows Over' and 'Proof'. After the nerve-wracking experience of starting work on their previous LP with little fresh material to hand, they were determined to keep inspiration constantly flowing. Touring continually since the previous August, the band made a firm point of writing whilst on the road. Chris told *NME* that they didn't want 'to sit around and get fat and arrogant. We want to work even harder. We've got about 27 new songs. But, of that 27, I would say maybe 26 won't ever be good,' Will explained to *mtv.com*. 'We always try to play the songs in sound check, but you can gauge a song much better when you're playing it as a performance rather than just as a practise. It's important that you start playing it and work out where the weaknesses are and work out where the strong points are, and so on. Use the audience like guinea pigs, you know?'

Also among the new tracks that Coldplay tried out were 'Gravity', the very rocky 'Marianne', 'Moses', 'The One I Love', and 'Poor Me'. This last song was played at their Indianapolis gig and 'seemed to be a look at how those with everything are still not happy', observed *hotandcoldplay.com*'s Lora Ruffner. Written for Gwyneth, 'Moses' is a powerfully rocking song, containing a blunt tribute: 'As Moses had power over the sea/You have power over me.' Although she refused to comment about her relationship with Chris, Gwyneth acclaimed 'Moses' as 'a great song' during a US TV interview, adding, 'I love those lyrics.' 'Moses' is about a man who feels overpowered by his love for a woman. But he also feels his own intense power surging forth to protect and console her with his understanding of her grief.

These powerful live performances provoked so much popular response that in early February 2003, only ten days into the schedule, the band announced a significant extension to the tour. 'It seems North American audiences can't get enough of Coldplay,' reported *mtv.com*'s Brian Orloff, announcing a further 45 dates.

Every one of these new dates would be in an arena, coliseum, or amphitheatre. As for the final, 18,000-seat show at Madison Square Garden, it was the most prestigious venue a band could secure in America. The gig sold out in 45 minutes. If Coldplay needed any additional confirmation of their status within the American music scene, this was it. Earlier in the year they'd taken a whole two hours to sell out the far smaller Irving Plaza.

Other prestigious gigs that were lined up included a show at Red Rocks, Denver, on the twentieth anniversary of U2's legendary show there, and another at the Hollywood Bowl. Coldplay had suddenly stepped up a league – they were preparing for superstardom in the US.

The announcement of this super-tour was accompanied by the news that Coldplay had been nominated for two Grammys: Best Alternative Music Album and Best Performance By Duo or Group for 'In My Place'. For their highest profile gig yet, the band would break off their tour in mid-February to play at the annual Grammy Awards, along with Norah Jones, Nelly and Bruce Springsteen. Ultimately, the single 'Clocks' reached Number Four in *Billboard*'s Adult Top 40 chart and peaked at Number 29 on the Hot 100. *A Rush* . . . was still in the US Top 30 six months after its release, and had recently been certified platinum. 'The quality of their album across the board has carried them,' observed Jonathan Cohen, reviews editor of the industry bible *Billboard*. 'They're sitting alongside acts like Foo Fighters and Nirvana.'

Playing down such hyperbole, Coldplay appeared unimpressed with their growing reputation. 'There's always someone who has absolutely no idea who you are and who thinks you're an idiot,' Chris told the *Hartford Courant*'s Eric R. Danton. 'There's always more people who don't know who you are than do, especially for us, obviously, 'cause we're not that big. Just when you start to think you're the next Bono, someone reminds you that you have to pick up your socks.'

However, Jonathan Cohen also felt that much of Coldplay's pre-eminence was due to the acumen of their US label, Capitol who 'know something the rest of the industry doesn't. Their track record for English bands is unparalleled. They seem to sign acts who develop and grow over time.' Capitol had nurtured Radiohead in the US, now they were beginning to push Leeds band The Music as heralding a new wave of young British talent. They also installed The Music as Coldplay's support, and, when *Esquire* asked Guy about the most interesting people he had met on the road, he cited the young band: 'They were great. Four whippersnappers from up north.'

Roy Lott, head of Capitol Records, told *NME* that the key to Coldplay's US success lay in the broad appeal of the themes their songs explored – 'Coldplay have lyrics which are universal. Some other British acts which haven't been a big success in America have lyrics which speak mainly to a British or European audience. Coldplay isn't like that.'

Back in Britain, *NME* ran a tour report under the headline, 'We're Like The Beatles In America'. The source for this unlikely comment was the usually reserved Jonny, who qualified his apparent boast by saying, 'Actually we're definitely not the biggest thing in America. I think Shania Twain is the biggest thing in America, but it's exciting at the moment. It's weird.' The *NME* observed that Coldplay were becoming the first band in a generation to achieve superstardom in America. Radiohead had managed to score significant US album sales, but had never played the huge venues that Coldplay were now booked into.

With Coldplay's sales success perceived by the British music industry as the sign of a recovery, major record labels were now showing greater flexibility in their approach to nurturing new bands. After all, Coldplay had gone on to become a great mainstream success without compromising their creative integrity. As Fierce Panda's Simon Williams told the *TrakMARX* website, 'Major labels now understand how to market alternative rock acts with the same degree of menace that they've always shoved pop acts down the kids' throats.'

In contrast to this surge of interest in guitar bands, Coldplay's attention was turning towards electronic and dance music, in particular to the work of Norwegian dance duo Royksopp. Following a request from Chris, the duo had produced a remix of 'Politik'. But Royksopp's Svein told Radio One that he was not sure if the mix would ever be released. 'I think it's basically for their laughs. I think it's the first time ever they had got remixes for the music. I've been told this might be a lie just to impress us!' What was the experience like for Royksopp? 'Doing a remix for someone like Coldplay, who have a really good vocalist and they also have quite appealing harmonies, to us it was all just fun,' said Svein. Upon reflection, though, his partner Torbjorn found this exercise to be a mixed experience. 'We really didn't find a way to deal with it. I personally think we went a bit far with that remix. Too far, if that's possible,' he told the *TOTP* website. When *Mvremix.com* asked if they ever thought their version would surface publicly, Torbjorn replied, 'Many DJs feel they have an educating aspect as well as an entertaining aspect and I think we may have gone a little too far on that educating aspect of that remix and a bit too low on the entertaining aspect.'

Torbjorn's use of the word 'educating' may help us to understand Coldplay's motivation in approaching Royksopp – the mix certainly helped the band to stretch their musical sensibilities, and to hear a wider variety of production techniques. Ultimately Coldplay must have found the experiment productive, because they later asked Svein and Torbjorn to remix 'Clocks' and gave the result a limited edition release.

13 February saw the presentation of the annual *NME* awards in London, for which Coldplay were heavily nominated. Coldplay and Oasis carved up the major awards, with both bands winning two each. Oasis beat Coldplay to the Best UK Band and Artist of the Year titles. However, Coldplay triumphed in the Best Album category, also beating the Vines, The Coral and The

Fairplay Concert, the Astoria, London, October 2002. 'Do you think this is a fucking karaoke?' Noel Gallagher hectored the sing-along crowd.

Streets. *A Rush . . .* was also voted Album of the Year in a further award decided by the *NME* writers. The awards night was also a very happy one for the band's close ally Steve Lamacq, who won Best Radio Show. Even Alan McGee was happy, as his latest charges the Libertines deservedly walked off with the Best New Band award.

Noel Gallagher butted in on Coldplay's *NME* interview, right after they won the Best Album award. 'Have you heard what they've just said about your missus?' he asked Chris. 'No, what did they say?' came the reply. 'Something about you not doing a Gwyneth,' laughed the monobrowed Manc.

Regardless of Noel's teasing, Chris was not inclined to emulate Gwyneth's Academy Awards ceremony tears. Rather, when asked how it felt to win Best Album, he marvelled, 'It's amazing, it's just the coolest thing. Who would have thought it. I said onstage, we could have gone into Shania Twain Territory, being a big band, so to get *NME* and *NME* readers still thinking we're cool is brilliant.' 'When we were young we always read *NME*, and all the things we dreamed of then are coming true,' added Jonny. Irrespective of the plaudits bestowed on the band, Chris's mother was most pleased when her son was voted the *NME*'s 'Sexiest Man In Rock'. When DJ Sara Cox asked the secret of his sensual appeal, Chris recommended, 'Start receding, get spots and wear the same jacket all the time.'

Just a week later, the mainstream Brit Awards were held at Earl's Court in London. Coldplay were nominated for Best British Album along with Ms Dynamite for *A Little Deeper*, The Coral for their eponymous debut, The Streets for *Original Pirate Material*, and Sugababes, for *Angels with Dirty Faces*. For Best British group, Coldplay were again nominated alongside Sugababes, in addition to Blue, the Doves and Oasis. The 2003 Brit Awards were never likely to be the most adventurous of ceremonies – 'It's a perennial problem for the Brits that they are required to salute the biggest earners. No money, no business, no Brits,' commented *The Mail on Sunday*'s David Bennun.

Drearily, Robbie Williams won Best British Male for the third time from candidates including Badly Drawn Boy, Craig David, David Gray and Mike Skinner of The Streets. Eminem was another very predictable winner, walking off with the Best International Male prize. The only winner who stimulated a broad consensus of goodwill was Ms Dynamite, who triumphed in the Best British Urban and Best British Female categories.

But Coldplay dominated the Brits ceremony, playing 'Clocks' onstage, and contributing much vitality to an otherwise largely predictable event – even though Justin Timberlake dutifully laid a hand on Kylie Minogue's bottom in a bid to inject a certain *frisson* into the proceedings.

The *NME*'s Steve Sutherland proclaimed that 'intensity and purpose are the attributes that raise Coldplay's songs above the rest of the game,' describing how the group stole Justin and Kylie's thunder 'by simply being so into their song.' Coldplay performed and then collected their two awards – but not everyone was wreathed in smiles. 'Like bands such as Travis and Manic Street Preachers before them, they seem to have sucked into the vacuum at the heart of British pop that's been created by the absence of a truly great group,' remarked *The Telegraph*'s David Cheal.

> **'Just when you start to think you're the next Bono, someone reminds you that you have to pick up your socks.'** *– Chris Martin*

Any possibility of a genuine controversy erupting at the Brit Awards was considerably lessened by a new ban on stars drinking alcohol until the after-TV show party. Making this attempt to stop the 'interesting' behaviour that had spiced up previous sluggish ceremonies, the organisers reckoned without Chris, who required no booze to act the goat. The cameras cut to our hero as Coldplay won Best British Group, but instead of his face, they caught his butt in the air and his legs in the splits. 'Coldplay tried desperately to pick things up,' *Dotmusic* noted. 'Chris Martin mouthed obscenities on his way to collect the award for Best Album and followed tradition by using the platform to voice his concern about impending war.' On receiving the award, Chris said, 'We think this is great, although awards are essentially nonsense. We are all going to die when George Bush gets his way – but it's great to go out with a bang.' Chris's comment was not the only reference made to the impending invasion of Iraq: Ms Dynamite performed a rewritten version of George Michael's 'Faith', which contained the lines 'there's got to be a better way' and 'I don't want blood on my hands.'

Guardian journalist Mark Lawson wrote an autopsy of the Brit protests two days later, in a broader piece about Britain's 'artistic battalions lining up against the planned attack: 'Given that the two most famous songs of the great icon and martyr of the pop industry are "Give Peace a Chance" and "Imagine", it's much less of a surprise to find so much "John Lennon–karaoke" going on from the recipients of the Brit awards. Given similar instincts among the record-buying generation, when Chris Martin tells his audience he's anti-war, he's almost certainly screeching to the converted.' While Chris was singled out as the main source of dissent, the sardonic Lawson's article also alluded to a rumour that Justin Timberlake would release an anti-war single – a sort of 'anti-Bush Band Aid'.

Coldplay weren't around long enough to read any of the post-Brits coverage – they had already left the country. The night after the ceremony, they flew on Concorde to New York, to rehearse for the Grammy Awards ceremony at Madison Square Garden. The band admitted to some nerves because, as Will explained to *mtv.com*, 'Playing at awards shows is always quite tough, because you've got a tough crowd. They're all musicians, and quite a few of them are great and some are not so great. It's not like you're playing in front of your fans.'

The day before the show was given over to a full-blown rehearsal. It broke the ice between the unacquainted participants and gave Chris, Jon, Will and Guy a chance to familiarise themselves with the venue, ahead of their forthcoming end-of-tour show.

The immensely complex rehearsals for the Grammys telecast were a microcosm of rock stardom, set against a background of slow-rising hoists, fast-dropping lifts and giant white video screens. Stars used the stop-and-start rhythm of technical adjustments to hold impromptu jams. Sheryl Crow and Kid Rock tore through a cranked-up cover of ZZ Top's 'La Grange'. An incredible one-night-only guitar-slingers' dream team of Bruce Springsteen, Elvis Costello, Dave Grohl, Steve Van Zandt of the E Street Band, Tony Kanal of No Doubt, and Pete Thomas of the Attractions powered its way through the classic 'London Calling', in fiery tribute to The Clash and their much-mourned frontman, Joe Strummer.

Unfortunately, Coldplay had little chance to jam or bond with their new peers. They were due to play 'Politik' accompanied by the full might of the 86-piece New York Philharmonic Orchestra. Their conductor was Grammy-winning composer/arranger Michael Kamen, who had helped Metallica to fuse metal and symphonic magnificence on their album *S&M*. (Sadly, a sudden heart attack in November 2003 would lead to Kamen's death at the age of 55.) Eschewing the 'easy option' of playing the song to a backing track, the band was pumped up for the occasion and all went well, with the grand orchestral backing creating a majestic sound. 'Coldplay frontman Chris Martin was all smiles at rehearsal's end,' noted the *Grammys* magazine.

The band weren't overly optimistic about their chance of winning Best Alternative Music Album two years in a row, Will told *mtv.com*. He also spoke of his ambivalence toward such prizes in general: 'We don't really care about awards that much unless we don't win. It's quite easy not to care about them when you get nominated, and when you win, you just go, "Oh Gosh." It's just an award, you know? But if you don't win, you think, "Why the hell didn't we win?"'

As with the Brits, America's looming attack upon Iraq cast a shadow across the event. While the stars rehearsed for the big show the following day, some newspapers published nervy, doom-laden pieces predicting political trouble at the ceremony. A senior executive of CBS, the US channel televising the awards, stated edgily, 'There is a time for political commentary. This is not one of them.' Chris's statement at the Brits ensured that the band were identified as potential dissidents.

Back in the UK, *The Daily Telegraph* ran a 'Grammy Award warning after Coldplay outburst' headline. The accompanying piece from Hugh Davies betrayed a state of some corporate panic: 'Television executives are worrying that the live broadcast of the Grammy awards in New York tomorrow – in which the British band Coldplay are nominated for two awards – could turn into an anti-war rally . . . There were reports that at least one of the acts performing at the ceremony was planning an anti-war gesture.'

It was also rumoured that Simon and Garfunkel were going to hold a one-off reunion in order to perform 'The Sound Of Silence' at the ceremony – although *The Telegraph* speculated that this apolitical 'Vietnam War-era ballad' about alienation might cause CBS some corporate discomfort. It was a great moment for Coldplay, to appear at the same ceremony with the musicians who had inspired them to sing harmonies on the Ramsay Hall stairwell during their student days.

On the night of the Grammy Awards, the tension was palpable. What kind of anti-war protest would these massed musicians make? What Coldplay did was to give a very powerful performance of 'Politik'. As Jon Weiderhorn reported: 'Against a backdrop of swirling green lights, vocalist

Coldplay win Best British Album and Best British Band at the Brit Awards, February 2003.

Chris Martin squinted, stomped and bobbed frenetically at a piano while singing such heartfelt lines as, "Give me strength, reserve control/Give me heart and give me soul," in a pained and vulnerable voice.'

The lyrics consist of humane appeals shouted aloud, in the implicit context of a world imperilled by man's destructive urges. This was arguably the night's strongest artistic response to the crisis, the perfect eve-of-war song.

The 'Best Alternative Music Album' Grammy went to a triumphant Coldplay, underlining the US music industry's esteem for the quartet. Thus far, they are the only band to have taken the award in two consecutive years. They also won 'Best Rock Performance' for 'In My Place' – the full promise of which had proven so difficult to capture in the studio. It was fitting reward for the track that had, to an extent, kept the band together when they doubted their second album could equal the quality of *Parachutes*. By carrying off two awards, 'Coldplay confirmed themselves as a band of genuine worldwide status,' declared *The Guardian*. 'Grammy Double Whammy From Coldplay', ran *PlayLouder*'s headline. But the band had no time to bask in their victories. The day after this taxing, euphoric Grammy show, they were off to Canada for the Ontario leg of their tour.

Irrespective of Coldplay's double triumph, the political dynamics of impending war had infected the Grammys. The *Guardian*'s Alexis Petridis remarked that when accepting the awards, Chris had been 'strangely silent' about the war. Australia's *SHM.com* made a satirical jibe with the headline, 'Look at the silent stars – they must be all yellow.' But the true reason for Chris's silence was explained by Petridis: 'Critics were quick to note that Coldplay are on the cusp of major US success, and that any anti-war sentiment might damage their career. But the reasons were more prosaic. CBS, who televised the awards had warned all prospective winners that if they attempted to mention the war, they would be taken off air, an act of censorship Coldplay's drummer Will

Champion later described as "absolutely disgusting – foul and totally fascist."'

A few musicians found small ways of subverting the ban during the telecast. Flaming Lips front man Wayne Coyne sported a blue plaster under his right eye, 'to draw attention to the fact that we are not supposed to talk about the war and peace. Stop the war. Let's find other ways. Hey, no black eyes.' More obviously, Sheryl Crow's guitar strap simply bore the legend, 'No War'. Will's politically explicit statement with its outright accusation of fascism could potentially have deprived the band of much mainstream airplay. The two US national radio networks, Infinity and Clear Channel, are notoriously conservative: the latter own 1,200 radio stations and reaches a staggering 54 per cent of the US population every week. 'Their power cannot be overestimated,' warned *The Guardian*.

A week later, the *Hartford Courant* published what it described as 'a fair description of how Martin sees the current standoff over disarming Iraq.' 'It seems to me that there's nothing like a war for a leader,' asserted Chris. 'I don't really know the ins and outs of it, but I'm not sure it's necessary to kill innocent civilians to get a few more votes in the Midwest, you know?' However, like many people then, Chris was disorientated by the endless stream of propaganda about the existence of an Iraqi arsenal of 'weapons of mass destruction'. 'But maybe I'm being very naive and cynical. But if Saddam Hussein really does have a lot of biological weapons, then obviously he's got to be stopped.'

> **'Playing at awards shows is always quite tough, because you've got a tough crowd. They're all musicians, and quite a few of them are great . . . It's not like you're playing in front of your fans.'** – *Will Champion*

One aspect that wasn't showing any sign of stopping was the worldwide sales of *A Rush . . .* which by March 2003 had reached 4.5 million copies. In Britain, 'Clocks' climbed to Number Nine in the singles chart. (The B-side of the UK release, '1.36', also featured some special guests: Ash's Tim Wheeler played guitar and TV comedian Simon Pegg provided backing vocals.) The UK tour and singles releases had propelled *A Rush . . .* back up to Number Two, seven months after its first release. *Parachutes* was also still hanging around at Number 48, 140 weeks after release.

Back on the road, Coldplay were delighted to be making a return to the ever-supportive city of Atlanta, where the last autumn's gig had been shorted out by typhoon damage. Chris reminded the audience that Atlanta was where the band saw their first-ever American tour take a hopeful turn: 'We almost gave up on finishing the dates here in the US until we came across you guys. So, in return for your hospitality, we want to bring out a special guest to do this next song with us – the best piano player ever – Elton John.' The stunned crowd at the Gwinnett Civic Centre went crazy, as Elton took his place at the piano and started to play 'Trouble'. He played the song perfectly, hitting every chord change and even incorporating a little bit of his signature style into the melody. Then he joined in on vocals. On this high, sustained note, the first leg of Coldplay's American tour approached its end. In early March 2003, the band flew back to England amid a climate of disintegrating international relations.

With America's NASA-style countdown to war now reaching the low numbers, preparations for an invasion were swift. Tony Blair had committed Britain to the conflict, and a million people marched in London in an expression of overwhelming popular opposition. Many people in the music world desperately wanted to reinforce this dissent.

One such was Glastonbury's Emily Eavis who organised *One Big No* – a benefit on Saturday 16 March 2003, determined to emphasise the popular opposition to the war, and to raise funds for the Campaign for Nuclear Disarmament (CND) and the Stop the War Coalition. Emily's co-organiser for the benefit, helping to put the bill together and arrange the venue and the publicity, was Chris's former girlfriend, Lily Sobhani. Emily appealed publicly for support for the event, stressing that it was one of the last opportunities musicians had to voice their opposition. 'War is inevitable,' she told the BBC. 'This is a very sensitive time. But we are hoping people can get a positive aspect out of this.'

For once, Emily's Glastonbury connection failed to open all musical doors. She had planned to use the Millennium Dome as a suitably massive venue to contain the anticipated massive protest from musicians. However, the event was 'downscaled to the 1200-capacity [Shepherd's Bush] Empire when she failed to recruit enough star names,' reported Caroline Sullivan in *The Guardian*. 'The raggle-taggle assemblance who donated their time on Saturday consisted of protest veterans such as Paul Weller, a couple of moonlighting lead singers and Ronan "To the barri-cades!" Keating. If it lacked punter appeal, blame the A-listers who refused to commit for reasons not unconnected to fear of alienating American record labels.'

The One Big No gig also featured Beth Orton, Faithless, Travis's Fran Healey and Ian McCulloch. Although he was not billed as part of the concert line-up, Chris Martin made a sur-prise appearance, playing three songs (including a version of Lou Reed's 'Walk On The Wild Side' with Ian McCulloch).

In a *Guardian* review that described his contribution as 'refreshingly honest', Chris admitted to the audience, 'My songs have nothing to do with war, they're all about the sad insecurities of a balding rock star.' Mac was more effusive, introducing one of his own songs, 'The Killing Moon', as the 'greatest song of all time'.

Events like One Big No decisively routed New Labour's 'Cool Britannia' quest for hipness. Tony Blair had recently mouthed a 'trendy-dad' soundbite claiming that he sometimes listened to his kids' Coldplay and Foo Fighters albums. Now, Chris had come out publicly against Blair and his government's policy on Iraq.

Offstage, Chris and Gwyneth were facing an ever-escalating frenzy of media interest, *NME* reported in April: 'Twelve photographers sleep on Chris's doorstep every night. Every tabloid car-ries a blurred snap of him holding a newspaper in front of fiancée [sic] Gwyneth's head', the report claimed, directly implying that the couple were now engaged.

One theme that supposedly permeated the coverage was the great advantage Chris had gained in dating a Hollywood star – in that it had suddenly made Coldplay a household name. 'As any-one including your mum knows, Chris's relationship with actress Gwyneth Paltrow has helped the band's profile, too,' wrote Adrian Grist and Emma Morgan in *Bang*. *Spin*'s Tracey Pepper agreed: 'It wasn't until after *A Rush . . .* was released and Martin began dating Gwyneth Paltrow . . . that Coldplay became a band your little sister, your mom, and even your grandma had heard of. Suddenly, they were being name-checked by Timberlake, Renee Zellwegger, Jake Gyllenhall, even P Diddy.'

Despite the media's insinuations, the five million copies that *A Rush . . .* had sold worldwide by this point (not to mention the multi-million sales on *Parachutes*) had nothing to do with Chris dating Gwyneth. 'Coldplay became big because we work hard and we think we're bloody good,' asserted Will. 'Reaching this level of success was not a surprise to us. Even as we worked on *A Rush Of Blood To The Head*, we sensed Coldplay was going to go into another league.'

Essentially, the only effect that 'The Gwyneth Factor' was having upon the band was unprecedented levels of tabloid coverage given over to their front man's relationship. Chris told *Spin*'s Tracey Pepper that people recognised him 'because of who my girlfriend is.' 'Part of the reason the press is intrigued by Martin's relationship is that they think he's otherwise boring,' Pepper observed.

The next media broadside to be fired at Chris was an unpleasant memoir. In the London *Evening Standard*, Emma Holland – the former Oxford student who had briefly been the focus of his affections – opted to go public with the tale of Chris's clumsy attempt at wooing her. Posing the question, 'How did the lovely but hopeless Chris end up with Gwyneth Paltrow, the very epitome of a sophisticated A-lister?' Emma set about undermining his new 'Rock's Sexiest Man' status. 'The thing I find most surprising isn't his fame or fortune, it's his new found success with the ladies,' she marvelled. 'Here, she recalls a geek in braces who barely knew how to kiss,' bellowed the *Standard*'s subheading.

> '**When we were young we always read** *NME*, **and all the things we dreamed of then are coming true.**' – *Johnny Buckland*

As the paparazzi staked out Martin's house and Gwyneth's flat, a war of attrition began to develop. *The Sun* ran headlines that backed up the *NME*'s assertion that the couple had got engaged. *New York Post* gossip columnist Cindy Adams wrote that they were planning a wedding in the Hamptons where Gwyneth's godfather Steven Spielberg would walk her down the aisle. In an interview on Virgin Radio's breakfast show Chris retorted, 'Everything that is written about Steven Spielberg and Chewbacca is a load of rubbish. Darth Vader is supposed to be giving her away. It is sad because it proves you can't believe anything you read.' Gwyneth also adamantly countered these stories: 'It's bizarre, they literally make things up,' she told *Celebrity Chatter* columnist Michelle Solomon. 'The weird thing is that someone will just lie and completely fabricate and make up a story and newspapers all over the world will pick it up. The next thing it's on radio and then I have my mother calling and saying, "Do you have some news?" It's just absurd. It can be very tiring.'

The Guardian's John Robinson tried to present Chris and Gwyneth's relationship as part of a fad for actresses hooking up with 'the New Indie Boyfriend'. 'He's been in vogue before, but it's been a while since we've seen him make such a strong resurgence . . . there's never been a better time for an independently wealthy and successful young actress, model or personality looking for a relationship to shop for a slouching Indie Man.' Other examples cited included Bert McCracken and Kelly Osbourne. But Chris was described as indie's biggest catch, 'Despite occasional odd behaviour and unshakeable fear of male pattern baldness, dishy Chris, 26, can still send a "shiver" down a maiden's neck.'

On the same day that Gwyneth made her denial of the wedding plans, the *Evening Standard* published Emma Holland's memoir. Ostensibly, the piece was a wincingly wry look at her own changing attitude toward Chris; at first rejecting his over-intense, comically clumsy advances – and then, once he was famous, finding that she was attracted to him after all – only to be allegedly rejected after one night. Such exploitative revelations can be viewed as a cynical attempt to cash in on Chris's celebrity status and raise the aspiring journalist's profile.

With the tense political climate unaffected by any protest action from either the general population or the rock subculture, Coldplay focused their energies on vital issues nearer to home. The Teenage Cancer Trust was holding a week long series of gigs at the Royal Albert Hall featuring Eric Clapton, Supergrass, the Doves and Madness. When invited, Coldplay readily agreed to perform, opening the week of gigs on 24 March with a memorable 90-minute show. Although their set included two new songs, 'Gravity' and 'Marianne', it was the old favourites that delighted Adam Webb of *DotMusic.Com*: 'Songs like "Yellow", "Clocks" and "In My Place" are a perfect synthesis of the personal and the communal, and in times like these we all need some meaningful collective soul-searching.'

David Cheal of *The Daily Telegraph* also found 'Clocks' compelling, 'with its driving, focused beat and hypnotic piano riff; the song then segued cleverly into "In My Place", which provided a lovely pop moment as the crowd sang along lustily, the Albert Hall came alive.' On the night, no performer was more vital and hyper-energetic than Chris. Here in the sanctum of *Last Night at the Proms* jingoism, he even seemed to bounce when seated at the piano. Cheal was enchanted, wondering at his 'Tiggerish feats of sustained boinginess'.

> **'Coldplay became big because we work hard and we think we're bloody good. Reaching this level of success was not a surprise to us.'**
>
> *– Will Champion*

Perhaps it was fortunate that Chris was in such good physical shape. Especially as the pugnacious Liam Gallagher was about to square up to him – albeit verbally. Two days after Coldplay's performance, Liam made a special guest appearance during Richard Ashcroft's Teenage Cancer Trust set. During Coldplay's gig, Chris had asked the audience to sing along with him against the war. Liam took exception with Chris for expressing anti-war views at an unrelated charity fundraising show, asserting, 'These gigs are about kids who have got cancer, they've got to fight a war every day of their lives. That's what we're all here doing this for.' Beyond that, Liam's tirade was colourfully gratuitous: 'Chris Martin shouldn't be using this cause to bang on about his own views on war. If him and his gawky bird want to go banging on about the war they can do it at their own gigs. That lot are just a bunch of knobhead students – Chris Martin looks like a geography teacher. What's all that with writing messages about "Free Trade" on his hand when he's playing? If he wants to write things down I'll give him a pen and a pad of paper. Bunch of students.'

The response from Chris, a massive Oasis fan, was appropriately light-hearted. Several weeks later when the band were playing their biggest ever UK shows, Chris ventured some gentle satire. On Oasis' home turf of Manchester, he dedicated 'Yellow' to Liam – 'the second best singer in the world'. During the Earl's Court gig, the lyrics of 'Everything's Not Lost' became, 'If Liam Gallagher's out to get you/Don't let it drag you down.'

Coldplay were just about to start a ten-gig tour across Europe, beginning with a show in Lille on 27 March and taking in Germany and Portugal before finishing in Barcelona on 11 April. For these dates, it had been arranged that, wherever the band went, they would be accompanied by a film crew. Coldplay and Parlophone had decided that now was the right time to produce their first live concert DVD. It would also include a Tour Diary documentary covering the European dates, as well as the band's early summer USA arena tour. 'When we joined them in Madrid, playing a bull ring with sawdust on the floor, they had been touring for about a year and a half in total, and it was like being parachuted into a maelstrom of activity,' said Tour Diary director John Durrant.

The challenge of shooting the tour footage with nine cameras on 16mm film was considerable. It was exacerbated by an over-abundance of interesting material: 'We shot over 150 hours, 200 almost, and we had to whittle it down to 40 minutes,' revealed Durrant. Such compression was made easier by the selective reactions of the band. 'There were certain bits that we were like, "Please get rid of that!" I think he very quickly knew what the good bits are while he was doing it,' explained Chris.

Although Coldplay were enthusiastic about the project, being constantly filmed did mean that they lost most of their relaxing 'off-duty' moments. 'It's very weird filming everyday life, 'cause you're like a slave to the camera and you're thinking all the time, "I better do something interesting," but sometimes you end up just sitting totally still, petrified about doing anything,' fretted Chris.

During pre-production, the band had definite ideas about the footage they wanted to secure. Their brief to Russell Thomas, director of the live concert part of the film, was 'intimate going to expansive' – spanning their career in microcosm, from club venues to arenas. They decided that shooting in an intimate venue would be ideal – Sydney's Horden Pavilion, one of the smallest venues on the summer leg of the band's forthcoming world tour. 'The reason we didn't film a big gig was we had to leave ourselves somewhere to go,' Chris told *mtv.com*. 'I always think *Live by the Sea*, Oasis' first DVD, was the right size, and then you see them at Maine Road and stuff.'

Another crucial reason was that they felt that fans would prefer it. 'There's lots of people that don't want to see us in a massive place . . . There's lots of people that hate us since we left the clubs and I understand why, so that's why we haven't gone for a stadium DVD first,' confirmed Chris.

Coldplay had had no other option but to make the transition to stadium rock. But, before three huge shows at Manchester Arena and Earl's Court, the group played one of their smallest gigs, a live session for BBC Radio One's *Mark and Lard Show*, in front of only 30 people.

Despite this emphasis on intimacy, the band were perfectly at home on the UK's largest stages. *Guardian* journalist Dave Simpson's five-star review of their Manchester Evening News Arena gig on 14 April called the show 'virtually a master class in the art of playing rock to stadiums'. He wrote, 'Three years ago, Coldplay's Chris Martin told a tiny Leeds audience to "remember this when we're massive." Now hindsight doesn't disguise the fact that he knew exactly where he was headed, Martin has coped with Coldplay's worldwide success by remaining unaffected, putting his efforts into simply doing his job better.'

The band were approaching their music with renewed gusto. At their Earl's Court soundcheck they crashed out a heavy metal rendering of 'Trouble' that thundered around the empty arena. Later, in their cramped dressing room, the documentary cameras discovered them locked in an acoustic session. The biggest surprise was seeing Will's guitar work: he had his instrument laid zither-flat on his knees, while his fingers carved intricate bluegrass out of the strings.

Once the show got under way, Chris triumphantly exclaimed, 'This proves geeky kids can win through!' The packed crowd roared in affirmation. 'You have to know that I got into it all for the love of music – and only ever for the love of music.' This rallying cry prompted the *Evening Standard* to christen him 'the modest man of pop', adding, 'despite earning millions as the frontman . . . and dating a Hollywood star, he has never played up to his cult status.' In agreement with the Earl's Court congregation, the *Standard* pointed out that Chris gave hope to every adolescent who felt they were a geek.

While performing as an icon for unfashionable outcasts everywhere, Chris found time to compose a song for one of his own heroes – Johnny Cash. Subsequently, Coldplay approached Rick Rubin, head of American Recordings, the label that had rescued Cash and lovingly promoted his career after Capitol summarily dumped him. 'Rick Rubin had us in and recorded it with all the band and all the guys who do Johnny Cash's records,' revealed Chris. In fact Cash was quite ill at that time, but when he was better Rubin intended to have him come in and record Coldplay's song. An exultant Chris declared to *Esquire*, 'If he's well enough to record it, it would be unbelievable. Fucking Hell!'

Toward the end of April, Ian McCulloch released his solo album *Slideling*, to which Jonny and Chris contributed in the place of Bunnymen guitarist Will Sergeant. Despite their assistance, *Guardian* reviewer Dave Simpson claimed they didn't 'vastly alter things for McCulloch musically', Mac's solo effort remaining of a piece with his recent Bunnymen work. 'Four songs – "Playgrounds And City Parks", the druggy "Love in Veins", "Sliding" and the fabulous "Stake Your Claim" – hold their own with the best of his canon. That one or two certainly don't is typical of one of pop's most flawed but fascinating characters,' enthused Simpson.

The previous four years had seen Coldplay step up to increasingly larger venues as their popularity grew. Now they headed for the biggest, most prestigious arenas in America, which could only continue to propel them to stratospheric heights. 'Madison Square Garden is a huge leap for them,' said *Billboard*'s Jonathan Cohen. 'But of any band, they can do it. They have the potential to have a long and interesting career. Chris Martin has a little bit of Bono in him.'

One major strategy for Coldplay's spring 2003 tour was to use it as a vehicle to promote the Make Trade Fair campaign. Oxfam would organise volunteers – over 150 in number – at the US shows. These teams would raise awareness by distributing postcards to the entire audience. It was hoped to collect thousands of signed cards calling on President Bush to stop dumping cheap, subsidised exports on poor countries. Oxfam's strategy was focused on the crucial upcoming conference of the World Trade Organisation in Cancun, Mexico, which was scheduled for September. Coldplay's mass of signatures would be delivered to George W. Bush just beforehand.

In addition, Chris submitted an article to *The Guardian*, hoping to shake the British social conscience. 'When I went to Haiti with Oxfam last year, I was shocked by what I saw,' he wrote. 'Battered, dusty cities full of crumbling, half-finished buildings. Shells of cars everywhere. Very few real roads. It looked like a war zone. It could be a beautiful Caribbean island, but it looks as if it has been burned to the ground.' And why was this? Chris continued, 'The EU and the US won't let them export their goods to us because it might unbalance our economy, yet we force Haiti to accept products it doesn't need, that it can produce itself. And it's disgusting, indefensible . . .' Once again, Chris reminded readers that their consumer choices were equated with a degree of political power. 'Going out there shattered my illusions about many Western companies. I love KitKats and Rolos but they're made by Nestle, the same company that is able to buy its coffee from peasant farmers for less than it costs to grow. They work incredibly hard, and they get nothing.'

By the time the piece appeared on 24 May, Coldplay were in Washington, playing the first date of the US leg of their tour. This show at the picturesque Gorge Amphitheatre followed right after three Canadian dates in Edmonton, Calgary and Vancouver. The constant travelling had the effect of muting Chris's obsession with his own mortality, a reccurring feature of his lyrics. 'I don't want to die,' he told *Esquire*, 'I want to record another album. Whenever I travel by plane at the moment, I think it's not going to crash because surely we'll be allowed to make another album.'

In late May, the band's distance from home meant that the presentation of a most distinguished British honour had to accepted by proxy. Coldplay were named Songwriters of the Year at the 48th Ivor Novello Awards. One of the top music industry accolades, the Novellos are presented to esteemed British songwriters, composers and music publishers. British comedian Al Murray, best known in his comic persona as the Pub Landlord, read out Coldplay's speech: 'The Ivor Novellos mean a lot of us and even our grandparents would be impressed with us winning this. We're not sure whether we deserve this – but we'll trust your opinions and say thank you very much.' Mike Skinner, aka The Streets, beat Coldplay to the award for best contemporary song, for his single 'Weak Become Heroes'.

Meanwhile, on Coldplay's biggest tour yet, fans in the US and Canada splashed out a total of $7 million to see their idols: almost 200,000 people spent roughly $35 per ticket to see them at a total of fifteen arenas. At the tour's opening date on 20 May at Edmonton's Shaw Conference Centre, Chris continued his tradition of paying tribute to local stars, by launching into an impromptu burst of Canadian Avril Lavigne's hit 'Sk8er Boi'. 'If the number of people singing along to Coldplay's songs are any indication, Coldplay have definitely made it,' reported the *NME*. Next up for conquest was the vast Shoreline venue in San Francisco.

As a venue for Coldplay it seemed odd, mused *San Francisco Chronicle* reviewer Yoshi Kato. 'Like many thoughtful artists, Coldplay looked to be richer in respect and admiration than massive popularity. So the idea of these sensitive yet passionate rockers filling up Shoreline's vast spaces appeared a bit far-fetched.' In the event, it turned out to be one of the summer's biggest sell-outs. The Shoreline audience was 'a trans-cultural melange of indie kids, older prog-rockers and fresh converts who discovered the band through their local modern-rock stations,' the *Chronicle* elaborated. 'But for veteran Coldplay fans, who have watched their group move from relatively intimate sets at Bimbo's and the Fillmore to the Greek Theatre and finally the 20,000-capacity Shoreline, this transition from inspired underdogs to rock stars probably carries a bitter-sweet aftertaste.'

> **'You have to know that I got into it all for the love of music – and only for the love of music.'** – *Chris Martin*

The huge sold-out concert represented another new achievement for the band. 'I've just been told that this is our biggest show ever, and if everyone here had voted for us we would have won *American Idol*,' quipped Chris. Throughout the gig, he repeatedly marvelled at the size of both audience and venue. Regardless, as the *Chronicle*'s Neva Chonin noted, the band were not dwarfed by their surroundings. 'Coldplay's expansive sound, in which even piano ballads seem built for cathedral recitals, is perfectly suited to huge venues, and on Friday it effortlessly filled the amphitheatre's sprawling space.' Chris dedicated the night's final song, 'Amsterdam', to 'my lady and my dad,' and threw out a final verdict on the evening – 'We thought there's no way we can be a soft rock band with short hair. We've proved that we can.'

Since opening in 1922, the Hollywood Bowl has become one of the most famous LA landmarks. With its onion-layered, art deco canopy, it is the concert venue equivalent of the Hollywood sign. It would also present Coldplay with an opportunity to perform in front of the movie industry's major players. The band were booked into the Bowl for a two-night stint and were watched by 36,000 people (all with perfect teeth, as *Q* observed). On the first night, the audience cheered for twenty minutes after Coldplay left the stage. Fans from all over the country who weren't able to get there could still hear this landmark show live, as it was broadcast on countless radio stations right across the US.

Everything was on a different scale now, with a police escort accompanying Coldplay from the hotel to the venue. Undaunted by the fuss, Guy indulged in an on-stage game of football before the Bowl's doors opened. 'This is totally the best thing that's happened to us,' marvelled Chris. 'The rest of the world is slowly catching on but, if it wasn't for the people in Los Angeles, we'd probably be playing cross-Atlantic boats. It's all quite Springsteen.' The band reached out further to the people of LA with an interview and performance for KROQ radio's influential breakfast show. During the interview, which took place at the House of Blues, Chris was asked about new songs. He replied, 'We've probably got half a good one, half a rubbish one.'

But this was typical self-deprecation. At the Hollywood Bowl gigs, the band debuted a new track, 'The World Turns Upside Down', which showed a distinct Bunnymen influence. The band also threw in a pristine cover of Justin Timberlake's 'Like I Love You' and Louis Armstrong's 'What A Wonderful World'.

Later, rather than indulge in any post-gig rock excess, Chris acquired some karmic credits in an incident that became the 'indisputable highlight' of the Tour Diary. 'After their career-high sell-out appearance at the Hollywood Bowl, Martin is seen rescuing a kitten that has somehow become trapped in the dressing room roof. Coldplay? Rescuing kittens? You really couldn't make it up,' marvelled *Q* reviewer Tom Doyle. Identifying Chris as the new St Francis of Assisi, *The Los Angeles Times* predicted he was 'about to be fitted for a halo' as the heir to 'St. Bono's crown'.

After the concert, the stars came forth to pay their respects. 'Everybody is here. I've just met Brian Wilson. Does life get any better?' Chris asked *Q*'s Nick Duerden. The former Beach Boy (who had spent years as a psychologically troubled recluse) had difficulty convincing the security guards that he was 'somebody'. Coldplay, on the other hand, didn't need to check Wilson's credentials. It was an encounter that blew the band away. 'That was a pretty big deal for all of us,' Chris told *Esquire*. 'We've already met most of the people that we love . . . The illusion of fame has been kind of removed, but occasionally someone comes in who you think, "Wow!"' 'I think he's a little more . . . fragile than he was,' commented Will. 'But he still has this amazing life in his eyes. We asked him if he enjoyed the gig. He said, "I fucking loved it!" Wow! How cool. He's inspired more people than most.'

> **'We thought there's no way we can be a soft rock band with short hair. We've proved that we can.'** – *Chris Martin*

Meeting Brian Wilson prompted the band to check out his back catalogue. *Esquire*'s Amy Raphael caught up with Coldplay just before their Cleveland, Ohio gig, sketching the backstage ambience. Will and Guy sat around on couches in the Portakabin, drinking beer and listening to the Beach Boys. Chris was happy enough simply to soak up the pre-gig milieu. 'I was just lying on the stage earlier trying to have a sleep,' he told Raphael. 'Looking at the venue emblazoned with our name, thinking: "How the fuck did we manage that?" To some people I must still be Chris who used to run around school with a stupid haircut acting like a twat. To others I'm Chris Martin of Coldplay and they're freaked out to meet me.'

By early June, *A Rush . . .* had advanced back up the *Billboard* charts after 39 weeks on sale, just hitting the Top 30. On 6 June, Coldplay faced another huge crowd at the Denver Red Rocks Amphitheatre. Both the date and venue were laden with significance, as their booking coincided precisely with the twentieth anniversary of U2's unforgettable performance there. On the night, an incredibly violent storm pounded down on the 9,500-strong assemblage. Huddled under umbrellas and improvised coverings, the soaked fans gave Coldplay an ecstatic, if damp, reception. When U2 had invited Coldplay to play at their Slane Castle show, Bono had segued into 'Yellow' at one point in tribute. Now Coldplay returned the compliment, working in a U2 reference –

June, 2003: 'Breakfast with Coldplay' at KROQ, the LA station that – along with ABC TV's use of 'Yellow' in promos – helped to break Coldplay in America.

'how long must we sing this song?' from 'Sunday Bloody Sunday' – while Jonny demonstrated his take on The Edge's distinctive riffing.

During Coldplay's maiden performance at Denver, 'Politik' was taped for inclusion on a ten-track anthology album entitled *Carved in Stone Volume Two.* The CD was intended to raise funds to help maintain the Red Rocks amphitheatre, which had been threatened with closure due to its high running costs. 'Politik' would appear alongside live contributions from R.E.M., Willie Nelson, Ben Harper and U2, with the aforementioned classic 'Sunday Bloody Sunday.'

On 13 June 2003, the tour reached its Madison Square Garden climax in front of an A-list audience that included Woody Harrelson, David Blaine and Mike Myers. Despite the frantic pre-gig tension, a harried Chris stopped momentarily to greet *Esquire*'s Amy Raphael: 'I'm stressed, man. Thanks for coming. Haven't you seen us enough times? I'm sorry, I've got nine things to do. Everyone forgets we've got a gig to play.' One of these nine obligations was to give an attentive welcome to Gwyneth's highly coiffured aunt and her partner. Another was to rehearse during the soundcheck with a young woman named Christy Roider, whose friend had bid $35,000 on her behalf at a charity auction held to benefit the Robin Hood Organisation (a charity for disadvantaged New Yorkers), so that Christy could sing 'In My Place' with the band at the home ground of the Knicks basketball team.

The band were totally stunned when David Bowie materialised backstage to wish them luck. 'He said he never usually goes to big gigs; the last time he came to the Garden was in 1972 to see Elvis,' revealed Jonny. 'What were we supposed to do after that?' Of course, Coldplay did their utmost – with Chris revelling in the mad unreality of it all. 'We're a young English band, and this is bonkers.'

Reviewing the concert for *Spin*, Tracey Pepper declared that Coldplay 'had transformed themselves from Radiohead obsessives into a critically-respected, celebrity-props receiving mainstream sensation.' *NME* agreed: 'They are now, without question, the pre-eminent British band of 2003.' However, keen to counter such runaway hyperbole, Chris told *Esquire*, 'It is still the beginning for us . . . I want to play nine nights at Madison Square Garden. One is not enough.' Likewise, when Pepper told him that the band were never off the radio at the moment, he responded with anxiety: 'It is too much, isn't it? Fuck. I'm sorry. I'd like to apologise if we're over-exposed. What a bummer. Well, we're fucking good, so we can't worry too much.'

The end-of-tour party after the Garden was held at Joe's Pub in the East Village, with the ever-versatile Will manning the decks. 'Rather surprisingly, given their overwhelming ordinariness, they also attract endless A-list celebrities,' commented Amy Raphael. 'No doubt Gwyneth is doing her bit, but it's more than that: Coldplay are cool in America.' The girls who squealed whenever Guy Berryman looked their way would certainly have agreed. The party was also a family occasion, where Chris's father and brother arrived in the company of film star Rachel Weisz. Jonny stood outside the pub, smoking and swigging beer: 'David Blaine was talking about suspending himself in a bubble above the Thames . . . very weird. Oh yeah, and Mike Myers. He is so shy. He can barely have a conversation. Unbelievable.' Later, Chris and Gwyneth arrived, dressed in their modest civilian clothes, and stayed only half an hour – taking a short break from their very happy private world.

> **'It is still the beginning for us . . . I want to play nine nights at Madison Square Garden. One is not enough.'** – *Chris Martin*

Coldplay could now allow themselves a sigh of relief. A major part of the world tour to promote *A Rush . . .* was at last behind them. In just three more months they would reach the end of this promotional forced march.

The band flew back to Britain just as the summer festival season was starting, headlining at Scotland's tenth annual T In The Park event. Coldplay performed the festival's closing set to a delighted 65,000-strong crowd. Ever-willing to give credit for a good turnout, Chris changed the lyrics of 'God Put A Smile Upon Your Face' to 'God gave you light and gave you dark/God gave you tickets for T In The Park.' It was an excellent festival, also including Coldplay's old pals the Flaming Lips, in a vital performance featuring a menagerie of people on animal costumes, REM, The Coral, Feeder, The Darkness, Sugababes, The Rapture and The Streets. It all bore testimony to a reawakening of Britain's live music scene, to which Coldplay had contributed with energy and passion.

Highlights from Coldplay's set were later broadcast on *Lamacq Live* – along with a radio documentary called 'The Ticking of Clocks' that Steve Lamacq had made while accompanying the band on their recent US tour. During the documentary, Chris went on the record about his relationship with Gwyneth: 'This is the only time I'm ever going to talk about this. When you have a high-profile girlfriend, people forget that really she's like, well, everyone, Jack Nicholson or the Pope – they're just people with parents and worries.'

Ahead of the band's mid-summer flight to Australia for the next leg of their world tour, several completed projects saw fruition. One of these was the 14 July release of Royksopp's 'Clocks' remix. Of the limited edition pressing of 1,000 copies of the disc, 120 were retained especially for the Coldplay fan club who were invited to purchase the song via their website. The disc also featured a version of 'God Put A Smile Upon Your Face' remixed by Def Inc featuring Mr Thing.

The original mix of the song was selected as the band's next US single, the video for which went into rotation on the music channels. Once again directed by Jamie Thraves, the black and white video intercut performance footage with a storyline about a businessman who bumps into a mysterious stranger with no shoes, and is then dismayed to discover himself gradually disappearing. As if to confirm Coldplay's penetration of American mainstream culture, the band also received an invitation to appear on the teen TV show *Dawson's Creek*. 'Me and Jonny said, "We don't mind, yeah, let's do it,"' Chris told *Q*. 'Will and Guy went apoplectic. So it was decided that "no" was the answer. But there weren't any tears.'

The second half of July was entirely taken up by appearances in Australia, where the band's live DVD was to be filmed. To coincide with their visit, 'Clocks' had been released as a single with a completely new track, 'Murder,' as its B-side.

One of the major dates on this leg of the tour was the Splendour in the Grass Festival, on 19 July at Byron Bay, New South Wales. Other acts due to appear included Powderfinger, The Living End and Superjesus. 'The signing of the British supergroup is a coup for organisers, who expect a capacity crowd of 12,500 people at the festival,' *Smh.com.au* reported. Such delight was in direct contrast to the doubts Coldplay had harboured during their first Australian visit – when they feared they might fail to provide the immense sound required for large outdoor shows. But now, free of these anxieties, Coldplay could relax: Chris might even find time for a spot of surfing. Gwyneth could also accompany her man on the tour, just as he went with her earlier in the year to film *Sylvia* in New Zealand.

Coldplay's Australian visit started with an intimate private gig at the Sydney Opera House, an hour-long, semi-acoustic set for just 150 people, recorded for the Australian cable channel MusicMax. 'We've been relegated to the basement,' joked Chris, on seeing the small Studio Room where they were to play. 'It was incredibly intimate – the band seemed happy to be there,' an unnamed fan told *nme*.com. 'There were a lot of lamps and the background was a black cloth with fairy lights all through it – it looked like stars . . . It felt like it was a really cosy little gig – it was such a privilege to see a band like Coldplay with so few people in a really special environment.' Christie Eliezer of *Australian Musician* commented that this micro-gig 'allowed Chris to exchange banter with the crowd, showing off what a funny and loving person he is.'

Next on the itinerary was a show at Melbourne's Rod Laver Arena on 18 July. At first, the Melbourne fans seemed unsure how to react to Coldplay in such a large setting. 'Initially the crowd did seem daunted' observed Eliezer. However, Chris broke the ice with his banter, joking that, unlike the Rolling Stones (then on their 40th anniversary world tour), they only had two good songs: 'The good songs [i.e. the hits] will come later, promise!' Chris also offered sedentary members of the audience $10 to stand up. Eventually, said Eliezer, 'they won the audience over, with Will providing a greater attack than is evident on the records.'

Whilst at the Splendour in the Grass Festival, Chris and Gwyneth found themselves badgered at every turn by paparazzi. The level of attention was assuming such nightmarish proportions that Chris even came down from his hotel room and paid some photographers the price they would secure for an exclusive shot – just to give the couple some peace. Although much of his concern was for Gwyneth's peace of mind, he needn't have worried. The actress was well used to this kind of trashcan-rummaging media interest. 'Shredders were made for girls like me,' she told Donna

T In The Park Festival, June 2003. Chris wears his Fair Trade message on his sleeve – or just above it.

Freydkin of *USA Today*. 'I sound like a complete jerk. I've been given this incredible life and now I'm complaining, but honestly, when people are stalking you to that extent, it's just awful . . . I've made it abundantly clear in all my actions and in the way I lead my life, I don't want to be a tabloid person. I'm not putting myself out there in a celebrity way. I don't go to this premier, party, opening.'

Chris was far less experienced in coping with media intrusion and, given his sensitive nature, it was always possible that, if exposed to enough provocation, he would react and provide the standard banner headlines. Unfortunately, that's precisely what happened – Chris had been surfing at Byron Bay with several friends when he spotted a photographer. 'They were innocuous photographs, and I don't know why he's upset,' press photographer Jon Lister said later. Allegedly, Chris walked up to Lister and demanded that he delete the pictures from his digital camera. 'I told him I was entitled to take pictures of him on a public beach but he wouldn't accept it,' Lister told *The Sun*, who published the photographer's version of events alongside his snaps. The argument grew more intense. 'He was pissed off, that's all there was to it,' Lister told *NME*. 'Somehow he wanted to get me back for it.'

Chris is then alleged to have picked up a large rock and bashed it into the windscreen of Lister's car and then let all the air out of its tyres. 'He didn't manage to break through the screen, but the window now has to be replaced,' said Lister to *The Sun*. 'If he'd just done the tyres I'd have laughed it off, but I have to get the screen paid for somehow,' he explained to *NME*. Lister made a complaint to the Byron Bay police, and at five o'clock that evening they duly turned up at Chris's hotel. Inspector Greg Carey confirmed, 'police interviewed the gentleman where he admitted he had lost his temper due to constant harassment by that journalist.' Carey added that the normal penalty for such an offence would be a warning, a bond or a small fine. On the other hand, although a custodial sentence was unlikely, the maximum sentence for malicious damage was five years' imprisonment.

Accordingly, Australia's *Daily Telegraph* reported that Chris would have to appear at the local Byron Bay Court on 8 October on a charge of malicious damage, although a plea of guilty would mean that he need not attend. Eventually, a Coldplay spokesperson confirmed that the band's lawyers would deal with the matter from London. She added that it would be 'very un-Coldplay' for the band to comment on the incident.

However, according to Reuters, shortly afterwards Chris joked from the stage at a Sydney concert that the only time he expected to see the police was when he met the 1980s band's former frontman, Sting. Before the final song of the night, Chris put his minor travails into their proper perspective, dedicating 'Amsterdam' to the Australian victims of the Bali bombing. Movingly, he spoke of a musician the band had met on a previous visit to the region, who had died as a result of the atrocity. 'Like U2, they made that great connection that we are all we've got, and we are all together,' noted *Australian Musician*.

But still, Chris continued to respond to questions about the Byron Bay fracas in a very human manner: 'It's recently come into my life, this thing, and it's a really odd thing, when people are following you around and making you mad. It's not a very big deal. It's a very First World problem,' he told Virgin Radio. But, as he explained to *Spin*, 'If someone was following you around all day, eventually you'd be like, "Please, will you fuck off and get on with your own life?"' Grinning, he added, 'It is great to let out aggression. Everyone wants to smash up a car. If I'd known how much trouble that tiny bit would get me in, I would've done more.' Chris eventually had to pay damages amounting to AU$2000.

Shortly after, Gwyneth gave an interview to the *Toronto Globe and Mail* that went some way towards explaining Chris's anger. The new gossip weeklies had made her life hell and, as *The Daily Telegraph* put it, 'even left the sweet and saintly Paltrow spitting in rage.' Recalling how the paparazzi had pursued her following her father's death, Gwyneth explained, 'In the darkest hour of my life, to be hunted like that, it's hard for me. I think, "I'm trying to fall back, please, isn't it clear? Can you please give me some room?" And they don't.'

The media's obsession with Chris and Gwyneth was 'driven by simple economics', noted *NME*'s news page. 'A photo of the pair in an intimate surrounding is worth at least £100,000,' and so was an intimate picture of an argument between them. Significantly, photos of either star alone would only fetch about £200. 'It appears that by attempting to keep some things in their lives private, Chris and Gwynnie are pushing up the value of photos of them together and dangling a carrot for the growing number of photographers hunting them,' *NME* concluded.

Chris's relationship with the press became as much of a story as his liaison with Gwyneth. 'Is Fame Too Much for Chris Martin?' asked *NME* on 2 August. The news article was accompanied by a hastily snapped picture of Chris cowering with his head in his hands, his huge, haunted eyes gazing straight into the lens. Others gathered to stick the boot into the soft flesh of Chris's nice-guy image. 'Well, well, well, apparently even the nice boy of British music has his wild side,' crowed *PlayLouder*. In *The Guardian,* Caroline Sullivan observed sardonically, 'So muesli-gargling frontdude Chris Martin has finally unleashed his inner rock-pig (we knew it was in there).'

Chris's reaction to the intrusion was that of someone who had reached breaking point following a series of such tiresome encounters. Clearly, the media pressure had got to him, to the extent that the press even pervaded his dreams. Shortly after the incident, Chris had a freakish nightmare about *The Sun*'s showbiz columnist. *The Daily* Star reported that Chris dreamt he was in a swimming pool accompanied by 'this girl I go out with that I never talk about,' and Cameron Diaz. Equally bizarrely, Dominic Mohan from *The Sun* appeared underwater with a camera. 'I was like, "What the fuck are you doing?!" I took the camera off him and threw it off this building and he got really angry with me and said, "I'm going to kill myself," and I was like, "Don't do that." He jumped down two storeys, but landed on the balcony, which was a great move. Then this guy attacked him and I threw a lump of wood and knocked him out and Dom thanked me.' 'This is proof that *Sun* columnist Dominic Mohan reaches the parts that other hacks cannot,' chortled *The Star*, adding, 'You sure it was a dream, Chris?'

The Horden Pavilion shows ended Coldplay's commitments in Australia, but the band's live impetus was maintained by gigs in Auckland, New Zealand, followed by the Fuji Rock Festival in Japan, and a performance in Thailand the following week. On the Auckland trip, radio presenter and fan Phoebe Spiers announced that if she got a Coldplay song dedicated to her from the stage during a gig, she'd pay for a Coldplay tattoo. The band called her bluff, dedicating 'Everything's Not Lost' to her, and she had the same words tattooed in a ribbon on her arm, crying, 'Goddamn me and my big mouth!' Such commitment worried Chris. 'I'm not sure if I want someone with a Coldplay tattoo,' he told *NME*, 'if we release a shit record or I get put in prison or something, then they'll be embarrassed.'

> **'If someone was following you around all day, eventually you'd be like, "Please, will you fuck off and get on with your own life?"'** – *Chris Martin*

By mid-August the band were back in Britain, and preparing for yet another festival appearance – this time at V2003. As publicity for the shows began to proliferate, so did reports that Chris and Gwyneth were planning to marry in the autumn – and, consequently, so did Chris's strenuous denials. 'We're not getting married in the near future,' he insisted to London's *Metro* newspaper.

Later that same month, Chris told *NME* that the success of their second album had given Coldplay many opportunities they had never thought possible. But he also cited the media pursuit of the couple as the dark side of the whole unique adventure.

It was an adventure that the band could now look back at with some satisfaction, especially now that the long period of touring behind the second album was nearly over. 'It's the end,' said Chris, of the V Festival gigs. The only commitments the band had before them now were several dates in Mexico City and a gig in Sao Paulo, Brazil, in early September. Since the Mexico trip coincided with the World Trade Organisation conference in Cancun, Chris and Jonny had been asked to deliver Oxfam's Big Noise petition to the head of the WTO.

In *Q*'s list of the 100 greatest gigs ever, Coldplay appear twice. The first show cited was their performance at the Meltdown Festival during the previous summer, the other was 2003's V Festival performance, 'the night they . . . bowed out of the public eye.' It was Coldplay's final gig of that particular stage of their collective career. It made their epic performance of 'Clocks', complete with green lasers boring into the crowd, all the more dramatic. Chris played short renditions of the Foo Fighters' 'All My Life' and Justin Timberlake's 'Rock Your Body', performing a cabaret of contortions at his black upright piano, which had the now-ubiquitous Make Trade Fair slogan chalked on it.

After sixteen months' straight touring, Coldplay announced they were going to take a year's break in order to 'reinvent' themselves. No more gigs, appearances or interviews for the foreseeable future. 'We've got to reinvent the wheel, basically,' Chris told *NME*. 'We have to hide away and get out of peoples' faces and cook things up again. We're not going to take any time off, we're just going to be working, working, working, like Mole in *The Wind in the Willows*!' On Saturday 16 August, the day before Coldplay's final V performance in Staffordshire, Chris announced, 'It's going to be the death of soft rock tomorrow night!'

'I agree with Chris,' added Jonny. 'It is the end of an era for the band. We've taken our songs as far as they can go and it's time for something different. I don't know what we're going to do. It's hard when you've been touring for sixteen months. Don't get me wrong – I love touring, but I just want to stay in a place for longer than a couple of days.'

TEN

REINVENTING
THE WHEEL

Coldplay had been seen simply everywhere, achieving exposure on a global level. Like the rest of the band, Chris was convinced they needed to retreat. On 23 August 2003, *NME* ran the speculative headline, 'Will Coldplay Quit?' The speculation had been stoked by a comment made by Chris on Virgin Radio: 'I'm not sure if we will come back . . . To be honest I'm petrified – it's really frightening being in England, I feel like everyone really hates us at the moment.' Given the rapturous response they had recently received at the V-Festival, the two Brit Awards they had won that year, and the reams of positive press, Chris's view seemed completely unwarranted, but unsurprising, given his anxious nature.

The band repeatedly vowed they would not be back unless they had some 'really amazing' new songs. Certainly, they had a solid cache of new material, such as 'Marianne,' 'Moses' and 'Ladder To The Sun'. 'We have got some amazing stuff but I'm just nervous about it,' fretted Chris.

Before the band could take a break from globetrotting, they still had a number of outstanding engagements to fulfill. At the end of August, Coldplay joined a roll call of the music world's biggest stars at the MTV Video Music Awards, held at Radio City Music Hall in New York. To the band, the MTV Awards were one more hurried stop on their way to Mexico and the final gigs of their gruelling world tour.

However, Madonna's schock tactics turned the show momentarily into a full-blown erotic phenomenon: dressed as a black-clad dominatrix, she ended her performance by kissing Britney Spears and Christina Aguilera full on the lips. That was a hard act for Chris and company to outdo. Coldplay performed 'The Scientist', which proved to be a daunting experience. 'I looked out at the crowd, and Eminem was looking at me, and I thought, "God, he's going to hate this." I lost all my confidence,' Chris told *Spin*'s Tracey Pepper, 'we were shit.'

Despite Chris's feelings about their performance, the event provided Coldplay with yet another awards bonanza. They clinched Best Group Video for 'The Scientist', beating B2K and P Diddy who were nominated for 'Bump, Bump, Bump', the White Stripes ('Seven Nation Army'), Good Charlotte ('Lifestyles Of The Rich And Famous'), and the Donnas ('Take It Off'). A second gong followed when Jamie Thraves won Best Direction in a Video. Coldplay and their video director had actually beaten two of the band's idols – Johnny Cash for 'Hurt' and Radiohead, who had been nominated for 'There There'. The Breakthrough Video award also went to 'The Scientist', which prevailed over such acts as Kenna, Queens of the Stone Age and Sum 41.

Coldplay at a farmer's cooperative in the state of Puebla, outside Mexico City, September 2003.

This hat-trick of MTV awards gave rise to a further crop of press articles about Coldplay and their escalating US success. Jonathan Cohen, *Billboard*'s reviews editor, told *NME* Coldplay had succeeded because they established a solid fan base with their debut album, reinforced through constant touring. 'They have spent oodles and oodles of time here. They've done club shows and radio station shows and bigger venue events – they have worked and worked.'

> **'Free trade is a great idea. It's just that we in the West do anything but stick to it.'** – *Chris Martin*

Tim Herbster, assistant music director for New York's Z100 radio station and DJ, told *Bang* magazine, 'The best way to sum up how huge Coldplay are in the US right now is that Justin Timberlake introduced them at the MTV Awards as "the number one rock act in the world." That's coming from the biggest pop star in the US. Respect – that's what Coldplay have.'

Kerri Cockrill, a marketing consultant for a number of US labels, told *Bang*, 'Coldplay are bigger than the White Stripes, Suede and David Gray because they can reach a wide range of audiences. Where David Gray will reach the College and Top 40 radio formats and the White Stripes will reach College and Alternative, Coldplay will reach College, Top 40 and Alternative audiences. They have a bigger slice of the pie.' This was why, she pointed out, 'Top 40 listeners in rural Iowa have heard of Coldplay and know a song or two; these folks may have heard of Radiohead but not know their music.'

The band's impact on American schedulers was expressed by Haley Jones, assistant programme director at San Francisco's KFOG: 'They have potential to hang around for a long time. They're smart adult rock. They're not too hard, and they're not too soft. They're perfect.' KFOG first playlisted the band with 'Yellow' in December 2000, and have never stopped airing and abetting Coldplay ever since.

Coldplay's broad appeal, radio-friendly output and constant Stateside gigging caused *A Rush Of Blood To The Head* to re-enter the Billboard Top Ten again, a full year after its release. To date, the album had sold 2.2 million copies in the USA. Even the perennially picky British music press agreed that the album exemplified a band at their peak. Reviewing Muse's new LP, *Absolution,* for *The Guardian*, Alexis Petridis observed, 'like Coldplay on *A Rush Of Blood To The Head*, Muse sound like a band who are at the top of their game.'

In mid-September Chris and Johnny headed south to Cancun, Mexico to support Oxfam's lobbying of the World Trade Organisation conference aimed at liberalising trade agreements. 'Cancun is a defining moment in global poverty reduction,' explained Oxfam campaigner Roger James, 'an opportunity to make a level playing field for world trade and stop unfair subsidies, tariffs and dumping.' Oxfam hoped that Coldplay's involvement would raise the media profile of an event that deserved much more coverage than any rock band.

Chris and Jonny's journey to Cancun represented the second stage of Oxfam's planned strategy for making use of the band's public profile. The first had raised general awareness of the Fair Trade campaign. 'The next step is to start meeting people who can actually do something about it,' Chris explained. 'Now is the first time that we as a band have been in a position to get those meetings.'

The signed cards that had been collected from Coldplay gigs earlier in the year added over 32,000 names to Oxfam's Big Noise petition. At the end of May, the group was told that the Make Trade Fair petition had a million signatures. Amazingly, this figure had nearly tripled by the time Jonny and Chris's met with the WTO's director general, Dr. Supachai Panitchpakdi, to hand him the document. It was hoped that such a massive demonstration of public opinion would encourage key decision makers to change global trade rules to work for the poorer countries, as well as the rich. When Chris was later interviewed by left-of-centre US magazine *Mother Jones*, Katherine Turman asked him, 'I know that when you met Dr. Supachai, you said, "You seem like a nice guy. Why is it so hard to get this problem sorted out?" How did he respond?'

'He said it was going to be difficult,' Chris replied. 'The great thing about the Cancun summit was, although it fell apart, it fell apart because the poorer countries are coming together and making a stand for themselves. What will come of that I don't know, but it's better than them just being walked over again.'

Aside from the disappointment of the summit's failure to produce a positive outcome, Jonny found himself cast as a victim of corporate muscle on a much smaller scale. Soon after arriving in Cancun, there was a knock on his hotel room door just as he was settling down for a good night's sleep. He was told that a terrible mistake had been made, that his beachfront room had been double-booked, and he'd have to leave and find other accommodation. With his usual calm, Jonny went along with this and found another, less salubrious hotel nearby. 'Perhaps his good-natured acceptance was misplaced,' *The Guardian*'s Cancun Diary suggested. 'The new occupant was from the US trade delegation.'

In front of the world's press, on Cancun's long expanse of beach, Jonny and Chris erected a large sign spelling out 'HOPE'. 'It's the first time I've been happy to see a long lens for a long while,' Chris wryly observed.

The irony of using Cancun's beautiful setting for the 146-nation conference was noted by Chris. 'That's what's so farcical,' he said, 'You come to a beautiful beach resort to talk about the world's poorest people.' 'We are in an incredibly privileged position and it is hard not to come across as a complete hypocrite,' added Jonny. 'Free trade is a great idea. It's just that we in the West do anything but stick to it,' observed Chris. The frontman demonstrated his commitment to the cause by taking every opportunity to hammer in the key point, that opening agricultural markets to free trade drives small farmers out of business, earning them less than it costs to produce their crops. 'This is an injustice,' he told *Ananova*. 'These people should be fairly rewarded for their work. We get fairly rewarded for ours.'

The band's unwavering support of Oxfam's campaign was recognised in *The Guardian*'s Cancun coverage. 'Coldplay have made the Make Trade Fair campaign one of the most high-profile campaigns among the young.' Conversely, *Bang*'s Adrian Grist and Emma Morgan had a more cynical interpretation of the band's motivation, insisting that their support for the Fair Trade campaign had done much for Coldplay's profile. Allegedly, an unnamed 'UK-based music industry consultant' suggested to *Bang*, 'Supporting Fair Trade makes the band look caring and sharing and altruistic. It's not like getting caught up in Amnesty International or Drop the Debt; they've chosen a worthy, *Guardian* reader type of cause but it's not going to rock the political boat.'

However, when asked in *Mother Jones* about his first ever experience of activism, Chris cited a Drop the Debt event in London. 'The great thing about Drop the Debt is that you have Bono and Thom Yorke and all these high-powered musicians actually going inside the buildings where decisions are made. I'm not sure how much George Bush is swayed by a hundred people standing outside his house. I'm sure he's more likely to be influenced by one person having a meeting with him.'

Chris's frustration at the motives ascribed to him was clear when *Esquire* pointed out how supporting conservation of the rainforests had a huge negative effect on Sting's image. 'Fuck it. People are cunts,' he exclaimed. But he admitted later, 'I do worry about people getting fed up with us. But fuck it; I am going to carry on supporting Fair Trade. Part of it is appeasing the guilt of being successful, I'm sure, but it's a good cause too.'

Lobbying for HOPE on behalf of the Fair Trade campaign – at the World Trade Organisation's conference at Cancun, Mexico, September 2003.

Chris and Jonny also went on to visit Mexico City, where Chris was photographed furrowing a poor farmer's acre with a rudimentary plough. *NME* reported that he came a little too close to one of the local poisonous snakes for comfort: 'I couldn't work here because of that. You have to deal with cheap foreign imports coming in, and then there's the snakes.'

Back in Britain, nominations for the Mercury Prize had rolled around again and Coldplay were once more included. The band also featured prominently among those chosen for the year's *Q* Awards – they were up for Best Act in the World, Best Single (for 'Clocks'), Best Video (for 'The Scientist') and Best Live Performance.

Typically, none of this positive attention made any visible impact upon Chris's insecurity. Tracey Pepper telephoned Chris to set up an interview – the occasion being that *Spin* had chosen Coldplay as its band of the year. Chris thanked her. There was a pause, then he asked, 'Is this going to be a story about how you've named us band of the year but take it back because we really don't deserve it?' Attempting to explain Chris's reaction, Guy told Pepper, 'That's who he is, I'm afraid. I think it stems from our British build-'em-up-cut-'em-down mentality. Once you're established in Britain, you become kind of uncool. But it's not such a bad thing to think everyone hates you. It makes you work harder.'

Intellectually and emotionally, Chris was perfectly able to distinguish his anxieties and neuroses from true distress and grief. For Coldplay, the saddest news since Will's mother's death came when they were told that their hero Johnny Cash had lost his struggle against the diabetes and associated ailments that were killing him. 'A sad day in Tennessee, but a great day in Heaven,' Cash's former co-writer Merle Kilgore told CNN. 'The "Man in Black" is now wearing white as he joins his wife June in the angel band.'

The Coldplay song and backing track that had been waiting for Cash all this while at producer Rick Rubin's studio would never receive its last crucial element – Cash's inimitable voice. 'He was someone who stood up for everybody and never got criticised for it, maybe because he lived it a lot more than people like me. When you're a musician you have to look up to these people,' Chris told Radio Five's Simon Mayo.

Chris's attempt to praise another musician closer to home rebounded on him. In early October he told Tracey Pepper that he felt he owed everything to Thom Yorke. She in turn let drop the bomb that Yorke had commented publicly that Coldplay were 'an example of how popular bands become lifestyle music.'

'What is lifestyle music?' Chris asked.

'It's music that loft dwellers listen to as they sip chardonnay and eat risotto – stuff like Norah Jones or Dido.'

'Oh, that's the worst.'

'Not to bum you out –'

'No, it's fine. Everyone hates us.'

Shortly after, Chris's eggshell confidence cracked a little further at the *Q* awards. 'A pop awards ceremony known as the *Q*s last night distinguished itself from many filling the calendar by sending Coldplay home empty-handed,' drawled Caroline Sullivan in the *Guardian*. This was, the paper pointed out, despite the fact that *A Rush . . .* had now sold five million copies and the band was actually 'one of the only young British acts selling records outside Europe.' Instead, it was Blur who won Best Album, Radiohead who won Best Act in the World, and Robbie Williams who clinched the Best Live act.

Since the *Q* Awards are mainly voted for by the general public, that year's results might indicate Chris's long-feared (or anxiously-awaited) popular backlash. However, it's just as likely that the awards indicated what Coldplay already knew full well – they needed to produce new material to qualify for continued recognition.

With this in mind, Chris and Jonny booked into a Chicago studio to begin producing demos for the band's third album. Simultaneously, half a world away in Australia, Chris's malicious damage case came to court. His lawyer, Megan Cusack, asked on his behalf for the charges to be dropped, and the case was adjourned until 21 November.

Chicago was selected by Chris as a base for recording because it was where Gwyneth was filming her new movie, *Proof*, which co-starred Anthony Hopkins. 'We went straight into the studio to get these ideas down in case we died or something before they were recorded,' Chris told *The Sun*. 'We've completed enough songs so that if our plane goes down, they can be finished.'

'I'm prepared to cut off my feet to make the next album amazing,' Chris told *Esquire*. 'I want to make a really up-tempo and emotional album. I'd like to write a song like "Trouble" crossed with "The Only Way is Up" . . . Yeah, I'd like to write a gay "Trouble",' he laughed.

Chris gave a compulsive account of the sessions to *NME*: 'We want to record and record and record. We've already started. We spend half of the night writing. The great thing about flying back from America is that you're up all night and you can just work.' The whole process reaffirmed the band's commitment to those dynamics that had pushed them forward in the music industry. 'It strikes me the more fame and success you get, the more you realise that the only thing that's really worth anything is the thing that made you want to get famous and successful in the first place. And that is writing tunes,' continued Chris. 'The answer is putting down your favourite new song or being with the people you love the most. It's not about the bling bling aspect. We've got some tunes, man. Let me tell you that!'

The break from touring at last allowed the band to enjoy some fruits of their success. In Chris's interview with *Esquire* he suggested that someone should go into HMV and blast all the great classic albums into space to ensure their immortality. In response, journalist Amy Raphael suggested that he should do it himself, given his new wealth. Chris laughed, 'My dad told me the other day that I was reported as being worth £5 million, which is way off. Way, way off. I do not have £5 million. Really, I don't.' However, the publishing catalogue that Chris has created looks set to net the band far more than that amount. In November 2003, a 'Salary Gallery' in *The Sunday Times* claimed that the band members had made £2 million apiece in the past year.

'Everyone assumes we're multi-millionaires because we've sold a lot of albums but none of us are rich enough to retire,' Chris told *The Sun*'s Victoria Newton. 'The most extravagant thing I've bought is 95 hooded tops all the same. It means I can hide when I walk out of my front door.'

Earlier on Guy, making light of his newly affluent status, had told *tripod.com*, 'I might buy a fridge.' He later had a better idea though, and invested his cash in some more advanced technology, converting two adjoining rooms in his London house into a control room and a studio. The performing area was fully soundproofed and acoustically treated, with a floating floor.

For his desk, Guy chose a TL Audio 32-channel VTC valve console, 'the only one of its kind available on the market,' he explained. The bassist didn't select one of the many digital desks available, because he planned to record onto Pro Tools: 'I wanted something which would give it a warmer, analogue sound.' Guy's motives for building a home studio were not entirely professional. 'It's also important to remember that this is also a hobby, something I do for enjoyment, without any pressure on making music. I'm really looking forward to having some people over, getting together with some friends and just playing . . . It's not inconceivable that the band might end up doing bits and pieces here as it's more than capable of handling it – anything is possible really.'

He used the sabbatical to hook up with his old pal Jim Ward from At The Drive In, his group having recently fragmented into two new bands: The Mars Volta and Sparta. *Playlouder* was 'startled to report' news of a collaboration between Jim and Guy. However, Guy didn't find it in any way odd. 'It's funny, but we both hate people who think we shouldn't do other kinds of music than the stuff we play,' he told *Canoe.ca* webzine. 'They're in it for the music and have so many things going on musically, and so do we.'

Likewise, Chris collaborated with pop-metallers Ash on a track for the soundtrack to their comedian friend Simon Pegg's 2004 zombie film, *Shaun of the Dead*. The song, used for the end credits, was a cover of the Buzzcocks' 1979 hit, 'Everybody's Happy Nowadays'. Chris also contributed to Ron Sexsmith's 'Gold in Them Hills' single. Sexsmith had opened for Coldplay on various occasions, and Chris's collaboration raised the profile of a much underrated musician.

Chris also gave a live performance for the American documentary *Mayor of the Sunset Strip*, which also included contributions from David Bowie and Brian Wilson. The documentary centred on KROQ's influential disc jockey Rodney Bingenheimer, whose long-running show was influential in introducing Coldplay to the West Coast audience.

At Christmas, the group made their cover of the Pretenders' '2000 Miles' available as a paid download for a limited period. The purpose of this exercise was to raise funds for the Future Forests and Stop Handgun Violence campaigns. BBC News reported that it was the biggest-selling legal download of the period January to March 2004 – even outstripping OutKast's massive hit, 'Hey Ya!'

Chris also embarked on a journey to the front ranks of UK street culture by collaborating with The Streets' Mike Skinner. A duet of Skinner's heart-wrenching account of being jilted, 'Dry Your Eyes', was recorded. However, by the time The Streets' new album, *A Grand Don't Come For Free*, was finished, *NME* reported that the track might never be heard publically. Skinner explained, ' I wrote the track and I thought that [Chris] would sound really good on it. I asked him to do it and he did. After that I really don't know. I don't think his record company liked it. But maybe he didn't like it. On the day he was happy with it. Well, maybe he wasn't, maybe he was lying to me and he walked out going, "This is not working." But it wasn't a massive stress. It would have been nice, but we re-recorded it and it sounds great.' Despite the absence of Chris Martin, the track was subsequently released as a single and hit the top of the British charts in July 2004.

> '**I do worry about people getting fed up with us. But fuck it; I am going to carry on supporting Fair Trade. Part of it is appeasing the guilt of being successful, I'm sure, but it's a good cause too.**' –
>
> *Chris Martin*

Chris undertook a further departure from the rock milieu by writing 'See It In A Boy's Eyes' for R&B star Jamelia, who is also signed to EMI. 'I absolutely loved every minute of being in the studio with him,' she told *NME*. 'It feels like we've created a new genre of music where we both stay true to what we do. I loved the fact that he brought out something completely different in me. His vocals on the track are really haunting. It's amazing that he could write lyrics from a woman's point of view and articulate feelings from a totally different perspective. I have always been a fan of Coldplay, and I am even more of a fan now.'

Chris later told Simon Mayo that he wrote the song thinking he could remain incognito. 'No one was ever supposed to know that I wrote it to be honest. The record companies kind of screw that up. My perspective is, I think she's an amazing singer and I had nothing to do for a week, so I thought, "I wonder if I could ever write a song for Jamelia?" This is what I'm saying – you've got to go for things in life haven't you? Jamelia then, in return, when she's an enormous global superstar, she might mention the words "fair trade" when she picks up an MTV award.'

On 3 November, the Flaming Lips headlined the Hammersmith Apollo, and Lips frontman Wayne Coyne was delighted that Chris turned out to watch them: he told Radio One, 'It was great, yeah! He's a really unchanged sort of guy. You can see how much he's moved by concerts and music and when you're around him you do really feel good about all the success they've had. He genuinely loves that communication that music does and thinks, "Wow, what a wonderful time we're having."'

Although Gwyneth had revealed that she was also a fan of the Lips during a publicity interview for *Sylvia*, the actress was less forthcoming about her feelings for Chris. Such discretion was particularly frustrating for the tabloids. Her relationship with the Coldplay frontman was, as she explained to *Vanity Fair*, 'sacred and so special that I feel talking about it is wrong.' Blythe Danner added, 'I think she is incredibly happy. And she's slowly coming to terms with her father's death. She puts one foot in front of the other now that the shock has worn off a bit.'

Speaking to *Esquire*, Chris reflected on the unwanted media attention: 'The main thing is, if you go out with someone . . . you belong to the tabloids. Basically, however, I'm not going to worry about anything today because we are going to make such a bonkers-ly brilliant record that I don't care. I don't care if it flops . . . well, I do care. Do you know something? Everything apart from the music is bollocks. So I don't care if people think I have sex with badgers.'

Unfortunately, it transpired that much of the music considered during their Chicago sessions was bollocks too. 'So far all we've achieved is managing to scrap 42 songs. I regard that as constructive destruction,' Chris told MTV news. 'But numbers are insignificant. You could say, "I've written twelve songs," and they could all be rubbish, or you could say you've written one song and it was "Bohemian Rhapsody". I'm glamorising it, but we were just in Chicago and we scrapped a lot of songs.'

Chris also told *Esquire* that he hadn't yet written the perfect song for Coldplay. 'We'll always be the band that wrote "Yellow",' he acknowledged, but confessed that he can't listen to the record because he hates the mix. As for Chris's views on his other songs, *Esquire* revealed, 'He thinks "Clocks" is close and maybe "Politik". He says "The Scientist" is "nice".'

Because the band was taking a break from live appearances, they didn't attend the MTV Awards in Edinburgh in early November, where they were shortlisted for Best Group. At the same time, Gwyneth mentioned that she also was planning to take a year's break from films. Emotional exhaustion after her year's heavy filming schedule and the loss of her father had changed her priorities. She explained, 'I worked so much in my twenties. I really burned the candle at both ends and I wasn't too picky about what I did. I think the combination of losing my father and turning 30 has completely shifted everything.'

'It's not such a bad thing to think everyone hates you. It makes you work harder.' – *Chris Martin*

On 6 November Chris accompanied Gwyneth to the UK premiere of *Sylvia* in Leicester Square. Afterwards, she stopped on the kerb to chat to the press while Chris jumped silently into a car. *The Mirror* described Chris's disappearance as 'stroppy', but by doing this he at least enabled Gwyneth to make the distinction for the media between her career and their relationship. She also told the media that Chris 'has more depth than any man I've ever met. I'm a lucky girl.'

10 November saw the release of the *Coldplay Live 2003* DVD. Asked by Katherine Turman whether he thought that Coldplay were better live, or in the studio, Chris responded, 'I feel we're a better studio band. Some days I think we're shit at both; other days I think we're great at both. But we couldn't have one without the other. At the moment, all I want to do is be in the studio all day, every day. But I'm sure in a year's time, we'll be itching to play live again.'

In his *Q* review of the DVD, Tom Doyle emphasised the polar contrast between Coldplay's Tour Diary and that of Radiohead: 'Radiohead have already set the bar for this kind of black and white, cinema-verite rockumentary . . . with the harrowing *Meeting People Is Easy* . . . [Coldplay's] Tour Diary might have been subtitled *Meeting People Can Be Really Very Pleasant Actually* . . . as Chris Martin later states of the band's grip'n'grin promo duties: "These people keep playing our music. We don't want to say, Fuck You."'

On the day of Chris's Australian court hearing, it was announced that the police had dropped the charge of malicious damage resulting from the Byron Bay incident. The official explanation of the decision not to proceed was that, 'Investigations indicated there was a degree of provocation causing the 26-year-old man's actions. Further basis for not proceeding was [that he] is a person of prior good character who admitted his guilt when speaking to the police, expressed his contrition and has since paid reparations for the damage.'

For Chris and Gwyneth, even more welcome news was soon to follow. On 1 December Gwyneth hosted the Music Has Power Awards at New York's Lincoln Center. Photographs of the gala first revealed her fuller figure, causing much press speculation. Shortly after, the couple visited a doctor's office on Manhattan's Park Avenue, where a photographer caught them acting like any other young, happy, *expectant* couple. The result was a cover feature in *Hello* magazine, under the byline, 'Intimate pictures confirm their "ecstatic" reaction to news of a summer baby.' In the shots, Gwyneth was killing herself with laughter while Chris, dressed in his smart 'doctor's appointment' clothes, bent his head to her stomach on the street.

Gwyneth described their early reactions to her pregnancy to Bernard Bale of *Ms London* magazine: 'we just looked at the screen, totally amazed . . . I don't think anything prepares you for the moment when you know you are pregnant. It is the sort of thing that happens to other people and you share in their joy, but when it's your own it's totally different. I keep thinking about this baby growing inside me and, while we already feel as if we have a family, we cannot wait to meet him or her.'

In *Rolling Stone*, Chris revealed that he didn't wait to meet his child face to face before starting one part of the infant's education. The expectant father subjected his unborn child to a programme of pre-natal music. Unsurprisingly, this kicked off with some U2: 'The first song on *The Unforgettable Fire*, "A Sort of Homecoming", I know it backward and forward – it's so rousing, brilliant and beautiful.'

The press emphasised the benefits that Chris and Gwyneth's clean-living lifestyle would have upon the health of their developing infant. But in a cover story for *Vanity Fair*, Gwyneth said that her pregnancy had also helped to heal the loss of her father: 'It's just amazing to know that I'm going to have something that's a quarter my dad.'

When it was announced that Chris and Gwyneth were 'pleased to confirm' their baby would be born in the summer of 2004, the couple's spokesperson refused to comment on the possibility that they might marry. Speculation about a wedding grew as the couple were seen out house hunting in Belsize Park, just north of Camden. The couple themselves would not be drawn. 'Getting married is a serious move,' she told *Ms London*. 'Of course, it is fun to have a new ring to show off and it's great to have a wedding with all your friends telling you how nice you look, but after all that there is a marriage and you have to make it work forever.'

Since August, when Ms Paltrow was spotted wearing what appeared to be an engagement ring, Chris had been denying reports that a wedding was imminent. The couple were widely expected to marry in New York that autumn, 'before the leaves and their loves turn,' as gushing *New York Post* columnist Cindy Adams put it. But by the beginning of December, still nothing had happened. Appearing on the BBC's *Parkinson* show, Gwyneth gave the impression that she was still waiting for a proposal. When asked if it would necessarily be from Chris, she replied, 'I'm the wrong person to ask. Ask him.'

The couple then travelled to Los Angeles, ostensibly so that Gwyneth could do some television publicity for *Sylvia*. On 4 December, *The Tonight Show* staff noted that Gwyneth seemed unusually excited to appear as a guest. An unnamed studio source told *People* magazine, 'She was chatting everybody up. People congratulated her, and she was very receptive and happy. She was very excited. She seemed a bit giddy.'

As it turned out, Gwyneth had good reason for jubilation. The very next day, the couple turned up together at a courthouse in Santa Barbara, California, to apply in person for a marriage licence. The licence allowed them to be married by a local judge at any time within 90 days. This news travelled the world fast: 'So no Hampstead wedding for them, then,' commented *My London* web magazine, asking, 'Are they already married? . . . Rumours are flying thick and fast that Gwyneth and Chris have apparently wed in secret.'

Next came word that the betrothed had got one over on the press by using the licence immediately they received it, to marry in secret. That the couple 'married quietly' was an understatement. 'The surprise nuptials included no family members, not even Paltrow's mom, Blythe

Danner,' marvelled *People* Magazine.

According to *US Weekly*, very early in the morning of 5 December, Chris and Gwyneth had someone else check them into the exclusive San Ysidro ranch in Santa Barbara: this enabled them to drive straight to the door of their honeymoon cottage in secret. At nine a.m. the couple drove to Santa Barbara's courthouse and queued to get their marriage license, paying an extra $2 to secure an officially confidential one. This confidentiality lasted only fifteen minutes, claimed *US Weekly*, for at 9.15 a.m. a Santa Barbara radio station apparently received an anonymous fax from the courthouse stating that the couple had just left. By this time, Chris and Gwyneth were driving back to their hotel cottage, to await the arrival of a judge.

Simply dressed and alone, Chris and Gwyneth took their vows before the judge in a ten-minute ceremony. By early evening they arrived at Santa Barbara airport, to fly off in a private jet for their honeymoon at the luxurious Esperanza Resort outside Cabo San Lucas, Mexico. As they waited to board the plane, some pressmen caught up with them, an American named Scott Cosman and Frenchman Nicholas Chirior. According to *Spin*, Britain's *The News of the World* and other news reports, Chris exploded as the photographers snapped away at Gwyneth: 'Gwyneth was behaving very strangely, going to great lengths to hide her left hand with her grey hoodie top. I have no idea why,' recalled Cosman.

Then, it was claimed, Chris went over to Cosman's car and scraped his key down the side of it – allegedly, Cosman confronted him over this. 'Then he turned on Nicholas,' stated the photographer. 'He smacked him right in the face, leaving Nicholas with a black eye.' Cosman's pictures were published in the *News of the World*, but no court action resulted from the incident.

Despite this scuffle, Chris and Gwyneth had largely succeeded in wrong-footing the world's press. *Now* magazine had predicted 'a classy, traditional wedding with most of Hollywood turning up to toast the new bride.' With all the media speculation that Spielberg might walk Gwyneth down the aisle, no one had been expecting an austere, lightning elopement. It was a reasonable assumption that this couple, who thought about marriage so conventionally, would want the full traditional wedding. The media also assumed that Chris and Gwyneth would express the importance they attached to the event in the accepted grand Hollywood fashion.

Chris had secured the absolute privacy and control he so clearly desired. What a real pity, though, that in order to protect themselves, the pair had to sacrifice the kind of celebratory wedding party that would have so suited them both, given their gregarious personalities. 'I guess you can say we eloped. It was great because we got married without any fuss. I'd have eloped even if I wasn't famous and ran a shop,' Chris told *The Sun*. 'Sometimes I think I'm like the Hugh Grant character from *Notting Hill* who runs the bookshop. Just an ordinary bloke who has extraordinary things happen to him.'

On Christmas Eve, two weeks after Chris's 'shock elopement' with 'the Hollywood beauty,' *The Sun* published Victoria Newton's rare and revealing interview with Chris. Fiddling nervily with his wedding ring, 'he was open, funny, and almost confessional as he talked about his life and the future for him, Gwyneth and the band,' reported Newton. Chris declared, 'I love the thought of having babies and I love being married.' He also emphasised, 'We're not the kind of people to do the red carpet thing and go to lots of showbiz parties. We're just normal people who want a normal life.'

With Chris 'n' Gwyn settling down into married life, the media obsession with the supposed strangeness of the match was diminishing, reflected in Newton's sympathetic description: 'In the flesh Chris is funny, charming and intelligent and cracks jokes to disguise his shyness. He is far from boring. He and Gwyneth . . . are the perfect match. They are polite and caring people whose talent has brought them wealth and fame. Chris says, "Everyone says my wife and I are miserable but we're not. We're happy people."'

Despite enjoying an idyllic honeymoon and reaping the awards of Coldplay's sustained success,

Chris and Gwyneth stop and pose for a photographer on a walk on Primrose Hill, near their London home.

Chris's tendency to veer between feelings of confidence and uncertainty remained evident. On the one hand, he airily commented to *Chart* magazine, 'I hate the fact that I have to look up to people. I don't want to have to look up to Paul McCartney. I'd rather just be on a level.' Then there's the Chris who still gets very nervous about the future: 'I'm always worried it could end tomorrow. There's no guarantee people are not going to get fed up with us,' he told *netmusiccountdown.com.*

Chris's insecurities about success were not manifested in self-important rock star behaviour. Just after Christmas Chris and Gwyneth turned up at the British Airways First Class check-in desk for a Gatwick flight to Mexico, *The Mirror* reported. Shaking off their public personas, they were dressed with casual scruffiness - Chris in dirty khaki pants and boots with a battered guitar on his back, Gwyneth in ripped jeans and old shoes. Initially, the check-in staff thought they were buskers or down-and-outs, stopping to ask for directions. It was only when they presented their First Class tickets (costing £10,474 each) that staff realised who they were. The check-in staff kept the pair occupied while hurried checks confirmed there was no dress code for the First Class section of the plane.

On Tuesday 7 January 2004, Coldplay entered the studio formally to begin work on their new album. The plan was to start at Parr Street in Liverpool, and then to move on to Air Studios, London. 'There's a real pressure on us now. We've become obsessed with trying to deliver something amazing,' Chris announced.

The *NME* pondered the next album's likely content: 'The group have been playing a handful of new songs live; working titles include "Gravity", "Poor Me", "Moses" and "World Turns

Upside Down". It's unclear if any of these will make it to the final record.' There was also more material left over from the last album's sessions, on a CD marked 'Songs for #3'. However, an interview Ken Nelson gave to VH1 revealed that this was not currently being considered by the band for the new disc, adding 'This is going to be a fantastic album. I actually believe it's going to be stronger than *A Rush Of Blood To The Head.*'

At the beginning of February, the nominations for the 46th annual Grammy awards were announced. Although Coldplay had no new album yet to be considered, they were still eligible for the Record of the Year for the single 'Clocks'. The Grammys were considered important enough to Coldplay's American career for them to suspend their intense recording schedule to attend the ceremony in LA.

The awards show began with Prince performing 'Purple Rain,' to mark the twentieth anniversary of his groundbreaking album and movie. Recent trends at the Grammys indicated that a single artist was likely to sweep the awards, as had been the case with Norah Jones a year earlier. This time, it was Beyonce Knowles, who captured five trophies for her solo album *Dangerously in Love*. Justin Timberlake won two, and took time out to apologise for his part in Janet Jackson's performance at the previous week's American football Super Bowl, where the fading diva's breast had been 'accidentally' exposed as he danced with her.

'Clocks' duly took the coveted Record of the Year award, beating both Beyonce and Eminem in the process. Chris dedicated the award to the late Johnny Cash – but also to Democratic Party Presidential nominee John Kerry, 'who hopefully will be your president one day.' This dedication to Kerry was Coldplay's considered response to the 'fascist' censorship at the previous year's event in New York. This time, instead of explicitly criticising an American regime, or US policies regarding Iraq or trade with the Third World, Coldplay expressed positive support for a less politically conservative presidential candidate. Obviously, it was a deft attempt to undermine youthful support for George W. Bush and his disastrous occupation of Iraq. Chris himself explained his action some weeks later in a Radio One interview: 'I mentioned John Kerry at the Grammys because someday, if he's president, maybe he'll say, "Maybe I'll meet with these Coldplay guys and find out what they have to say about Fair Trade."'

The day after the Grammys ceremony, John Mercurio of CNN's Political Unit commented that Coldplay's endorsement 'put Kerry (or at least his twenty and 30-something aides) over the top last night . . . Kerry couldn't have drawn better publicity if he had staged a wardrobe malfunction with Justin Timberlake.' Subsequently, Kerry's campaign organisers adopted 'Clocks' as a theme. At a campaign event on 23 February at the Alhambra Ballroom in Harlem, ABC News reported, 'the event concluded with Coldplay's "Clocks". But regardless of front man Chris Martin's endorsement of Kerry, the Grammy-winning song was quickly skipped for Stevie Wonder's "Sir Duke".'

The band then returned to the studio to concentrate on 'trying to make the best thing that anyone has ever heard'. In an interview on BBC Radio Five Live in mid-March, Chris revealed their ambitious philosophy: 'Why not try and be Einstein, even if you're never going to make it.'

In April *nme*.com reported that Coldplay might undertake a major tour in the New Year, citing as their source Ian McCulloch's interview on the *Gigwise* website. Mac had been talking about his band's latest work, 'The stuff we've been doing is amazing, mega, fantastic. But Chris has asked us to support them on a massive tour in the New Year.' Subsequently, the *Daily Star* quoted an unnamed source who alleged that Chris had angrily blasted Mac, saying Ian had jeopardised the band's chances of supporting Coldplay. However, any talk of gigs proved to be entirely speculative, as a Coldplay spokesperson confirmed that no specific tour dates had been planned.

There's no specific plan for many of life's positive occurrences – and this proved to be the case with one interview about Coldplay that spring, given by none other than Alan McGee. McGee pointed out that he rarely gives interviews, but a request to be interviewed for this book became an exception to his rule.

Surely, few single tags have stuck to any group as firmly as the startling phrase 'music for bed-wetters'. I asked McGee if he was surprised at the extent to which his comment had been applied to the band. 'Yes I was, and if I had probably known that four years later, or three years later, some-body was still going to be in this office asking me questions about "music for bedwetters", I prob-ably would never have said it. It was an off-the-cuff, kind of like bizarre Northern remark, really. And just to go on the record, I have nothing personally against anyone in Coldplay. It's like, I don't like their music but, you know . . . I think the thing got out of hand when the manager said that I had used them deliberately to make millions of pounds on the stock market, which is complete rubbish, because basically anybody who knows anything about me knows that if I don't like some-thing I say I don't like it, and if I do like something I say I like it. That was the point – you know, and then when he said that then there were personal remarks exchanged both ways and during that time it all got carried away. But I have nothing against them. I don't get off on their music but eight million people do, so good luck to them.'

> **'I love the idea of having babies and I love being married.
> We're not the kind of people to do the red carpet thing and go to
> lots of showbiz parties. We're just normal people who want a
> normal life.'** *– Chris Martin*

You said to me on the phone that if someone told you they'd be selling eight million records that you'd be very surprised.

'Yeah, obviously I would have been, but then against that I was surprised when Oasis sold mil-lions of records as well. So it's not as if I'm some great visionary or seer. You know, I'm surprised that The Darkness sell a million records. So that wasn't me dissing Coldplay – it's surprise that the mainstream have taken to them in such a big way.'

Asked if he thought there was any particular reason why Coldplay had done so well, McGee replied, 'I think Coldplay went over and did the right things at the right time and their music – though obviously I don't get off on it, two to three million Americans do, and they did the right tours at the right time, they were obviously well-managed and the records are well-made – you know, respect, at the end of the day. It is an incredible pressure when you are selling that many records and they seem to be adjusting and adapting to it pretty well.'

You said that rock needed very big characters. What if I were to put it to you that Chris Martin is the kind of huge character that can bash in a windshield with a rock and still refer to *The Wind in the Willows*?

'It's completely subjective what you're talking about now – and everybody's got their own def-inition of what they want out of a rock 'n' roll band. Coldplay don't give me particularly what I want out of a rock 'n' roll band, but then again I do manage the Libertines so they give me what I want. But that's subjective, and that's not to say that the Libertines are better than Coldplay or Coldplay are better than the Libertines, because, you know, that is a matter of personal opinion.'

McGee continued, 'I just wanted to say really that it was not personal, and it got a bit out of hand on both sides but, you know what, two years later you look back and go, what the hell was any of that about? Good luck to them. It's like they're British, sell loads of records – respect. It's just not my kind of music.'

The obvious softening of McGee's earlier hostility toward Coldplay may have been indicative of the end of an era for the band. The band had carved an individual niche within the music scene and gradually silenced their critics, or those who accused the band of being Radiohead/Travis copyists.

Unlike their music press brethren, the tabloids were less liable to change their spots. On 2 April 2004, Chris was accused of kicking a photographer outside San Lorenzo's restaurant in Knightsbridge, London. He and Gwyneth had been out to dinner there. After their meal, Chris protectively sent the now heavily-pregnant Gwyneth home ahead of him in a taxi, but one of the gathered press throng, Alessandro Copetti, ran after her cab.

Coldplay's spokesperson told *BBC Online* that Copetti became 'very aggressive' in his pursuit of a picture. *NME* quoted the band's spokeswoman as saying, 'Naturally enough for a man whose wife is heavily pregnant with her first child Chris's sole concern was to ensure that Gwyneth got into the cab safely and was not impeded or harassed in any way. As they were not leaving together he followed the taxi for a short distance to ensure she was safely on her way when at the same time the photographer ran after the taxi, tripped and fell in the process.'

Initially, the Metropolitan Police would only confirm that 'an allegation about an attack' was made. Countering the Coldplay spokesperson's claim that he had tripped, Copetti insisted that Chris kicked him from behind.

> **'Everyone assumes we're multi-millionaires because we've sold a lot of albums but none of us are rich enough to retire.'** – *Chris Martin*

The following day, Copetti filed a common assault complaint against Chris. A police spokesperson said Copetti had received minor cuts and scratches and that a formal statement would be taken 'in due course'.

Regardless of the constant hassle of photographers 'just trying to make a living', Chris insisted he wasn't going to be driven out of town. 'London is and always will be, our home,' he told *The Sun,* 'We've got no intention to live in America. I sometimes get fed up with the attention we get here, but that would never make me give up my home. I feel very protective towards my wife. But I'm no different to anyone else. Sometimes I react, but I don't go around punching photographers.'

It had been widely supposed that Chris and Gwyneth's baby would arrive in June. But, on Friday 13 May, after what Chris described as 'a long labour', Gwyneth gave birth to their baby daughter at the private St John and St Elizabeth Hospital in St John's Wood, north west London.

'We are 900 miles over the moon, and we'd like to thank everyone at the hospital who have looked after us amazingly,' exclaimed the ecstatic new father. Later, the couple happily posed with their child for photographers. Gwyneth looked tired but radiant, and in love twice over; Chris, his child's head cradled in his big, thin, pianist's hands, looked hugely content but thinner than ever.

Gwyneth had already hinted to *The Mirror* that she might put her acting career on hold to raise her child, making the same choice as her mother, who 'turned down every fantastic movie there was. She turned down these amazing things that would have made her a huge movie star.'

Inevitably, the birth received extensive international coverage, with *People* magazine running a cover shot of the joyful family. There was almost universal astonishment at the couple's choice of name for their little daughter – Apple Blythe Alison Martin. It gave rise to a bumper crop of fruity headlines, such as *The Mirror*'s 'Bananas Gwyneth Calls Her Baby Apple'. Surprisingly though, the name 'Apple' isn't so rare in the couple's professional circle – Coldplay's US booking agent Marty Diamond has a daughter of that name, as does Peter Farrelly, who directed Gwyneth in *Shallow Hal*. 'It's a very cool name,' Chris told *Hello* magazine as he left their Belgravia flat, passing gifts left by well-wishers, which included a large basket of apples.

To celebrate Apple's arrival Coldplay filmed a spoof glam-rap music video, which was shown on their website for one week only. The band donned Darkness-style glam-rock wigs, to perform as 'the Nappies'. Chris, bespectacled and bare-chested, trumpeted his devotion – 'I'll be there through the thin and the thick/I'm gonna clean up all the poo and the sick.' Legendary Beatles producer Sir George Martin introduced the performance from the mixing desk of his Air Studios in London, respectfully toupeed for the occasion.

The video represented something of a release for a man who'd had to exercise public caution about his relationship for too long. When it came to marrying, Chris had opted for a private event, but for the birth of his child, as *The Guardian*'s John Robinson pointed out, he chose to go large and 'well, mad . . . A crazy mixed-up kid smelling of crisps he certainly is, but even by his own high standards, this is barmy behaviour,' Robinson gawped. Recovering a little, he noted, 'He is, perversely enough, though, only doing the same kind of thing that rock 'n' roll legends habitually do when confronted with an event as beyond their traditional remit as fatherhood.' The other greats had performed with slightly more grace than the Nappies, but the songs were much less fun: John Lennon's 'Beautiful Boy' for his son Sean, or David Bowie's 'Kooks'.

Whatever the calibre of Coldplay's nappy-rash rap, it's not the kind of spoof that a band puts out when they are experiencing recording difficulties. Another sign that things were going well was that the band decided to set up a webcam in the studio. The aim was to treat fans to behind-the-scenes footage of the quartet at work, feverishly straining to surpass *A Rush . . .* 'There are four clips of us sweating and strumming on and we'll add more each week,' Chris explained on the band's website.

Outside Chris's house, on a dry day in London in late May 2004, a paparazzo managed to take an unusual new photograph of the band. Chris held Apple to his chest, Jonny Buckland wheeled the buggy, and Guy Berryman and Will Champion made up a strong rearguard. *The Sun* reported an observer as saying, 'It was a real 21st century sight, all these new men taking care of baby. It seemed a million miles from the traditional life of a famous rock star.'

But that's the point. Coldplay aren't traditional rock stars. They are a unique symbiosis of four talented individuals, each of whom share a love of music and a desire simply to be true to themselves. Which, on reflection, is what every rock 'n' roller should be shooting for.

Some years earlier, the hot sun and salt spray of an Australian beach had lulled Chris into sooth-saying mode. 'I'm just waiting 'til I'm about sixty and that's all I'm gonna do . . . surf;' he claimed. 'I won't have to tour and write songs.' Until then, we've got plenty to look forward to.

SELECTED DISCOGRAPHY

Singles/EP's

Safety (EP):
*Bigger Stronger/No More Keeping My Feet On The
Ground/Such A Rush*
(Hilton Grove UK) *May 1998*

**Brothers And Sisters/Easy To Please/
Only Superstition**
(Fierce Panda UK) *April 1999*

The Blue Room (EP):
*Bigger Stronger/Don't Panic/See You Soon/
High Speed/Such A Rush*
(EMI UK) *October 1999*

Shiver/For You/Careful Where You Stand
(Parlophone UK) *March 2000*

**Yellow/Help Round The Corner/No More
Keeping My Feet On The Ground**
(Parlophone UK) *June 2000*

**Trouble/Brothers And Sisters/Shiver
(Jo Whiley Lunchtime Social)**
(Parlophone UK) *October 2000*

**Sparks/Careful Where You Stand/Yellow
(Jo Whiley Lunchtime Social)/See You
Soon/Yellow (Video)**
(UK Promo – Parlophone) *October 2000*

Acoustic
*Sparks/Careful Where You Stand/Yellow/
See You Soon*
(UK Promo – Free with the *Independent On
Sunday* 29/10/2000)

Don't Panic/You Only Live Twice (Live)
(EMI Sweden) *March 2001*

Trouble – Norwegian Live EP
*Trouble/Shiver/Sparks/Yellow/
Everything's Not Lost*
(EMI Norway) *April 2001*
*All tracks recorded live at Rockefeller Music Hall,
Oslo 01/12/2000*

Mince Spies EP
Have Yourself A Merry Little Christmas (Radio
One Session)/Yellow (The Alpha Remix)
(Parlophone UK) *December 2001*

In My Place/One I Love/I Bloom Blaum
(Parlophone UK) *August 2002*

The Scientist (Radio Edit)/1.36/I Ran Away
(Parlophone UK) *November 2002*

**The Scientist (Radio Edit)/The Scientist
(Video)/Lips Like Sugar (Live)/Interview**
(Parlophone UK CD/DVD) *November 2002*

Clocks/Crests Of Waves/Animals
(Parlophone UK) *March 2003*

**Clocks (Video Edit)/Politik (Live)/In My Place
(Live)/Interview/Gallery**
(Parlophone UK CD/DVD) *March 2003*

Clocks/Yellow
(Capitol USA)
June 2003

Clocks EP
*Clocks (Radio Edit)/Crests of
Waves/Animals/Murder/In My Place (Live)/Yellow
(Live)/Clocks (Video)/In My Place (Video)*
(Toshiba Japan) *August 2003*

God Put A Smile Upon Your Face EP
*God Put A Smile Upon Your Face/Crests of
Waves/Animals/Murder/In My Place (Live)/Yellow
(Live)/Clocks (Video)/
In My Place (Video)*
(EMI Asia) *December 2003*

Albums

Parachutes
(Parlophone UK) *July 2000*
(Nettwerk USA) *November 2000*

*Don't Panic, Shiver, Spies, Sparks, Yellow, Trouble,
Parachutes, High Speed, We Never Change,
Everything's Not Lost
Life Is For Living* (hidden track)

(Japanese version issued with two additional tracks
– *Careful Where You Stand* and *For You* – EMI
Asia August 2000)

A Rush Of Blood To The Head
(Parlophone UK) *August 2002*

*Politik, In My Place, God Put A Smile Upon Your
Face, The Scientist, Clocks, Daylight, Green Eyes,
Warning Sign, A Whisper, A Rush Of Blood To The
Head, Amsterdam*